T

John Paul II

John Paul II

Man of History

EDWARD STOURTON

Hodder & Stoughton
LONDON SYDNEY AUCKLAND

The right ... hor of
the W ... ith
t

British Library Cataloguing in Publication Data
A record for this book is available from the British Library

ISBN 0 340 90816 5

Typeset in Baskerville by Avon DataSet Ltd,
Bidford-on-Avon, Warwickshire

Printed and bound in Great Britain by
Clays Ltd, St Ives plc

The paper used in this book is a natural recyclable product made from wood grown in sustainable forests.
The hard coverboard is recycled.

Hodder & Stoughton
A Division of Hodder Headline Ltd
338 Euston Road
London NW1 3BH
www.madaboutbooks.com

Contents

Acknowledgements

This book would not have been written without Judith Longman of Hodder and Stoughton, who first proposed the idea to me. It has turned out to be a thoroughly enjoyable experience and I am extremely grateful to her for persuading me that it was worth attempting. The speed with which her team at Hodder worked to turn the finished product into a published book was awe-inspiring. She and my agent Vivienne Schuster have been wonderfully supportive throughout.

I owe a general 'thank you' to the BBC bosses who have encouraged me to cover John Paul and the Church over the years, and a particular one to *Today* and the other BBC programmes which kept me in Rome during the memorable days of John Paul's last illness and the conclave to elect his successor. My BBC colleague, Gilly Orr, used her fluent Italian and irresistible telephone manner to do some invaluable research during the final stretch of writing, when I most needed help. Ewa Ewart, television producer and friend, translated the extracts of Karol Wojtyla's poetry I have quoted with sensitivity and clarity.

Since my wife Fiona spends her working days editing programmes it was especially generous of her to give so much of her spare time to my manuscript; she read, improved and reassured at every stage. I am also grateful to my children – Ivo, Eleanor and Tom – for managing to sound so enthusiastic about the project, and to my step-daughter, Rosy, for putting up with it.

Introduction

John Paul II had a passion for apologies; he said sorry to Jews, Galileo, women, the victims of the Inquisition, Muslims slaughtered by the Crusaders and almost everyone else who has suffered at the hands of the Catholic Church in its long and not always glorious history. In the same spirit I shall begin with an apology of my own.

In a book I wrote about Catholicism in 1998 I suggested that John Paul II was in the twilight of his reign, an increasingly irrelevant figure who had lost his appeal for the world's editors. 'He still manages to find his way into the newspapers,' I declared loftily, 'but it tends to be on the inside pages.' It was just after the Monica Lewinsky affair, and I noted that the story of Bill Clinton's Oval Office carry-on had broken during a papal visit to Cuba: 'The American networks chartered planes to fly their anchormen off the island and back to Washington. It told a sad truth about the place to which this sometime superstar of the Cold War had sunk in the news rankings.' Oh dear. Six years later, as I began writing this book, I found myself looking at a very prominent headline in the *Guardian*: 'Bush takes a tongue lashing from the Pope over Iraq,' it said. And there was a picture of our man, frail certainly, but speaking with arresting directness on what was undeniably the top news story of the year. And several months after that I was standing in St Peter's Square on a warm spring evening listening to tens of thousands of voices joined in prayer for the dying man in the papal apartments above us, and reflecting that there has probably never been a public figure who managed to turn the manner as well as the fact of his death into a news story in quite the way John Paul did.

The death of Ronald Reagan in June 2004 brought John Paul's longevity into focus. He moved into the papal apartments in the Vatican two years before the former governor of California won the keys to the White House, six months before Margaret Thatcher entered Downing Street and nearly seven years before Mikhail Gorbachev came to power in the Kremlin; François Mitterrand was still toiling away to turn the French Socialists into an election-winning machine when Karol Wojtyla was elected Supreme Pontiff, and Helmut Kohl was licking his wounds after failing in his first bid for the office of German Chancellor. And of that remarkable generation of leaders who presided over the end of the Cold War, only John Paul remained an active presence on the world stage into the twenty-first century.

Yet his papacy could be characterised as history's longest death watch. The assassination attempt which brought him down in St Peter's Square was in 1981, and in 1992 surgeons at the Gemelli Hospital in Rome had to open up the scars to remove a cancerous tumour from his colon. The following year he tripped over his robes and dislocated a shoulder, and in 1994 he slipped in his bathroom and broke his hip. During a visit to Croatia in September that year he was in so much pain that he had to abandon his traditional practice of kissing the ground whenever he arrived somewhere new, and that autumn he resorted to carrying a cane in public. In the decade after that his health was a subject of constant and often feverish speculation. One Friday in 2003 officials at Westminster Cathedral in London became so convinced that a papal death was imminent that they hired a choir to cover for the weekend; the Cathedral's own singers were on tour, and the word from Rome suggested that John Paul might not make it through until the Monday morning. In 2004 there was a rumour that a delegation of the men in grey suits – or perhaps, to be strictly accurate, one should say the men in scarlet cassocks – was on the way round to St Peter's to suggest a relaxing retirement somewhere obscure in the Tatra Mountains. But no one quite dared to play Brutus. And John Paul lived through so many death scares in the final years of his life that at the end many people found it quite difficult to believe that he would actually die. When the news came through that he had finally decided not to return to hospital for treatment and I was despatched to Rome by the BBC, I had been due to spend a couple of days staying with a former priest as part of the research for this book. I telephoned to apologise for the change in plan and my host insisted that he would keep the bed made up as he was quite sure it would turn out to be a false alarm, remarking rather wearily that he had had a Polish parishioner of John Paul's generation to whom he had administered the last rites on no fewer than four occasions.

And in the meantime the biographies came and went. Jonathan Kwitny called his *Man of the Century*, meaning, of course, the twentieth century; we are in a new century now, and John Paul seemed to feel he had just as much to say to this one as he did to the last (sadly, Jonathan Kwitny himself, wonderful writer that he was, has now died). The Conservative American intellectual George Weigel claimed a degree of finality with '*The* Biography of Pope John Paul II' on his title page. The hubris is understandable; Weigel spent twenty years studying and writing about John Paul and was commissioned to produce his book by the man himself, during an evening of 'the freewheeling conversation that John Paul's openness invites . . . over roast chicken and a good local red wine' at Castel Gandolfo. The result was a unique level of access to the Vatican and a tome which runs to nearly a thousand pages.

But between the publication of Weigel's work in 1999 and his death in 2005, John Paul faced an agenda which could readily provide enough material for another, equally weighty doorstopper of a book. The Church was struck by what has been arguably its gravest crisis since the publication of *Humanae Vitae*, the birth control encyclical, in 1968: the paedophile priests scandals which touched dioceses from Boston to Poland have done profound damage to the institution, and the impact of the sense of betrayal they have left among ordinary Catholics will endure for many years to come. The Church's contraception ban came under pressure as never before as the AIDS crisis deepened in its severity. Outside the Church – and John Paul was never shy of mixing it on the geopolitical stage – Osama bin-Laden's terrorists went about their grisly work, and America invaded Iraq. And, of course, the beginning of a third Christian millennium provided John Paul with an opportunity for a veritable outpouring of his views on church and world affairs, and on human destiny in the widest sense of the phrase.

So part of the point of this biography is simply to catch up; to try to give some sort of shape to the final years of John Paul's pontificate. But this is above all an attempt to make sense of what must by any standards rank as a truly remarkable life – to find what those who sell political messages these days call 'a narrative' that draws together the cluttered decades of unrelenting activism and intellectual effort. When George Weigel addressed a congregation at Westminster Cathedral on the paperback publication of his book in 2001 he gave a snapshot of John Paul's life in statistics: '670,000 miles travelled on 84 papal trips . . . that is, 2.8 times the distance between the earth and the moon . . . 3,078 addresses and homilies delivered . . . 13 million people met in audience . . . 15,000 intimate personal encounters . . . 159 new cardinals appointed'. John Paul had, he said, 'beatified 798 men and women and canonised 280 new saints', and 'The printed record of his teaching . . . covers ten whole linear feet of shelf space in libraries.' The final statistical record was no doubt even more impressive (I confess I have not done the sums), but what do those figures actually mean, and is there a story that ties them all together?

John Paul was, famously, a bundle of paradoxes; he defied every attempt to put him in an ideological box, and he could be equally bewildering to his admirers and his detractors. How could the great champion of liberty in Eastern Europe be such a ferocious witch-hunter in his own Church, ruthlessly rooting out and punishing dissent? Why did this arch-reactionary in cultural and sexual matters publicly berate George Bush, the most socially conservative president America has known for years? How did a man with first-hand experience of Nazi aggression in the 1930s wind up as a near-pacifist in the twenty-first century? What on earth are we to make of a professed intellectual with a string of academic works to his name who was so deeply attuned to the world of peasant cults, shrines and mysticism? Why did the great

4

ideological enemy of Marxism become one of capitalism's most trenchant critics? How could someone who showed such a clear grasp of modern methods in the way he communicated be so determined to preserve some of the most anachronistic characteristics of the institution he led? The list goes on, and behind all the questions lies the profound paradox of a man who was self-evidently inspired by a love of humanity, yet remained obstinately wedded to teachings which sometimes caused great suffering.

The way John Paul wanted us to make sense of what he did is to look for the hand of Providence. The attempt on his life in St Peter's Square happened on the feast of Our Lady of Fatima, which commemorates the Virgin's appearance to some Portuguese peasants in 1917; she revealed three 'secrets' which seemed to predict much of the suffering of the twentieth century, including, apparently, the murder of a pope. John Paul always attributed his survival that day to the direct intervention of the Virgin and 'a motherly hand which guided the bullet's path', enabling the 'dying Pope' to halt 'at the threshold of death'. In the millennium year he visited Fatima to beatify the three visionaries – one of the bullets fired at him has been set in the Virgin's crown at the shrine – and the Fatima connection cemented his conviction that his life and career were an expression of the Divine Will making itself felt in history. However silly that may sound to those outside the Church, most Catholics would probably at least be willing to keep an open mind on the question – and the election of a Polish pope at such a critical moment in Central and Eastern Europe's history was, after all, a most unexpected and very remarkable thing.

But John Paul's habit of seeing his life in providential terms added to the inevitable tendency to treat him as an institution and not a human being. The papacy is so hedged about with history, symbol and tradition that those who hold it are bound to seem distant from the world we ordinary mortals inhabit, and it is all too easy to see them in caricature terms; to many of John Paul's admirers he was a plaster-cast saint, and to many of his detractors he was an irredeemably wicked old man in a funny white suit. When he was elected, Fr Mieczyslaw Malinski, who had known Karol Wojtyla since they were pious young men together in the days of the Nazi occupation of Krakow, wrote an instant biography. It is a moving book because it chronicles – without really meaning to – the way Fr Malinski feels he is losing his old friend to the institution of his high office. He interviews the priest who served as Karol Wojtyla's chancellor when he was the Archbishop of Krakow, and is surprised to be asked if he can secure a signed photograph of the new pope; 'Goodness,' he reflects, 'how wonderful it all is and how things have changed. Father Marszowski must have seen the archbishop a dozen times a day on one matter or another, and now he is asking for a signed photograph.'

The best source for any biographer looking at Karol Wojtyla's life before his election is a remarkable document published under the modest title *Kalendarium of the Life of Karol Wojtyla*. The work of a Marian Polish priest, it is huge – it was originally written in Polish, but my English edition runs to nearly a thousand pages – and contains 'a chronological record of facts, documents, testimonies (verified) and statements by Karol Wojtyla himself, in which he spoke of his life on various occasions – all this without any "connective" narrative'. The first edition came out early in the papacy, and the author found his admirably rigorous approach coming under increasing pressure as the years passed. 'As printed accounts of the life of the Holy Father multiplied,' he writes, 'persons relating their recollections tended more and more to repeat things they had read as if they themselves had been an eyewitness ... I was very sceptical of stories which seemed excessively uplifting.' Fr Malinski acutely predicted that something like this would happen to his own reminiscences; after meeting his old friend as pope for the first time he wrote, in somewhat maudlin mood,

> People would be asking me what it was like, what he was like ... and I would have to think up some comment to describe the indescribable and relate something that could never be related. I knew that I would be angry with those who made me do so, and whatever I told them would impoverish me forever. For every time I was asked the same questions I would play the same record, repeating the same words in the same tone. I

would know what most interested and affected people, what they wanted and expected me to say – and I would repeat it over and over again, distorting it more each time. And in the end I would come to believe that what I was saying was the whole truth, whereas the reality was so much richer, so much greater, so much more beautiful.

I interviewed Fr Malinski many years later, and there was indeed something rote-like and resentful about the way he delivered anecdotes which I have since encountered many times in other tellings.

The tendency of Karol Wojtyla the man to disappear behind the legend of John Paul the Great has become even more pronounced since his death. Some of the cardinals who in the final years of John Paul's life were willing to voice discreet reservations about his record and nuanced comments on his character were simply overwhelmed by that huge outpouring of devotion they encountered when they gathered in Rome to bury him, and with the push for canonisation serious criticism has become almost impossible from within the Church. But the full picture is, in Fr Malinski's phrase, 'so much richer', and part of the purpose of this book is to look beyond the caricatures to the man himself, and to recapture some of that sense of excitement that rippled round the world when, in the early days of his papacy, Karol Wojtyla became the first pope ever to let us see his humanity.

Or perhaps it would be more accurate to say that we thought we were seeing his humanity – so bewitched were we by that 100-megaton smile, the actorly gestures and the sheer zest for life and leadership which shone forth from the dusty grandeur of the Vatican in the late 1970s. André Frossard, a French journalist who conducted one of the earliest and most revealing interviews with the new pope, recalls the new enthusiasm for their faith which many Catholics felt in those first days of this papacy. Remembering the moment when John Paul appeared for the first time on the steps of St Peter's 'with a big crucifix planted in front of him like a two-handed sword' and told the crowd 'Be not afraid', Frossard writes,

We had learnt that he came from Poland. My impression was
rather that he had left his nets on the shore of a lake and that
he came straight from Galilee, on the heels of the apostle Peter.
I had never before felt so close to the Gospel. For the words 'Be
not afraid' were doubtless addressed to a world in which man
fears man, fears life as much, if not more than, death, fears the
savage forces he holds prisoner, fears everything, nothing and
sometimes even his own fear; but they were also, or might have
been, the exhortation of a disciple in the dawn of Christianity
to his brothers called to bear witness, and while the new pope
spoke, the memory of Nero's circus on which St Peter's is built
rose again from beneath the marble.

And yet, as Frossard himself notes, the man who inspired such
hyperbolic flights of Catholic triumphalism did 'not like talking
about himself'. The way John Paul allowed little bits and pieces
about himself to dribble out over the course of his two and a half
decades in office is intriguing. Gobbets of memory and emotion
are slipped into highly structured interviews or writings on such
abstract theological subjects as the nature of priestly vocation.
Rise, Let Us Be On Our Way, which came out in 2004, is perhaps the
most fascinating and the most frustrating of these offerings. Much
of it is a meandering musing on the role of a bishop, and it has
the rambling character that one might expect from an elderly
man chatting to his grandchildren about the moments that might
make sense of his life. But age is a remarkably effective editor, and
when you set the events John Paul has chosen to reflect upon in
the book against the record of his life it provides some valuable
insights into what has really mattered to him. The last of these
books, *Memory and Identity*, is certainly not the 'autobiography' it
was said to be when it came out just before John Paul's death, but
despite the rather ponderous reflections on such matters as
'Nation and Culture', it too tells us a good deal about the way his
mind worked.

So while this is, of course, the story of a man who witnessed
history in the making and made it himself, it is also, simply, the
story of a life; of a young orphan who sneaked off to the boiler
room of a Nazi chemical factory to study at night, of an energetic

priest and teacher who took parties of young people on hiking tours and talked to them about sex in the mountains, and of an ardent, budding philosopher who bewitched a beautiful Polish American academic. It is the story of a man capable of sudden and terrifying rages – thumping the table and shouting when one of his bishops dared to suggest a change in the celibacy laws. But it is finally the story of a man who in old age and infirmity showed such patience and endurance that, in the last of his many incarnations, he became an icon of the Christian response to suffering.

And this book is also, if I am honest, a way of reflecting on my own experience of my religion. The two John Pauls were elected when I was in my second year at university, so this one was pope throughout much of my adult life. Any serious conversation about what it has meant to be a Catholic in the late twentieth and early twenty-first centuries inevitably comes back to him. A generation of Catholics – my own children among them – have grown up knowing no other leader of their Church. I took my three children to Rome just before Christmas in 2003, and we emerged from St Peter's on an Advent Sunday morning in time to see the frail figure at that famous window, addressing a somewhat sparse and drizzled-upon crowd. All three – they were in their late teens and early twenties, and I would not describe them as pious – paused and watched and listened, straining to catch the voice that whispered of eternal truths in a foreign tongue.

1

Childhood

Karol Wojtyla spent much of his life thinking, writing and speaking about sex and the family, but he grew up without very much experience of either of these things. His tutors in the school of life were harsher: modest means, grief, a strong sense of duty and an overwhelmingly heavy burden of history. Only by appreciating the depth of the divide that separates our comfortable world from the one in which he spent his early years can we come close to understanding this titanic but bewildering figure.

On 13 April 1929 the future pope learnt that his mother had died. He was just short of his ninth birthday, a schoolboy in the provincial town of Wadowice. He was in class when it happened, and his father, Karol Wojtyla senior, came to the school to report the news but left without speaking to his son – it fell to a woman teacher to pass on what had happened and offer consolation.

Karol Wojtyla's feelings about this episode, and indeed about his mother's place in his childhood, remain opaque. One version of the story has him responding to the news of her death with the terrifyingly precocious and pious words, 'It was God's will' (this is the kind of detail that needs to be approached with caution because of the significant body of sometimes questionable mythology that has inevitably grown up around the future pope's childhood). He later told a friend that he had cried privately on his mother's grave, and ten years after her death he wrote a poem about her. Like much of his writing at the time, it is pretty dreadful as a piece of literature – the adolescent Karol Wojtyla wrote freely about his own feelings and ideas without any hint of the embarrass-

11

ment that acts as a poetic prophylactic for most of us – but it is affecting nonetheless.

> On your white grave
> White flowers of life are blooming
> Oh how many years have gone already
> Without you here!
> Oh how long have you been gone!
> Over your white grave
> Closed for so many years
> Something unfathomable is rising
> Something as incomprehensible as death itself.
> On your white grave
> My darling departed mother
> Here is a prayer from a loving son
> May you rest in eternal peace.

It is as if the young Karol knows that the death of a mother requires strong emotion but cannot quite work out how to express his feelings or, indeed, precisely what they are. In the end he takes refuge in conventional piety.

In adult life he said very little about his mother. In one of his autobiographical reflections he remarked simply that he 'does not have a clear awareness of her contribution' to his religious upbringing, which 'must have been very great', and he also regretted that 'I was not old enough to make my first communion when I lost my mother, who did not have the happiness of seeing the day to which she looked forward as a great day.' We know Emilia Wojtyla was frail – she succumbed to kidney failure and congenital heart disease – that she was the daughter of a saddler from Krakow, and that she took in sewing to help with the family finances. Beyond that she is something of an enigma. The temptation to trace some of the future pope's views on women – particularly his passionate devotion to the Virgin Mary – to the absence of a mother figure in his youth is strong, and plenty of biographers and commentators have given in to it.

Karol Wojtyla's elder sister died in infancy, so he never knew her. The death of his elder brother Edmund – when Karol was twelve – set the seal on a certain emotional austerity in his home life. Edmund's death sounds especially distressing. The two Wojtyla boys had developed a close relationship when Edmund ('Mundek', as he was nicknamed) graduated from the Jagiellonian University in Krakow and began practising as a doctor in a hospital closer to the family home in Wadowice; Mundek is remembered by his colleagues as charming and popular, a natural hero figure to the younger boy, and he used to take Karol to football matches. But in the winter of 1932 there was an epidemic of scarlet fever, and the twenty-six-year-old Dr Wojtyla contracted the disease from a patient. He was dead within four days (John Paul later remarked that 'antibiotics would have saved him') and spent his last hours in physical anguish and, according to a senior doctor at the Bielsko Hospital, existential distress; 'Why me? Why now?' he is reported to have demanded on his deathbed.

The emotional tone of the minutes of the next Municipal Council Public Session in Bielsko suggest a man capable of inspiring great affection. 'He contracted the deadly disease at the bedside of a severely ill patient whom he attempted to wrench from the claws of death, alas, in vain,' they record. 'For his dedication and extraordinary conscientiousness, he paid with his young life.' The tribute to his qualities notes that 'He was happy that his dreams were fulfilled, his dreams to be able to render support to his honourable father, whose pride he was, and for his beloved younger brother, to fill the void that was created by the premature death of their mother.' The minutes conclude with the observation that 'The Members of the City Council, following the example of the chairman, rose from their seats and listened to this speech attentively.'

It would be surprising if this sad parade of death through Karol Wojtyla's childhood had not had a profound impact on him. Carl Bernstein and Marco Politi argue in their biography *His Holiness* that it was the well-head of his theology; 'The idea of the hand of God, in his unfathomable wisdom giving and taking away, the idea of Judgement awaiting everyone now suddenly, unexpectedly, took hold in the consciousness of Karol Wojtyla,' they argue. 'From this moment on the parts of the Bible that would preoccupy him were the apocalyptic accounts of the Four Last Things – death, judgement, heaven and hell.' This verdict perhaps goes rather further than the facts allow, but John Paul himself acknowledged, in a speech at the Jagiellonian University fifty years later, that 'These are events that became deeply engraved in my memory, my brother's death perhaps even deeper than my mother's death – equally because of the special circumstances, one may say tragic ones, and in view of my greater maturity at the time.'

When the French journalist André Frossard asked John Paul about his childhood, in that first really full interview with the newly elected pope, his response was as eloquent in its reticence as it was in what he actually said. 'He asserted at first that my little question implied many others of a very personal nature,' Frossard recorded, 'that he would not go into the details into which autobiographies so easily sink and that he would stick to essentials.' The pope then digressed into a characteristic philoso-phical reflection on '"inner time" which is not the time indicated by clocks, and on the disproportion familiar to us all between the psychological length of childhood and the fragmentary memories which it leaves us' before cutting to the chase and allowing himself a very brief childhood reminiscence which consists almost entirely of the most heartbreaking litany of loss. 'Quite soon,' he said, 'I became a motherless only child.' Drawing on his experience as a priest preparing couples for marriage, he observes that boys often look for the image of their mothers in their fiancées, and tells Frossard that 'There comes a moment . . . when boys brought up by their father (however well and tenderly) make the painful discovery that they have been deprived of a mother.'

The same interview puts beyond any doubt the absolutely central role of his father, Karol Wojtyla senior, in the formation of his character. 'Almost all my memories of childhood and adolescence are connected with my father,' he told Frossard. Karol Wojtyla senior spent most of his professional life as a non-commissioned officer in the army of the Austro-Hungarian Empire, which means that the pope who led the Catholic Church into the twenty-first century was brought up by a man whose view of the world took shape in the nineteenth.

The Hapsburgs had ruled a jumble of Central European peoples for more than six hundred years, holding the hereditary title of Holy Roman Emperor from 1437 until it was abolished under Napoleon, and parts of Poland came under their control in the eighteenth century when the country was partitioned. The army in which Wojtyla served included Poles, Czechs, Slovaks, Croats, Slovenes, Bosnians, Italians, Ruthenes and Jews as well as Austrians and Hungarians. Karol senior almost always appears in uniform in the family photographs, and they reveal a dapper if somewhat severe figure who looks a little as if he might have stepped out of some sad Chekhovian provincial drama. His life story belongs to those confusing bits of history that tend to be taught at school under titles like 'The Rise of Nationalism and the Causes of the First World War', and in both time and spirit he was much closer to the world of Bismarck, Gladstone and the Tsars than the world of George W. Bush.

The Wojtylas seem to have hovered between the peasant class and the *petit bourgeoisie* – Karol senior's father was a tailor and farmer, and he worked as a tailor himself for a while before being called up for military service. When he married the frail Emilia in 1904, it is said that her family looked down on his origins. But army life suited him, and he clearly impressed his commanding officers: 'extraordinarily well developed, with a righteous character, serious, well-mannered, modest, concerned about honour, with a strongly developed sense of responsibility, very gentle, and tireless,' says his army file. He was promoted to warrant officer, specialised in accounting, and was praised as a 'very fast typist' in his efficiency report. When the Russians broke through the front in the early days of the First World War and shelled Krakow and Wadowice he evidently distinguished himself – he was awarded the Iron Cross of Merit with wreath – but beyond that there is no evidence that he saw action.

The end of the Great War brought the collapse of the Dual Monarchy of Austria-Hungary, and Poland was reborn as an independent nation at the Treaty of Versailles in 1919. Many officers and soldiers who had fought for the Empire simply transferred to the newly formed Polish army, and for Karol Wojtyla Polish independence brought a bonus; he was commissioned as a lieutenant in the 12th Infantry Regiment, a significant step upwards in society. But the newly independent nation nearly disappeared again before it had time to breathe the air of freedom. In 1920 it faced invasion by the Bolshevik forces of Lenin. Against any reasonable odds, Marshal Pilsudski, Poland's brilliant military commander, defeated the Soviet army at the gates of Warsaw itself; the battle took place on the feast of the Assumption of Our Lady, and became known as the Miracle on the Vistula. Karol Wojtyla senior was too old to go to the front by this stage, and remained at work behind his desk in the town of Wadowice, where his regiment was garrisoned. It was here that his third child, the future Pope John Paul, was born – Emilia went into labour on the day of Marshal Pilsudski's triumphant reception by the people of Warsaw, and the coincidence of Karol Wojtyla's birth with that of the modern Polish nation-state has been made much of by those who share his predilection for the providential view of history.

Though it is difficult to avoid the conclusion that Karol senior was slightly cold, the memories of those who knew him – and inevitably most of the testimony comes from witnesses who were children at the time – suggest a more cultured, thoughtful and complex figure than the average quartermaster serving out his time in a provincial regimental town. He was largely an autodidact – his formal education had ended after three years at high school – and in middle age his two passions were prayer and books. The culture of the Austro-Hungarian Imperial Army in which he had served was German; that was the official language, and the officer corps drew its inspiration from the traditions and past triumphs of the Hapsburgs. Perhaps as a deliberate reaction to that, Karol senior had developed a special interest in Polish literature and history, and the memories of one of the boys who used to bring homework back to the Wojtyla apartment from time to time suggest that he was an engaging story-teller; if the boys were studying a period of the Polish past that interested him, 'Tales of Polish bravery unfurled, martyrdom and resurrection rambling out from the hoard of his reading'.

'From my earliest childhood,' Pope John Paul wrote as an old man of eighty-four, 'I have loved books. It was my father who introduced me to reading. He would sit beside me and read to me, for example, Sienkiewicz and other Polish writers.' The writings of Sienkiewicz must have had particular resonance for someone of Karol senior's background, and it is easy to see why they were so popular in the Poland of the 1920s and 1930s, when the country was desperately trying to secure its independence. Henryk Sienkiewicz, who won the Nobel Prize for literature in 1905, was Poland's answer to Walter Scott (whom he much admired), and his principal stock-in-trade was romantic nationalism.

Many of his sprawling adventure stories – with titles such as *With Fire and Sword* – are set against the backdrop of an earlier Polish struggle for survival, its seventeenth-century wars against the Russians and Ukrainians, the Swedes and the Turks. Reading the books today it is impossible not to smile at some of their Mills and Boon moments – 'the princess raised the lashes of her eyes, and her glance fell upon the face of the lieutenant like a bright, warm ray of the sun' – or to be startled by the most unpolitically correct view they take of war and religion – 'May the God of mercy grant such a holy war for the glory of Christianity and our nation,' declares one Polish aristocrat at the prospect of fighting the Tartars, 'and permit me, sinful man, to fulfil my vow so that I may receive joy in the struggle or find a praiseworthy death!' But they are gripping stories and would have fired the imagination of most young boys, especially when read aloud by a soldier father. Like some of the other Polish literature which influenced the future pope as an adolescent – which I shall return to later – Sienkiewicz's writing is inspired by the idea that history demonstrates a direct link between Polish nationalism and the interests of the Roman Catholic Church. And it is shot through with a strong sense of the supernatural – here, for example, is his description of the steppe in *With Fire and Sword*:

Night came down upon the Wilderness, and with it the hour of ghosts. Cossacks on guard in the stanitsas [a Cossack settlement] related in those days that the shades of men who had fallen in sudden death and in sin used to rise up at night and carry on dances in which they were hindered neither by cross nor churches ... It was said, too, that the shades of mounted men coursing through the waste barred the road to wayfarers, whining and begging them for a sign of the holy cross. Among these ghosts vampires also were met with, who pursued people with howls.

The future pope listened to this spine-chilling stuff in a tiny apartment just off the main square of Wadowice. There were three rooms, a kitchen, a bedroom and a parlour, strung together like train carriages on the upper floor of a two-storey building. There was no bathroom – the luxury of running water had yet to arrive in the town. A curved metal staircase led up from a courtyard at the back, and the windows looked across the narrow alley that separated them from the walls of Wadowice's main church, the Church of Our Lady of Perpetual Succour. There was a holy water stoop at the door of the apartment so that people could bless themselves as they came in and out, and a small altar where the family said prayers each day.

Religion was always central to the Wojtylas' family life, and became more so as death reduced its numbers. John Paul once said of his father,

> The violence of the blows which had struck him had opened up immense spiritual depths in him; his grief found its outlet in prayer. The mere fact of seeing him on his knees had a decisive influence on my early years. He was so hard on himself that he had no need to be hard on his son; his example alone was sufficient to inculcate discipline and a sense of duty.

The papal memory is corroborated by that of one of his friends, who later said of Karol senior, 'He had great personal discipline and he demanded the same from his son,' adding to the impression of a somewhat severe household with the observation that 'Their financial situation was such that they had to live frugally.' Karol senior was generally respected in the town but appears to have had only one close friend, a Mr Banas who ran a snack bar. A member of the Banas family has given this account of the young Karol's daily routine:

After the death of his mother, the rhythm of his life at home was very structured; school, dinner in the milk bar of Mr and Mrs Banas . . . two hours of play, homework, in the evening a walk with his father. Games; playing ball, running; on rainy days Ping-Pong in the Catholic Home. He did not take vacations away from home.

Father and son would say the rosary and read the Bible together, and the habit of prayer communicated itself from one to the other. The younger Karol stopped at the church in Wadowice before and after school each day as a matter of routine, according to the contemporary just quoted. Another of his school friends remembers doing homework with him in the Wojtylas' kitchen. Each time Karol finished his task in one subject he would, before moving on to the next, excuse himself and leave the room. 'Once,' his school friend later remembered, 'the door to the next room was ajar, and I saw that Karol was on the *prie-dieu* praying.' When he was thirteen he put himself forward as a candidate for membership of his school's 'Sodality of Mary'. He was admitted two years later and elected president in 1936.

But it would be wrong to think of Karol Wojtyla as some kind of emotional freak, nurtured only by stern fatherly love, Polish high romanticism and intense religiosity. Almost all the contemporary accounts of his childhood portray him as an outgoing boy with a keen interest in the world around him. A priest who taught him when he was ten years old remembers him as 'a very lively boy, very talented, very sharp and very good' who 'showed great loyalty to his friends' and avoided trouble with his teachers. Fr Figlewicz makes particular mention of Karol's optimistic nature but adds the acute observation: 'upon closer acquaintance one could detect the effects of his being orphaned at an early age'. There was a terrifying incident in the Banas snack bar which, though very nearly fatal, suggests he had a healthy familiarity with the anarchic world of small boys. The local police officer used to give his revolver to Mr Banas for safe-keeping when he came in for a drinking session, and on one afternoon Banas junior pulled it out of the till and pointed it at his school friend Karol; 'I was only joking, of course,' he later remembered, 'but before I knew it I'd pulled the trigger and the gun went off. It was pointing straight at Karol, and it's a marvel I didn't kill him. The bullet missed him by a hair's breadth and broke a window.'

The young Karol was tremendously sporty. For his 1983 biography the BBC journalist David Willey talked to a school friend who remembers that Karol Wojtyla 'kept goal in the school soccer team and was a deft hand at ping-pong. There were afternoons of compulsory sports at school, volleyball or basketball in the summer and skiing in the winter.' He earned the nickname 'Martyna' – a famous soccer star of the time – because of his prowess as a goalie, and there is a story – slightly at odds with most of what we know of his home life – that he and his father would push all the furniture to the wall of one room in their flat and play football with a rolled-up rag. Karol Wojtyla's athleticism endured well into adulthood and was of course seized upon hungrily by the profile writers when he became pope. It seemed a reflection of a certain capaciousness of personality not usually associated with great prelates of the Roman Church.

Notoriously elliptical in his early philosophical works, John Paul becomes almost childlike in the simplicity of his style when writing about this period of his youth from the distance of age. 'I remember,' he says in *Threshold of Hope*, his written interview with the Italian journalist Vittorio Messori in 1994,

> above all, the Wadowice elementary school, where at least a fourth of the pupils in my class were Jewish. I should mention my friendship at school with one of them, Jerzy Kluger – a friendship that has lasted from my school days to the present. I can vividly remember the Jews who gathered every Saturday at the synagogue behind our school. Both religious groups, Catholics and Jews, were united, I presume, by the awareness that they prayed to the same God.

Karol Wojtyla's relationship with Jews and Judaism is one of the brightest and most attractive threads in this remarkable tapestry of a life, and it begins with his childhood friendships.

Jerzy Kluger's father was a lawyer with an imposing house on the market square, and he was acknowledged as the leader of the

town's Jewish community. Dr Wilhelm Kluger was also an enthusiastic champion of Jewish integration, a tireless diplomat in the
service of good relations between Jews and Catholics, and a
determined believer in a Polish future for the country's Jewish
community. His wife's family, the Hupperts, were Jewish grandees
who owned a substantial amount of property in Wadowice
and had given the town its public park. Old Mrs Huppert,
Dr Kluger's mother-in-law, was well known for her regular
afternoon walks in the company of Canon Prochownik, the parish
priest, which were taken as a public symbol of the amity between
the Jewish and Catholic communities in Wadowice, and at the
town's annual regimental ball the colonel of Karol senior's
12th Infantry Regiment would always open the dancing with her
daughter, Mrs Kluger. By and large Wadowice seems to have
reflected the best aspects of the long and highly ambiguous
relationship between Jews and ethnic Poles.

It seems likely that there were Jews in what is now Poland even
before Christianity arrived there. The first formal recognition of
their status comes in the General Charter of Jewish Liberties,
which was introduced in 1264 by the rather charmingly named
Boleslaus the Modest, and from the Middle Ages onwards Jews
were welcomed into Poland by the kings and nobility of the old
Polish–Lithuanian Commonwealth – often they were fleeing from
persecution elsewhere in Europe. In the early sixteenth century
Jewish immigration was encouraged as a matter of policy by
Sigismund I, and the Jewish community was given both royal
protection and a considerable degree of autonomy, governing its
own affairs under a system of elected Elders. Jews became a
separate 'estate' of the realm, like the nobles, clergy, peasants and
burghers.

During the Reformation Poland earned a general reputation
for religious tolerance which was reflected in the soubriquet 'the
state without bonfires', and one of the great Krakow rabbis of the
sixteenth century is reported to have observed that 'It is better to
live on dry bread, but in peace, in Poland.' When the first Polish
Republic was formed in 1569 there were some 200,000 Jews in
Poland – by the time the Republic ended in 1795 the figure was
800,000. And the expansion of the Jewish community continued

steadily. In the nineteenth century the lands of the partitioned Poland contained, in the words of the historian Norman Davies, 'the main reservoir of Jewish manpower and intellectual dynamism in the world', its Jewish population at one point accounting for an astonishing four-fifths of world Jewry.

A group calling itself the Congress of Poles of the Jewish Confession met in the year before Karol Wojtyla's birth and declared that 'The Poles of the Jewish Faith, penetrated with a sincere feeling of love for Poland will . . . serve their country as devoted sons, and will always be ready to sacrifice their lives and fortunes for its benefit and glory.' Many Jews volunteered to fight in Pilsudski's legions, fired by optimistic hopes for their future in a free and independent Poland, and in Wadowice the presence of Karol senior's 12th Infantry Regiment played a rather surprising part in encouraging good relations; Jewish soldiers were given the right to leave the town's barracks for the Sabbath, and they would be marched in formation through the streets to pray in the synagogue, returning to their quarters on Sunday.

Karol Wojtyla's experience of life in Wadowice reflected the high level of Jews in the population as a whole. There were some 2,000 Jews in the town, a fifth of the pre-war population. The Wojtylas' landlord, who ran a shop below the apartment, was Jewish, and so was one of the first girls for whom the future pope developed a fondness, a near neighbour called Regina Beer, or Ginka for short. There is no doubt at all about the depth of Karol Wojtyla's affection for his Jewish school friends. Much later in life Jerzy Kluger wound up working in Rome and would frequently be asked to lunch and dinner at the Vatican and the pope's summer residence of Castel Gandolfo. There is a touching story of a visit to Italy by another Jewish friend from Wadowice days, Poldek Goldberger, who, like Karol Wojtyla, played goalie in the school matches; he was also an enthusiastic musician, and a piano was driven out to Castel Gandolfo so that the two of them could spend an evening playing and singing old Polish songs.

If relations between Jews and Catholics in Wadowice had been entirely harmonious, then Karol Wojtyla's close friendships with Jews would be unremarkable. In fact there is ample evidence that he made a positive choice to cherish these relationships despite an underlying tension between the two communities which existed even in this apparently tolerant town. The story of the friendship between Jurek and Lolek – the nicknames by which Jerzy Kluger and Karol Wojtyla were generally known – has been told at length by the writer Darcy O'Brien in *The Hidden Pope*, and he paints a picture of a society in which good community relations had to be preserved through determined efforts by leading figures on both sides.

Anti-Jewish feeling was especially marked among the peasantry who worked the land in the surrounding Carpathian countryside; the old blood libel – that Jews stole and murdered Christian children so that they could use their blood at the Passover supper – was alive and well out in the sticks, and the wealth of urban Jewish families like the Klugers and the Hupperts was an object of resentment among people whose way of life had not changed very much since the Middle Ages. Not far from Wadowice there was a place of pilgrimage called Kalwaria Zebryzdowska, the work of an early seventeenth-century squire of Krakow. Struck by what he supposed to be the place's resemblance to Jerusalem, he established a monastery on a hillside and then constructed a series of chapels – twenty-four were built by 1617 – to re-create the setting for Christ's Passion. Tens of thousands of pilgrims would visit the site every year (including the Wojtylas, who went regularly) – and a highpoint in the 1930s was a Passion Play with distinctly anti-Semitic undertones. It portrayed Jews as Christ-killers, and because the pilgrims joined in the performance, walking the Stations of the Cross themselves and becoming caught up in the action, it stirred strong feelings. Incidents of violence against Jews and Jewish property, usually committed by young peasants fired up with perverted religious fervour and vodka, were a routine feature of Holy Week in the area.

Some of the efforts to keep this kind of thing in check were rooted in the past; many of the landed grandees in the region had often used Jewish agents to administer their estates and manage their businesses, and there was a tradition of turning to so-called 'Jewish Uncles', counts and princes who would use their power to protect Jewish families they had come to value. As anti-Semitism grew and spread during the 1930s and the old social structures felt the pressure of twentieth-century change, community leaders turned to more opportunistic and increasingly desperate measures to keep the peace; Jerzy's father Wilhelm showed the sensitivity of his antennae in this area when a young but already famous Jewish tenor, Moishe Kussawiecki, arrived in Wadowice to complete his military service in 1937. Dr Kluger arranged for him to substitute for the cantor in the town's synagogue, and invited several Catholics – including the future pope and his father – to hear him sing. It was an unprecedented gesture: the performance was memorable, the young Jewish musical superstar wore his Polish uniform and his military forage cap instead of a yarmulke, and it was by all accounts a brilliant diplomatic stroke.

There were two anti-Semitic boys in Karol Wojtyla's class and there were a couple of anti-Semitic teachers at the school too – one taught physics, the other geography, which, in Darcy O'Brien's words, 'gave him ample opportunities to discuss concentrations of wealth, demographics, and so on, encouraging the two hostile students to join in'. Other teachers – notably a Professor Gebhardt – actively tried to counter this kind of thing. Professor Gebhardt encouraged Jerzy Kluger to talk about anti-Semitism in debates on current affairs. O'Brien describes these occasions like this:

'There is an international conspiracy of world Jewry,' one of the anti-Semites would say again and again. 'Jews are foreigners. All you have to do is look at them and hear them talk!' The boy was repeating the line adhered to by Roman Dmowksi, head of the National Democratic Movement, who, with other right-wing politicians, was expressing interest in a German scheme to remove Jews to Madagascar. His cohort always nodded in agreement but said nothing much himself; he was the sort of fellow who would sooner hit someone than speak.

'Who is a foreigner?' Jurek would snap back. 'We are all Poles.'

'Jews speak Yiddish. They have no nation.'

'Do you hear me speak Yiddish? My Polish is every bit as good as yours! And by the way, what was your grade in Greek?'

Yiddish was in fact forbidden in the Kluger household – and Jurek was bright, so we can be reasonably sure that his own marks in Greek were impressive.

As Karol Wojtyla grew from childhood to adolescence he was forced to confront the fact that his friendship with Jews was not simply personal – it was a public declaration and, although he would probably not have seen it in quite these terms, a political act. School football games were often organised between teams of Jews and Catholics, and although they were by and large good-natured, the occasional shout of 'Get the Jew' from the Catholic team hinted at the potential for things turning nasty. Karol Wojtyla, however, often cheerfully offered himself as a substitute goalie on the Jewish side if they were short of players. When Jurek and Lolek took the exams which would allow them to graduate from the Wadowice primary school to the town's high school, Jurek rushed into the parish church where the future pope was serving at mass, desperate to pass on the news, and an elderly woman ticked him off for entering a Catholic church. Lolek's reported response to this incident was to ask, 'Why? Aren't we all God's children?' It is a somewhat precocious comment on ten-year-old lips, and this may be one of those pious legends that was embellished after his elevation to the papacy, but there is more than enough persuasive evidence that in his loyalty to his Jewish friends Karol Wojtyla was driven by a characteristic stubbornness about doing what he believed to be right.

In 1930 Karol Wojtyla was taken by his father on a pilgrimage to Poland's national shrine, a place called Jasna Gora, which translates as the Luminous or Shining Mountain. Just short of half a century later he would be there again as pope, telling a million of his countrymen and women that he had come to 'listen to the beating heart of the Church and of the motherland in the heart of the mother'. It was one of those arresting mystical images that spring from the mind of Wojtyla the poet as much as Wojtyla the preacher, and there was more of the same kind of thing to come – much of it spoken in a voice broken with emotion. Anyone who wanted to understand Poland, he said, must come to Jasna Gora to 'know . . . how history is interpreted in the heart of the Poles', where they could hear 'the echo of the life of the whole nation in the heart of its mother and Queen'. It is certainly true that anyone who wants to understand Karol Wojtyla must at least try to understand Jasna Gora; a cardinal who had known him since the 1970s offered me the rather arrestingly phrased view that the pope was 'brought up by Poland' and he mused that the Polish influence on his thinking had become, if anything, more rather than less marked as the years went by.

Jasna Gora is the sort of place that is almost guaranteed to annoy non-Catholics, a monument – if viewed with sceptical eyes – to the way the Church plays on the credulousness of the poor and ignorant to shore up its power and wealth. The Paulite Monastery of the Luminous Mountain stands above Czestochowa, an industrial town in the pleasant limestone hills of the Krawkowska–Czestochowa Jura. The high fortress walls and the slender tower of the monastic church give it an unmistakable silhouette and are an eloquent expression of the two roles – military and religious – it has played in Polish history. The monastery was founded in 1382 and the early building work that remains is massive in character and clearly defensive in its function. The baroque ornament which was undertaken later is extravagant in the extreme – the vaults of the church covered in rich plasterwork, its walls painted like coloured marble and its altars tricked out with marble, gilding and white plaster statues. The monastic library is entirely panelled with intarsia, the fifteenth-century Italian technique of making mosaics in marquetry, and the pale golden woods used by the monastic cabinet-maker make it the most satisfying space I have ever sat in to read a book. It is immediately apparent that a very great deal of money has been spent on all this ostentation, and the sophisticated nature of the craftsmanship on display – much of it aping foreign styles and techniques – is a stark contrast to the crude simplicity of the peasant homes which even today dominate the surrounding countryside.

But it is the Chapel of the Nativity of the Virgin, or Chapel of the Miraculous Picture as it is also known, that is most likely to enrage a passing humanist or Protestant purist. Built into the high altar is the silver-covered icon which has made Jasna Gora a place of pilgrimage for six centuries: the Black Madonna of

Czestochowa, an image of the Virgin and Child of the type known in Byzantine art as the *Hodegetria*. *Hodegetria* means 'she who points the way', and icons of this kind are usually associated with miraculous powers – the Black Madonna has them in spades. The walls of her chapel are hung with 'votaries', a jumble of pictures, presents, rosaries and crucifixes left by pilgrims who believe that she has answered their prayers. The image is protected by an ebony and silver cover; for much of the day it is concealed behind a silver screen, which, to the sound of a trumpet fanfare, is raised to reveal the sacred image to the gaze of the faithful. There is a fenced-off area around the altar to allow supplicants for the Madonna's help to walk round and round it on their knees. The monastic treasury and sacristy nearby are stuffed with an astonishing array of jewel-encrusted gold monstrances, chalices, candlesticks and crucifixes which have been brought as gifts by rich and noble pilgrims over the centuries, and the collection of embroidered liturgical vestments goes back to the fifteenth century. Rather like a Barbie doll – although this would not be a wise comparison to make while you are there – the Black Madonna has her own sets of clothes – 'votive garments' – which are changed with the liturgical calendar.

She has been given an especially illustrious provenance; the image is said to have been painted as a family portrait by St Luke the Evangelist, on a piece of wood taken from the Holy Family's dining table. First brought to Czestochowa in 1384, the icon was torn down and attacked with swords in the monastic courtyard during a Hussite rebellion in 1430; it was restored, but the Virgin still bears two deep scars on her left cheek in memory of that attack. The incident which gave the Black Madonna her unique place in the Polish national consciousness occurred in 1655, during the last of Poland's wars with Sweden.

Charles X of Sweden's invasion of the Polish Republic that year was quite unexpected, and he very quickly managed to take Warsaw and Krakow, persuading a large part of the Polish army to defect. Before long the only remaining point of serious resistance to Swedish dominance was the fortress monastery of Jasna Gora, to which the Swedes duly laid siege, no doubt attracted by the large amount of pilgrim booty which they knew was stashed away within the walls. The Swedish army was 9,000 strong, well equipped with the necessary cannon and mortars, and presumably arrived expecting a reasonably easy victory over the monks.

But they failed to consider the power of the Black Madonna. They made the mistake of pressing home their attack on the feast of the Transfiguration of the Virgin, and encountered a resistance which, according to the Polish chronicles of the event, can only be ascribed to divine intervention. 'The cannon-balls bounced off the walls and tiles or flew over the church roof, causing no damage', and within the monastery 'a grenade which landed and exploded in a baby's cradle did not hurt him'. Muller, the Swedish commander, was said to have seen 'a Lady in a shining robe on the walls, priming the cannon and tossing shells back in the direction from which they came'. After more than a month of this kind of thing the Swedes were forced to give up and go home, and it proved a turning point in the war. The Polish Republic lived on for another century and a half. 'Of course,' says the chronicler, 'no heretic will believe that cannon-balls were repulsed from the walls of Jasna Gora by supernatural means . . . But all that I have described is true, though Swedish chroniclers are silent about these events, suppressing their shame and . . . the need to praise God for the successful defence.'

The likely response of the secular modern historian to this interpretation of events is not difficult to imagine, but even to a believing Christian who is prepared to give the supernatural the benefit of the doubt from time to time it poses all sorts of awkward questions. The history of the icon of the Black Madonna is, to put it at its mildest, murky. St Luke never knew Jesus, much less Mary, and probably wrote his Gospel in Rome at least half a century after the crucifixion in Jerusalem, so the idea that he had access to discarded items of the Holy Family's household effects is implausible; the scholarly consensus puts the image's creation at some point between the sixth and thirteenth centuries. The concept of the Virgin as a sort of warrior goddess is worrying, and the idea of monks sallying forth and slashing away with their swords – as they are said to have done periodically when the Swedes showed signs of weakening – scarcely accords with the modern understanding of the monastic vocation. Nor, come to that, does the acquisitiveness of the monks of Jasna Gora, which seems to have endured until the present day; I filmed there for a television documentary in the late 1990s, and was startled by the determination with which the procurator (the monastic finance director) negotiated a 'facility fee' for our work there.

None of these sceptical thoughts, however, would have occurred to the recently bereaved and imaginatively impressionable ten-year-old who made a pilgrimage to Jasna Gora in 1930. The events of 1655 are dramatically described in those works of Sienkiewicz he had heard read by his father. The siege of Jasna Gora is seen through the eyes of one Kmita, a knight who arrives to warn the monks of the Swedes' intention to take the monastery. Kmita goes first to the Chapel of the Black Madonna and witnesses the collective ecstasy as her screen is drawn back to reveal her to the crowd:

> All at once a thunder of trumpets and drums roared, and a quiver passed through all hearts. The covering before the picture was pushed apart from the centre to the sides, and a flood of diamond light flashed from above on the faithful.
>
> Groans, weeping, and cries were heard throughout the chapel. *'Salve, Regina!'* (Hail, O Queen!) cried the nobles, *'Monstra te esse matrem'* (Show thyself a mother); but the peasants cried, 'O most Holy Lady! Golden Lady! Queen of Angels! Save us, assist us, console us, pity us!'
>
> Long did those cries sound, together with sobs of women and complaints of the hapless, with prayers for a miracle on the sick or the maimed.
>
> The soul lacked little of leaving Kmita; he felt only that he had before him infinity, which he could not grasp, could not comprehend, and before which all things were effaced.

The pilgrims at Jasna Gora can be pretty fervent even today, and the scene the ten-year-old Karol Wojtyla saw was probably not so very different from that described by his favourite bedtime author. For most children brought up in Western Europe in the twenty-first century it would be bewildering and perhaps rather frightening, but when Karol Wojtyla stood before an 'infinity which he could not grasp', it was an experience sanctified by literature. What is more he would – like most Catholics even today, and certainly almost all the Polish Catholics of that generation – have been perfectly comfortable with the idea of divine intervention in human affairs in a visible or tangible way; so when he looked around at the votive offerings cramming the walls he would not have seen the tawdry trappings of credulousness, but would have felt inspired by the yearning of all those thousands of souls who had come to Jasna Gora over the centuries hoping for an answer to their prayers.

The Black Madonna is a prominent presence in the works of another Polish writer, the high priest of Polish romanticism and messianism, Adam Mickiewicz. The future pope may have been too young to have read Mickiewicz on his first visit to Czestochowa, but he was to become one of Karol Wojtyla's favourite authors in adolescence, and a love of his work endured into Pope John Paul's old age. Mickiewicz's best-known hero, Pan (an honorific roughly equivalent to 'Lord') Tadeusz, apostrophises his divided country thus:

> My country, thou
> Art like good health, I never knew till now
> How precious, till I lost thee. Now I see
> Thy beauty whole, because I yearn for thee.
> O Holy Maid, who Czestochowa's shrine
> Dost guard and on the Pointed Gateway shine
> And watchest Novogrodek's pinnacle,
> As thou didst heal me by a miracle . . .
> So by a miracle thou wilt bring us home.

The idea that the Black Madonna had a special role to play in Poland's national history took root after the mysterious events surrounding the lifting of the Swedish siege in 1655, and there was an attempt to give this belief a kind of objective reality when, in 1717, she was crowned 'Queen of Poland' at a ceremony attended by 200,000 people, an astonishing number at that period. Half a century later she again played a part in one of the epic struggles of Polish nationalism when the Polish leader Kasimierz

Pulaski led a revolt against Catherine the Great's forces and made the Jasna Gora monastery the site of his heroic last stand. It is a commonplace of Polish history that during the years of partition and foreign domination the Black Madonna embodied the spirit of the Polish nation and kept the very idea of Poland alive.

Karol Wojtyla made regular pilgrimages to Czestochowa throughout his youth – most of his Catholic contemporaries in Wadowice would have done the same – and it is impossible to overstate the importance of the Jasna Gora experience in the formation of his mind. The legends surrounding the place had all the power of the very best children's stories, but they came with the authority of adult endorsement. What is more, the literature and history that he was beginning to lap up at school and at home confirmed their truth: these were not mere peasant superstitions, but the subject of Poland's greatest writing and the cornerstone of her politics and the sense of national identity that drove them. This mixture of religious fervour, poetry and nationalism must have been especially intoxicating to a child growing up in a Poland which was enjoying its first experience of freedom over a century. Those puzzled by the paradox of a pope who combined John Paul's high intellectualism with his apparently easy-going acceptance of the supernatural will find part of the answer on this most numinous – to Polish Catholics, at least – hilltop.

Karol Wojtyla's early interest in the theatre was closely associated with a family who supplied some of the warmth missing from his own home. The Kotlarczyks ran Wadowice's theatre; their apartment was close to his school, and Karol Wojtyla gravitated towards them because he was 'trying to find friends and close family'. By the time he had become a teenager he had been drawn into the Kotlarczyk family circle and had become a passionate theatre-goer and would-be actor. He was soon performing regularly with the Kotlarczyks and in school productions, and he had a spectacular ability to learn lines. On one occasion he played both male leads in a drama by the Polish author Julius Slowacki; a member of the cast was suspended by the school authorities for threatening a teacher, and although there were only forty-eight hours before the first performance, Karol Wojtyla revealed that he had already stored the part in his head during rehearsals.

This new world seems to have given him the first opportunity to escape beyond the sphere of his father's influence. He would often drop in at the Kotlarczyks' after school to be fed and to listen to Mieczyslaw Kotlarczyk, the father of the household and the manager of the family's theatre, talk about performance techniques. Karol senior would pick him up from the apartment after work, but he never once stopped in to exchange pleasantries with the family who had been looking after his son, and no one can remember him attending any of Karol junior's performances.

The development of this adolescent enthusiasm coincided with Karol Wojtyla's first serious relationships with girls. He was close to two in particular – the headmaster's daughter, Halina Krolikiewicz, and his neighbour, Ginka Beer, who was a couple of years older than him – both shared his thespian passion and both were very beautiful. Jurek Kluger describes Ginka as a Jewish beauty with 'stupendous eyes and jet black hair, slender, a superb actress', and Halina is remembered as 'heart-stoppingly attractive in face and figure' (she went on to have a stage and television career).

The relationship between Karol and Ginka reflected the age difference between them; she acted as his drama coach, mentor, and perhaps to some extent as the elder sister he never had. Karol and Halina distinguished themselves as the stars of their generation, and would frequently be paired as the male/female lead. At his school graduation ball it was with Halina that Karol Wojtyla danced; their closeness continued at university, and perhaps inevitably there has been plenty of prurient speculation about the nature of the relationship. Halina later categorically denied even a platonic romance: 'I never dated him – never,' she said. However, in the week of John Paul's death in 2005 the now retired and widowed actress told a Berlin newspaper that he was the 'love of my life'. The article was accompanied by a publicity photograph of her in her stunning prime, seductively parted lips tipped towards the camera.

The pope is one of the very few public figures whose past sex life is – arguably at least – a legitimate focus for journalistic enquiry. We would think it reasonable to ask whether the Chancellor of the Exchequer had a background in city finance or a history of dodgy tax returns, because he makes the financial rules within which the rest of us live and work, and his experience and probity in the field are both relevant to our confidence in his ability to do the job. The pope is responsible for the rules which are supposed to regulate the sex lives of hundreds of millions of Catholics. As a young man Karol Wojtyla seems to have appreciated the force of this line of reasoning as it can be applied to the celibate Catholic priesthood in general, and in the introduction to *Love and Responsibility*, his 1960 book on sexual ethics, he tackles it head on. 'It is sometimes said that only those who live a conjugal life can pronounce on the subject of marriage, and only those who have experienced it can pronounce on love between man and woman,' he writes. 'In this view, all pronouncements based on such matters must be based on personal experience, so that priests and persons living a celibate life can have nothing to say on questions of love and marriage.' Not so, he argues: 'in their pastoral work they [priests] encounter these particular problems so often, and in such a variety of circumstances, that a different kind of experience is created, which is certainly less immediate, and certainly "second-hand", but at the same time very much wider.'

Karol Wojtyla's view of sex and his wider understanding of the relationship between experience and moral theology are issues I shall return to often, because they are central to an understanding of who he was and what he did. As far as his teenage relationships are concerned, the social mores of the period would make it extremely surprising if they had been consummated. In the 1990s he wrote a reproachful letter to one of his biographers, a Carmelite priest, who had suggested that as a young man Karol Wojtyla 'regained' grace through confession. 'To regain implies that I had lost, through grave sin, the grace of God,' he wrote. 'Who told you that I had committed grave sins in my youth? It never happened. Can't you believe, Father, that a young man can live without committing mortal sin?' As a denial of past sexual indiscretion it is perhaps slightly coy, but a denial it would seem to be, and there is absolutely no reliable evidence that suggests we should take it at anything other than face value. Equally, there is nothing in the accounts of this period of his life to suggest that he was awkward about girls or found them difficult to deal with, and there is certainly no hint of incipient misogyny in his intense friendships with Ginka and Halina.

In 1936 Ginka Beer left school with the intention of studying medicine in Krakow; her experience was to provide Karol Wojtyla with his first direct insight into the ugly side of the Poland beyond his world in Wadowice. The government had set an unspecified quota for Jewish students and she was turned down – Jews had typically accounted for a quarter of the student body at the Jagiellonian University, but the proportion quickly dropped to 8 per cent. Ginka's headmistress, a formidable woman who had fought with Marshall Pilsudski's legions and won Poland's highest military honour, travelled to Krakow herself to argue the case and eventually prevailed, and that autumn Karol Wojtyla was at the train station with Ginka's friends and family to wave goodbye when she set off for student life in Krakow.

But she was back before the academic year was out. Her roommate had a communist boyfriend and he had been found by the police hiding out in their digs. Both girls were reported to the authorities, and Ginka had been forced to withdraw from the university. Perhaps even more disturbingly, however, she told her parents that she had encountered widespread anti-Semitism from her fellow undergraduates. It confirmed her parents' growing conviction that Poland was no longer safe for Jews, and they decided that the family should leave for Palestine. They managed to secure Ginka one of the coveted work permits which the British mandate authorities then required from immigrating Jews, and sent her on ahead (they never joined her as planned; Ginka's mother died in Auschwitz, her father was killed in the Soviet Union).

Ginka's account of her farewell to her neighbours the Wojtylas is vivid:

There was only one family that never showed any racial hostility towards us, and that was Lolek and his Dad . . . I went to say goodbye to Lolek and his father. Mr Wojtyla was upset about my departure, and when he asked me why, I told him. Again and again he said to me, 'Not all Poles are anti-Semitic. You

know I'm not!' I spoke to him frankly and said that very few
Poles were like him. He was upset. But Lolek was even more
upset than his father. He did not say a word, but his face went
very red. I said farewell to him as kindly as I could, but he was
so moved that he could not find a single word in reply. So I just
shook the father's hand and left.

Karol senior's fundamental decency – an important counterpoint
to that coldness that seems to have lain at the core of his character
– shines through, but even more striking is the tongue-tied
emotion of his son. No doubt the future pope was indeed ashamed
of his anti-Semitic compatriots, but his reaction might also have
something to do with the fact that he was a seventeen-year-old boy
saying goodbye to a very pretty girl of a similar age.

The Beer family's experiences reflected a sharp and general
decline in Jewish security throughout Poland as the 1930s
advanced. The roots of modern Polish anti-Semitism lie in
a complex interaction of social and political trends in the
late nineteenth century. The spread of nationalism generally
throughout Europe made the politics of identity more prominent, and in Poland the development of Zionism alongside a
resurgent Polish nationalism exacerbated inter-ethnic tensions.
The impact of Poland's continued repression by foreign powers
in the years before the First World War had the effect of
putting the lid on a boiling saucepan. 'In the age of rampant
Nationalism,' as the historian of Poland Norman Davies puts it,
'inter-communal solidarity was badly hampered. So long as
the Empires of the partitioning powers remained in place, the
numerous nations of the region were trapped like rats in a cage,
where it was easier to bite one's neighbour than to break down
the bars of the common servitude.' And the hopes of a new
future for 'Poles of a Jewish Confession' which I have referred to
above finally foundered in the aftermath of Marshall Pilsudski's
death in 1935.

Pilsudski was an overwhelmingly dominant figure in the Polish
Republic which was born in 1919, and his legacy when he left
the stage was mixed. His reputation as the military saviour of the
nation in 1920 had given the army a powerful position in

the nation's political life which paved the way for the 'era of the colonels' when he died. Anti-Semitism acquired more and more semi-official respectability; government decrees like the cap on the number of Jews allowed to attend the country's universities were accompanied by economic boycotts against Jewish businesses, doctors and lawyers. John Maynard Keynes was prompted to describe Poland as 'an economic impossibility whose only industry is Jew-baiting'. Anti-Semitism became a sure way to sell newspapers and a cheap way to popularity for politicians. Jews were widely associated in the public mind with the left – an especially damaging association in the light of Poland's recent conflict with Soviet Russia – and to its great shame the Roman Catholic Church joined in the ugly game. Cardinal Hlond, the Archbishop of Gniezno and primate of Poland, wrote the following notorious passage in a pastoral letter:

> There will be a Jewish problem as long as the Jews remain . . . it is a fact that the Jews are fighting against the Catholic Church, persisting in free thinking, and are the vanguard of godlessness, Bolshevism, and subversion . . . It is a fact that the Jews deceive, levy interest, and are pimps. It is a fact that the religious and ethical influence of the Jewish young people on Polish people is a negative one.

Those words were read out from church pulpits in 1936, the year of Ginka Beer's painful discovery that not all Poles were as tolerant as her neighbours the Wojtylas.

In May 1938 Karol Wojtyla took his final secondary school exams. The results were almost repulsively exemplary:

> He received the following final grades in the subjects under examination: Religion – Very Good, Polish – Very Good, Latin – Very Good, Greek – Very Good, German – Very Good. He also received the following final grades in these subjects studied in the years 6 through 8: History and Current Polish Affairs – Very Good, Introduction to Philosophy – Very Good, Physical Education – Very Good, Hygiene – Very Good. The State Examinations Commission has found Karol Wojtyla to be

mature and adequately prepared to pursue higher studies, and hereby confers upon him this Secondary School Diploma.

It was, as we should say today, straight As – although it is interesting to note that the subjects he had studied included not a single discipline in empirically based science. At the end of May Karol Wojtyla was chosen to give the students' address on behalf of the graduating class of the Wadowice Gymnasium – his high school diploma, with seal, was presented on his registration at the Jagiellonian University of Krakow on 22 June.

The decision that the future pope was, like his brother, to study at the Jagiellonian meant that Karols father and son both decamped to the city of Krakow – there was little to hold the older man in the threadbare life he had lived in Wadowice. They set themselves up in dank quarters – a basement flat close by the banks of the River Vistula. They were tenants of Emilia Wojtyla's family – her brother and two of her sisters owned the building and lived on the top floor – and the Wojtylas' area of the living quarters was known locally as 'the catacombs'. Despite the fact that the future pope shared some of the most dramatic years of any period in history with his uncle and aunts, they do not feature in his or anyone else's recorded memories of the period.

The Anschluss – Hitler's annexation of Austria – took place a month before Karol Wojtyla's final high school exams. Hitler and Mussolini met to cement their friendship in the week before he sat down to the papers which would produce such stunning results at the Wadowice Gymnasium, and on 18 May, as he awaited his results, the Nazis introduced compulsory physical exercise in Vienna. In June, as the Wojtylas prepared for their big move, the new rulers of Austria insisted that all Austrians who wanted to marry must prove their Aryan ancestry, and later that month Jewish employees in the country were given fourteen days' notice of redundancy. There was a report of an unusually high number of suicides among Viennese Jews on 5 July, and on the 22nd of the month the government in Berlin issued an edict instructing Jewish citizens to carry special identity cards.

With the decision to move to Krakow, Karol Wojtyla had taken an unwitting step towards the heart of what was about to be humanity's most dreadful holocaust. His past belonged to an unimaginably distant era; Wadowice knew little of the trench horrors which dragged most of Europe into the twentieth century, and with its cosy provincialism, its horse-drawn carts (there were fewer than half a dozen motor cars there in the 1930s) and its determinedly fostered social solidarity the town really belonged to the nineteenth. But the twentieth century was about to hit Krakow like an express train.

At eighteen Karol Wojtyla is clever, holy, and a lover of life. And – this judgement was offered by someone who came to know him well in later life – there is a steely sliver of his father's coldness settling in his soul.

2

A Young Man in Wartime

Pull any image you please from your mental file marked 'Nazi Atrocities' and you can almost certainly give Karol Wojtyla a plausible place in the picture. Think of columns of refugees along country roads being attacked from the air by German planes, of Jews being rounded up and confined to ghettos, of deportations to the concentration camps, of the knock on the door in the night and random acts of officially sanctioned murder on the streets by day; the late pope lived these things. The Nazis ruled the area of Poland they designated as the 'General-Gouvernement' with far more savagery than they used in their Western conquests like France and Belgium, and the occupation there continued for longer than it did anywhere else in the East. So to live in the General-Gouvernement for the years of the Second World War really was to live in the heart of the darkness that engulfed Europe – and Krakow was the capital of the General-Gouvernement.

The Karol Wojtyla who turned up at the Jagiellonian University in Krakow a year before the war began is remembered by his contemporaries as a somewhat singular figure – not quite odd, but definitely out of the ordinary. His relatively humble origins attracted more comment in the cosmopolitan city; a student who sat next to him in lectures remembers that he turned up on the first day 'in cotton drill cloth', and describes him as 'always poorly dressed, giving the impression of a village boy, socially unpolished but of strong character'. There is an attractive photograph of him at this period standing between two pillars of the Jagiellonian's Collegium Maius, his cap at a jaunty angle over one eye and his overcoat slightly too big, very much the young student eager for life.

He was uncompromisingly high-minded; the list of courses he signed up for included the Principles of Polish Etymology, Elements of Polish Descriptive Phonetics, Polish Medieval Literature and Old Polish Literature, Introductory Russian and a variety of lectures and seminars in the theory and practice of drama, poetry and the novel. One fellow student remembers him taking part in 'heated, emotional' discussions which would spill out into the hallways after their seminars on contemporary literature had ended. Another recalls a class at which Wojtyla presented a report on 'Mme de Stael as a Theorist of Romanticism': 'The treatment was very comprehensive,' he observes, with what one hopes is a degree of irony, 'the author continued to present it over several succeeding sessions.' And the *Kalendarium*, that invaluable collection of first-hand evidence about the pope's early life, gives us another glimpse of Wojtyla's stubborn insistence on doing what he believed to be right: a contemporary who was not part of his close circle of friends stated, 'I remember that Karol Wojtyla often accompanied Anka Weber and played a particular role with regard to her. As I perceived it then, and as I perceive it now, he protected her, a Jew, from potential aggression.'

His exam results in June 1939 include the first recorded lapse from his straight A performance as a student – he was graded merely 'Satisfactory' in Old Church Slavonic. But the *viva* examination in Descriptive Grammar was concluded with the usual 'Good' grade, and he joined happily in a party given by one of his classmates at her parents' home. 'There was some wine and we danced to the gramophone,' one of the other guests recalled. 'He danced along with the rest of us, but he was more interested in conversation than in dancing.' The picture of a young academic in the making is endorsed by Pope John Paul's own memories. In the reflections on this period he published in 2004 he mused that 'but for the outbreak of war and the radical change that it brought, maybe the prospects opening up for me through academic study would have absorbed me completely'.

Almost every young man in Europe that summer must have given at least a passing thought to the possibility of war, and young Poles had especially good reason to consider the likelihood that they would soon be asked to bear arms in combat; Berlin's propaganda machine was pressing German claims on Danzig, the Polish city of Gdansk, and in April Hitler had renounced the Polish–German non-aggression pact. But Karol Wojtyla never seems to have expressed any enthusiasm for the idea of serving his country as a soldier. Like everyone else he had enrolled in the Academic Military Legion when he arrived at university, received his uniform – four-cornered cap, cloth jacket, infantry trousers and puttees – and had gone through his six-day introductory training course. But because of his university studies he was formally exempted from military service by the prefect of Wadowice early in his academic career, and, with what in retrospect looks like a certain flair for dramatic timing, he handed back his Academic Legion uniform on 30 August 1939, just two days before the German invasion of Poland. There is no record of what his soldier father, Karol Wojtyla senior, made of this, and the future pope's own thinking on the question of military service at the time remains obscure. But it is a striking characteristic of his life during this period that despite giving every sign of personal courage he remained determinedly non-violent.

The darkest chapter in Poland's history began with a deadly piece of pantomime: the Nazis staged a fake Polish invasion of Germany. On the evening of 31 August 1939 a *Sturmbanfuehrer* of the Nazi Security Service, disguised as a Polish officer, led an attack on a German radio station in Upper Silesia. His unit included a dozen convicted criminals who had been promised an amnesty in return for taking part in the operation; once they had been allowed to overpower the station guards and broadcast a few patriotic words in Polish they were mown down by SS machine-gunners. When the local police turned up, the pile of corpses in bloodsoaked Polish uniforms provided the necessary evidence of Polish aggression, and Hitler had the provocation he wanted for a full-scale invasion. Just before six the following morning German troops poured over the border.

It is entirely in keeping with Karol Wojtyla's character that on the morning of 1 September 1939, amid the unfolding drama of the beginning of the Second World War, he was doggedly pursuing his own agenda. It was the first Friday of the month, and that meant making his confession – so he walked from the damp apartment he shared with his father to Krakow's Wawel Cathedral. His confessor was Fr Kazimierz Figlewicz, who had given him religious instruction as a child in Wadowice and had since been transferred to Krakow. 'The morning air raids on Krakow caused a panic among the workers at the Cathedral,' Fr Kazimierz later remembered, 'so I had no one to serve mass.' Karol Wojtyla was roped in to perform the role, and his first wartime mass was completed 'amid the howl of sirens and the blast of explosions'.

There were air raids on Warsaw, Lodz, Czestochowa and Poznan as well as Krakow – Germany deployed some 2,000 aircraft against the 400 of the Polish air force. History has marked down the German assault on Poland as the world's first experience of a new kind of warfare: 'Blitzkrieg', an all-out attack launched with bewildering speed and overwhelming force. The people of Krakow would have had no frame of reference or collective memory for understanding what was happening to them. Karol Wojtyla and a young friend occupied themselves loading handcarts for neighbours who thought that they and their possessions might be safer in the suburbs. The future pope's friend recalled that as they worked they were caught in an air raid directed at a nearby radio station: 'Karol remained calm. Even during the worst explosions we did not exchange a word. Eventually his calmness spread to me.'

Calm or not, the Wojtylas decided to do what civilians had often done in the region's many wars; they packed up a suitcase and headed away from the front. Like most Poles in the first days of the German invasion, they would have believed that Poland's allies would soon come to her aid so that they could return home. The news reaching the outside world from the areas coming under German control at this stage was anything but encouraging. *The Times* newspaper concluded that 'The German army has won a striking military success, but has also sown a bitter harvest of hate' because of the way its troops were conducting themselves. In one village, it was reported, 'the Germans lined up the population, women, children and old men, chose every twelfth one, and shot them'. Hitler Youth brigades moved in behind the army and *The Times*' special correspondent painted this picture of the way they went about their work: 'Under their charge long rows of aged Jews, with black beards and astrakhan hats, are seen at work in the streets. Often they have no picks and shovels, and have to dig with their bare hands.'

The Wojtylas' attempt to flee was compromised by the physical condition of Karol senior, who by now was frail and heading into a somewhat premature old age. For some of the way out of Krakow Karol junior was able to beg a lift in a military truck for his father, but for the most part they just walked, like thousands of others. At one point their refugee column was strafed with machine-gun fire from a low-flying German plane. *The Times* of 20 September reported the incident as one 'which will linger long in the memory of those left alive in a column of refugees trudging from Krakow, over whom a German aeroplane flew; the 'plane dived, and machine-gunned the column without mercy.'

The attempt to escape the German advance was of course futile, and the tens of thousands of refugees clogging up the roads all over the country made the task of the Polish army even more difficult than it was. The stream of refugees trying to get into Romania – 'a pitiable caravan of human sorrow and misery', in the words of one British newspaper report – stretched twelve miles and was estimated to number 80,000. The Polish army had only 150 tanks to face a force of 2,600 deployed by the Germans, and serious Polish resistance collapsed with terrifying speed. Those romantic stories of dashing Polish cavalry charging German Panzer units on horseback were probably less widespread in reality than they have become in the telling of those early September days, but they accurately reflect the hopelessness of the Polish position.

Polish eyes turned to Britain. The British prime minister, Neville Chamberlain, had given Poland an unconditional guarantee of help in the event of a German attack. It was a gesture to deter Hitler rather than the basis for a genuine military alliance – and in retrospect it looks like the diplomatic equivalent of the last throw of the gambler's dice – but on the morning of Sunday 3 September Britain duly declared war on Germany. Cedric Salter of the *Daily Mail* was in the lobby of the Hotel Europejski in Warsaw when the news was announced on the radio. 'Silence,' he later wrote, 'held through the playing of an inordinately large number of verses of "God Save the King", and then pandemonium was let loose.' Salter joined the crowds spilling into the streets to show gratitude for this act of solidarity.

> By the time they had arrived opposite the British Embassy the crowd must have numbered a hundred thousand madly shouting men and women. Shamefacedly, looking as if he had been caught wearing a white tie with a dinner jacket, Sir Howard Kennard shuffled unhappily on to the balcony and agitated a self-deprecatory fin before diving back indoors for shelter. This exhibition of the traditional well-bred gaucherie was exactly to the crowd's liking, they having become acquainted with it through the cinema.

The *Mail*'s correspondent found himself next to an elderly man with a somewhat uncertain grasp of English: 'Grasping me by the hand, with tears standing in his eyes, he murmured again and again "Gott straf England." I had not the heart to correct him.'

Anyone British is bound to feel a certain awkwardness reading this account today. If Sir Howard Kennard had any idea of the official thinking of his government in London – and he presumably did – he had good reason to perform a shamefaced shuffle. General Ironside, the Chief of the Imperial General Staff, had promised that the RAF would match anything the Luftwaffe did in Poland with raids on Germany. In fact the only things dropped by the RAF over Germany were pamphlets; Bomber Command staged what were called 'truth raids' on Frankfurt, Munich and Stuttgart, dropping leaflets in German which set out the British view of Hitler's aggression. The bellicose Tory MP Leo Amery urged the air minister, Kingsley Wood, to drop incendiary bombs on the Black Forest as a reprisal for the attacks on Polish cities; 'You can't do that,' came the reply, 'this is private property.'

Near the San River, over a hundred miles east of Krakow, the Wojtylas heard the news that finally ended all Polish hopes: the Russians had invaded Poland from the east. The country's fate had in fact been settled before the fighting even began, when Molotov and von Ribbentrop, the foreign ministers of the Soviet

Union and Germany, signed their infamous pact in Moscow. In a secret protocol they agreed what was effectively a new partition of Poland; the protocol set out the boundaries of their respective 'spheres of influence' and, foreshadowing Poland's disappearance from the map, the two parties agreed that 'The question of whether the interests of both parties make desirable the maintenance of an independent Polish State . . . can only be definitely determined in the course of further political developments.' On 17 September 1939 Stalin sent his forces into Poland to claim his share of the spoils. Karol Wojtyla senior was exhausted by this stage, and the idea of fleeing into the arms of the Russians was anything but appealing. Father and son retraced their steps to Krakow.

Karol junior had kept up his friendship with Mieczyslaw Kotlarczyk, his theatrical guru and frequent host in Wadowice days, and in a letter to 'Mieciu' that September he paints a picture of the life the Wojtylas found on their return home. '"*Vita Cracoviensis*",' he writes, already displaying his life-long weakness for the Latin tag, 'consists of standing in line for bread, of (rare) expeditions to find sugar; also of morbid longing for coal and for reading.' In fact the Nazis had something altogether nastier than the inconvenience of food queues in mind for the vanquished people of Poland.

Northern and western Poland were simply annexed by Germany, and Karol Wojtyla's childhood home of Wadowice became part of a territory known as the 'New Reich'. The east was occupied and absorbed by the Soviet Union, and the central and southern areas between were designated as a German colony of uncertain status under the title of the General-Gouvernement. Hans Frank, who had been Hitler's lawyer, was installed in Wawel Castle as governor-general, ruling from what, in a phrase guaranteed to be especially offensive to Polish sensitivities, he insisted upon referring to as 'the ancient German city of Krakow'. He made no secret of his game-plan; 'From now on,' declared Dr Frank, 'the political role of the Polish nation is ended. It is our aim that the very concept of Polak be erased for centuries to come. Neither the Republic, nor any other form of Polish state will ever be reborn. Poland will be treated as a colony and Poles will become slaves in the German Empire.' His instructions to his subordinates were even more chilling:

> The Pole has no rights whatsoever. His only obligation is to obey what we tell him. He must be constantly reminded that his duty is to obey.
>
> A major goal of our plan is to finish off as speedily as possible all troublemaking politicians, priests, and leaders who fall into our hands. I openly admit that some thousands of so-called important Poles will have to pay with their lives, but you must not allow sympathy for individual cases to deter you in your duty, which is to ensure that the goals of National Socialism triumph and that the Polish nation is never again able to offer resistance.
>
> Every vestige of Polish culture is to be eliminated. Those Poles who seem to have Nordic appearances will be taken to Germany to work in our factories. Children of Nordic appearance will be taken from their parents and raised as German workers. The rest? They will work. They will eat little. And in the end they will die out. There will never again be a Poland.

Today it seems extraordinary that anything like ordinary life could continue in these circumstances, but on 2 November 1939 Karol Wojtyla registered for a second year at the Jagiellonian University. His good friend from Wadowice days, the headmaster's daughter Halina Krolikiewicz, said later, 'We students were so naïve we thought we would be able to complete our studies.' They were soon disabused of this notion. Three days after Karol Wojtyla's registration for a second year of studies an event took place which made it all too clear that Dr Frank was in deadly earnest. Here is a near-contemporary account of what happened from *Poland, Yesterday, To-day, To-morrow*, published in Britain in the spring of 1940:

> The German authorities asked all the members of the teaching staff of the University to attend a conference at which a German professor was to explain the German attitude towards the Polish scientists. The German lecturer began in the most vulgar

manner to slander Polish scholars and Polish science, whereupon the Polish professors indignantly left the lecture hall.

At the front of the University a number of heavy lorries were already waiting. All the 160 professors and lecturers were arrested and severely manhandled, in particular Kazimierz Kostanecki, a former President of the Polish Academy of Science; Frederic Zoll, the distinguished jurist; Wladislaw Konopczynski, the leading Polish historian; Tadeusz Lehr-Splawinski, the noted philologist; and Adam Kryzanovski, the famous economist, who has since died at the hands of the Gestapo.

All the professors, among whom many are septuagenarians, were deported to Germany and interned in a concentration camp. The fact of the arrest of the entire professorial body of one of the most ancient and famous universities in Europe, the University of Krakow, founded about the middle of the fourteenth century, has shocked the conscience of the entire civilised world.

With this action the Nazis declared war on the life of the mind in general, and the life of the Polish mind in particular. The impact on Karol Wojtyla, for whom intellectual activity was the supreme passion (perhaps, at this stage of his life, even more important than religion), must have been profound – this was altogether more shocking than being bombed and strafed from the air. The Nazis had first taken physical possession of Poland, and they now sought mastery over the inner life of its people. It was a strategy that would have made perfect sense to the future pope, precisely because he held the disciplines of learning and thought in such high regard. The evenings reading the Polish Romantics at his father's knee had taught him that the soul of a nation lives in its literature; the closure of his university and the deportation of its teachers demonstrated that Poland's enemies had learnt that lesson too.

Karol Wojtyla's cultural zealotry perhaps explains what in some ways seems a slightly eccentric reaction to the horror of life under the Nazis: he started writing plays. Vast numbers of Poles of his age were engaged in a military struggle against Germany. Troops who had escaped the invasion made their way to France, and by the spring of 1940 Poland had an army of 80,000 and a sizeable air force abroad, while at home the first serious underground resistance movement was formed as early as 27 September 1939. But none of that was for Karol Wojtyla. 'I am not a cavalier of the sword,' he wrote to his friend Mieczyslaw Kotlarczyk, 'but rather an artist.'

Karol Wojtyla's letters to his theatrical mentor at this period provide an illuminating insight into the way his thinking was evolving. Here is an account he gives of his life on 28 December 1940:

> Would you believe that I am virtually running out of time! I read, I write, I study, I think, I pray, I struggle with myself. At times I feel a great oppression, depression, despair, evil. At other times as if I am seeing the dawn, the aurora, a great light. I wrote a drama or, more precisely, a dramatic poem entitled *David*, in which he wears biblical robes and a linen shirt from the time of Piast [ninth century] and a crimson cloak of a Polish nobleman. In it I have bared many things, many matters of my soul.

It is very much the voice of a young would-be intellectual, caught up in the drama of his own consciousness. *David* has not survived, but the aspiring playwright's next offering, *Job*, which was finished in the spring of 1940, has been preserved. He himself described it in one of his letters as 'a new drama, Greek in form, Christian in spirit, eternal in substance, like *Everyman*. A drama about suffering,' adding, in a rather touchingly immodest moment, 'Some people here quite like it.' But not even his most enthusiastic fans would describe this as a crowd-pleaser today; the cast list includes such characters as Eliphaz the Temanite and Bildad the Shuhite, and it is very long on declamation and debate and very short on action. The title page is explicit about the relevance of Job's story to the Poland of 1940; it declares:

The Action Took Place in the Old Testament
Before Christ's Coming.

The Action Takes Place in Our Days
In Job's Time
For Poland and the World.

The Action Takes Place in the Time of Expectation
In the Time of Longing
For Christ's Testament
Worked out
In Poland's and the World's Suffering.

Karol Wojtyla's synopsis of the play – again in a letter to Mieczyslaw Kotlarczyk – gives us an idea of the way he was internalising and rationalising the traumatic experience of the Nazi occupation. After being told of a series of terrible disasters (herds of oxen stolen, servants slaughtered by bandits, sons killed by a collapsing roof while feasting, etc.) Job

> receives a visit from three of his friends. A dramatic exchange with them begins to develop the idea that suffering is not always a punishment but can sometimes be, often is, a presage. This is what Job thinks when, after initial rebellious impulses, his reflections lead him to the conviction that there exists the Highest Justice, all embracing Harmony. But he still cannot understand why he, the just one, is the object of God's punishment. He is helped by the young prophet Elihu. Having learnt of Job's misfortune (Job is his friend) Elihu comes to him and in his presence has a prophetic vision; he sees Christ's Passion, the Garden of Olives, Mount Calvary.

The young playwright had the very best authority for this kind of interpretation of the history he was living through in the works of his all-time literary hero, the high priest of Polish Romanticism, Adam Mickiewicz. Writing in the early nineteenth century, during the period of Polish partition, Mickiewicz developed a spiritual theory of history which drew heavily on the Christian theology of redemption. Just as personal suffering could prepare the soul for the glory of salvation, he believed, the suffering of a nation could prepare it for a messianic role in world affairs. Poland, he wrote, was the nation loved by Christ, peopled with those who 'believe, who love, and who have hope'. Its subjugation was merely a step towards the day when, as 'a Lazarus among nations', it would be reborn to fulfil its destiny as the country with 'the heritage of the future freedom of the world'. That view of history must have been powerfully sustaining during the days of Nazi occupation, and Karol Wojtyla both read and indeed performed Mickiewicz's works throughout the war. Their influence endured for far longer; one of his most dramatic sermons on his first visit to Poland as pope began with a quotation from Mickiewicz.

Karol Wojtyla's use of theatre as a weapon against the Nazi occupation was not simply a cerebral affair. He and some of his friends – including his old girlfriend from Wadowice days, Halina Krolikiewicz – began to stage clandestine performances in a private home. It was an extremely risky enterprise – the German crackdown on cultural activity was being rigorously enforced. The last Polish performance at Krakow's Julius Slowacki Theatre took place on 11 November 1939, and thereafter it was taken over by the Germans. A month later the governor-general, Hans Frank, ordered the seizure of all Polish art collections. Tapestries from Wawel Cathedral were moved next door into the royal palace he was using as his residence, and carved medieval altars were shipped back to Germany (a Rembrandt and a Leonardo disappeared altogether, to be found five years later at the Frank family home in Germany). By trying to keep a small flame of Poland's pre-war cultural life alive with their amateur dramatics, Karol Wojtyla and his friends routinely risked imprisonment or death.

It was during the writing of *Job* that Karol Wojtyla met one of the most influential but peculiar figures of his early life, a mystic tailor called Jan Tyranowski. As pope, John Paul remembered him as 'one of those unknown saints, hidden like a marvellous light at the bottom of life, at a depth where night usually reigns', but to modern ears Tyranowski sounds, frankly, rather creepy. He was a slight, stooped figure who at the relatively young age of forty already had 'decidedly greying' hair. He had trained as an accountant but gave it up because it apparently did not suit his delicate temperament, and when Karol Wojtyla met him he was supporting himself working as a tailor, running his business from a one-room apartment near the Wojtylas' home. His voice was high-pitched – 'almost a falsetto' in the words of one who knew him – and there is a photograph of him propped up in bed, dressed in white between pressed lace sheets. He is said to have taken a vow of celibacy, and there were rumours of a period spent in a mental hospital.

Tyranowski used to spend time hanging around at his local church, St Stanislaw Kostka, trying to talent-spot young men who would make suitable members of his secret prayer group, and Karol Wojtyla's frequent presence at mass there marked him down as a candidate. The group was known as the Living Rosary, and its members – all ardent Catholic young men – would be invited round to the tiny apartment on Rozana Street for spiritual instruction. Tyranowski (known as 'the Master' to the members of his group) had a well-developed taste for religion at its most mystical and contemplative, and he introduced Karol Wojtyla to the works of the sixteenth-century Spanish priest known as St John of the Cross. This is not the place for a detailed examination of St John's thinking, but it is tough stuff. 'To reach union with the wisdom of God, a person must advance by unknowing rather than knowing,' he wrote.

> They are ignorant who think it is possible to reach this high state of union with God without first emptying their appetite of all . . . things that are a hindrance to them . . . possessions, joy, knowledge, consolation, rest . . . Until the appetites are eliminated, one will not arrive, no matter how much virtue one practices. For one will fail to acquire perfect virtue, which lies in keeping the soul empty, naked, and purified of every appetite.

Karol Wojtyla lapped it all up. 'He [Tyranowski] disclosed to me the riches of his inner life,' he wrote as pope, 'of his mystical life. In his words, in his spirituality, and in the example of a life given to God alone, he represented a new world that I did not yet know. I saw the beauty of the soul opened up by grace.'

Not all the members of the Living Rosary were quite so sure. Mieczyslaw Malinski eventually became a priest and the future pope's close friend, but the first time he was approached by Jan

Tyranowski he was extremely dubious. Malinski gave me this
account of their meeting:

> I was in the habit of going out to morning mass during the
> German occupation . . . such were the times we lived in that
> leaving your house in the morning you never knew whether you
> would be back in the evening. You could get shot in the street or
> be taken to Auschwitz. That was how it was. Outside the church
> there was a man waiting for me, wearing a black overcoat, his
> wavy hair brushed back. 'May I accompany you?' he asked. My
> immediate reaction was that he was from the Gestapo and had
> come to arrest me. When I agreed to his company he said he
> too was going to Madalinskiego Street. How did he know where
> I lived?

Once the misunderstanding had been cleared up Malinski joined
the group, but did not entirely like what he found. 'I came to
enjoy our meetings less and less,' he said, and he found Tyranowski
difficult to deal with: 'There was something bossy about his
manner, and I kept wondering what he really wanted of me.' He
recalls a world of 'thorough discipline and self-control', in which
'Every moment of the day was organised for activity or relaxation',
and each day's prayers, reading and thoughts were recorded in
notebooks.

Mieczyslaw Malinski had good reason to feel anxious about being
approached by a stranger outside a church; the Nazis viewed the
Catholic Church – like the universities – as a target in their
campaign to eradicate the Polish national spirit, and the young
men who joined the Living Rosary were taking a real risk by
becoming involved in clandestine religious activity. In October
1939 the papal nuncio in Berlin presented the German government with a protest from the Vatican about the treatment of the
Church in occupied Poland; in the first six weeks after the German
invasion, it said, 117 religious houses and 211 churches had been
closed, the pastoral activities of seven bishops had been restricted,
and 193 lay and religious members of orders had been arrested on
political charges. As time went on it became apparent that the true
picture of the Church's life under Nazi rule was even grimmer. In

the spring of 1940 the religious publishing house Burns and Oates brought out a book in London, edited by Gertrude Godden, designed to raise awareness of the way the Nazis were 'attempting to monopolise the soul of Poland'. With a foreword by Cardinal Hinsley, the Archbishop of Westminster, who compared the Nazi regime to 'the barbarism of Genghis Khan', the book collates some of the stories that had begun to emerge from Poland:

> The Bishop of Posnan was interned and all his clergy were forbidden to say mass; many of the clergy were shot in the market square of the town. In Tarun the heavy work of reconstructing the bridge over the Vistula was carried out by the forced labour of prominent Polish citizens of the town, who were treated with ruthless brutality. A Catholic prelate was compelled to take part in this work, and being old and exhausted fell into the river; workmen tried to save him, but the SS Nazi guards stopped them, and themselves shot their victim dead in the water. At Gniezno, the seat of the oldest Polish Archbishopric, a See founded in the year AD 1000, and the religious capital of Poland, Canon Fablocki was shot. In Gdynia all the churches were closed . . . Mere imprisonment, or straightforward shooting, did not always satisfy the Nazi authorities when they found the clergy in their power. The Bishop of Lodz was grossly maltreated, and forced to clean the streets in front of his own cathedral, amid the jeers of the SS, i.e. the Nazi Black Guards, who are the spearhead of Hitlerism, and a crowd of young people from the local German minority.

And so it went on. By the time the war was over it is estimated that 3,646 Polish priests had been sent to concentration camps, of whom 2,647 were killed.

Against that backdrop, Karol Wojtyla's experience of being a member of a secret religious group was intense and life-defining. It may go some way to explaining the sympathy he has shown as pope for the more secretive groups that operate within the Catholic Church today. Many Catholics from the more liberal European churches have, for example, been puzzled by the patronage he has extended to the conservative spiritual movement Opus Dei, because they see something of the cult about the way it operates. But John Paul's response to the taste for discipline and discretion which is associated with Opus Dei would naturally be coloured by the memory that those were precisely the virtues which allowed him to find nourishment in the Living Rosary under Nazi rule.

The fact that Karol Wojtyla's adult understanding of his faith developed during a period of religious persecution had a profound impact on his view of the Church, and it is a subject I shall return to later. But it is worth noting here that on top of the direct experience of the Nazi repression he could see around him, it is also likely that he was beginning to hear similar stories from the Soviet-occupied zone in eastern Poland. The historian Norman Davies argues that 'In many ways, the work of the Soviet NKVD proved far more destructive than that of the Gestapo' in the early days of the war because 'Having longer experience in political terror than their German counterparts, the Soviets had no need for wasteful experimentation'. He reproduces an NKVD list of people subject to deportation which is revealing of the mindset of the Soviet secret police. It begins – of course – with '(1) Members of Russian pre-Revolutionary parties – Mensheviks, followers of Trotsky, and anarchists', and proceeds in an orderly and precise manner to '(13) Persons active in parishes; clergymen, secretaries, and active members of religious communities; (14) Aristocrats, landowners, wealthy merchants, bankers, industrialists, hotel and restaurant proprietors'.

Quite why restaurateurs were in such trouble is not clear, but the Soviet ideology with regard to the Church was very similar to that of the Nazis. The Catholic media – *The Tablet* in London, *Osservatore Romano* and Vatican Radio in Rome – began to record stories of churches being used as stables and cinemas, and *The Times* reported, more gruesomely, that 'the bodies of clergy were seen hanging from trees' by one of their informants. On 29 January 1940 the Polish Press Bulletin in London published this:

The following programme for Poland of the Soviet 'Union of Militant Godless' is reported in Lvov:
1 All churches and ecclesiastical establishments on Polish territory occupied by Soviet troops must be liquidated.

2 All clergymen and other persons belonging to the Churches must give up religious practices.

3 All properties of the Church shall be confiscated for the benefit of the State.

4 Throughout the whole area of occupied Poland branches of the Association of Soviet Godless shall be established forthwith.

5 An atheist journal, to be the official organ of the Godless, is to be published in the Polish language for distribution among the Polish population.

6 Soviet wireless stations on territories occupied in Poland shall include in their programmes appropriate atheist propaganda in the Polish language.

It is also reported that the Soviet government has placed large grants of money at the disposal of the Union of Militant Godless for the prosecution of their work in Eastern Poland.

So wherever Karol Wojtyla looked he saw a suffering Church. And while the public face of Catholicism, which had been so much part of the weave of his childhood life in Wadowice, was suppressed, Jan Tyranowski taught him that the Church can be built in the mind and the soul, whatever is happening in the world outside. It was a very powerful lesson. Father Wojtyla, in a reminiscence about his mentor published in 1949, wrote, 'He knew about the supernatural gifts deposited by Divine Grace in the depths of the human soul, and he wanted to bring forth this internal godliness in man. He wanted to discover it and make it apparent to each of his young companions. He wanted to discover this resource within man, the resource that we must continue to discover.' Towards the end of what was a very lengthy article he includes an acute observation on the way Tyranowksi's inner life allowed him to distance himself from the realities of Krakow life in the 1940s: 'It is worth noting that Jan's demeanour, for example the way he wore his watch, his expressions, all of the many details that reflect the social environment, were totally consistent with that environment. The entire difference was within.'

Karol Wojtyla's time as a manual labourer – which allowed the hagiographers great play with the idea of a 'worker priest' when he became pope – began in September 1940, almost exactly a year after the German invasion. The Nazis had passed a decree that all men between fourteen and sixty must work or face deportation, and Karol found his job at the Solvay Company through one of those connections which became so essential to survival during the occupation – it seems his French teacher had a friend who had a friend with a way into the company. But his first job there was scarcely a sinecure. The quarry was a daunting place; he and his fellow workers toiled away beneath 65-foot walls of limestone. One team of men blasted large chunks out of the rock face with dynamite; a second was given the task of breaking them up into manageable lumps which could be loaded onto trams to be taken away and used in the production of soda. Karol Wojtyla worked with the tram team. He put a brave face on what must have been a pretty brutal first encounter with a way of life he had never known before; after his first month in the quarry he wrote to his friends in Wadowice, 'Currently I am a labourer. I do physical work in a quarry. Don't be alarmed! So far I am not actually splitting rocks. I'm just laying the tracks of the tramway . . . Time flies when you're working. You become a fuller person.' The evidence of others working in the quarry is that the future pope did in fact work for a while with a pick-axe in his hands breaking rocks, and life in the open air must have become rather less appealing as autumn turned to winter; the temperature in the winter of 1940–1 dropped to thirty degrees below zero Celsius. Most of the journey to work was across open country; Karol Wojtyla would leave home each morning at 7.00 a.m. and walk for an hour in his wooden clogs to reach the quarry, working through until 4.00 p.m. On one occasion he saw a fellow worker killed when a splinter of rock pierced his brain while he was working a saw.

A number of other displaced students from the Jagiellonian University were employed by Solvay, and there is evidence that the German director of the plant 'paid the Gestapo to turn a blind eye to the high concentration of young Polish intellectuals' there. A selection of memories from those who worked with Karol Wojtyla were collected in an album called *The Nest from which I Came*, which was presented to him when he was an archbishop in the 1960s. I spent a summer working on a building site as a twenty-year-old to pay off my university debts, and the kindness showed to Wojtyla and his fellow exiles from the intellectual life will strike a chord with anyone who has done anything similar. A track worker, Jan Zyla, recalled that

> Several students had been hired into the plant . . . When they were assigned to me, manager Krauze told me to look after these people, that they could be useful, that I should not over-tire them with hard work. I put them to work digging holes, filling in under the tracks, levelling the track bed, filling under the crossties, stretching the track to a new layout. Karol Wojtyla, the present Archbishop, worked well, fulfilled his duties gladly; when he had a free moment at noon he read books. We talked about how we wanted the war to end, how we wanted to survive when it seemed we were to be crushed.

There was one grumpy reminiscence in the collection from a worker who seems to have had a rather dim view of the students who were 'using this place to hide out'; the engineer of a steam locomotive, he remembered simply seeing 'Karol Wojtyla walking about the quarry with a shovel'. The most touching of these shafts of light into this period of the pope's past comes from Franciszek Labus, a blaster to whom Karol Wojtyla was assigned in the spring of 1941 – it was a kind of promotion to lighter work organised by Mr Krauze, the plant manager. Speaking as a very sick man of ninety, Mr Labus recalled that

> He was so young when he came to work, I felt sorry for him; he was not suited to anything. I thought to myself, the best thing for him would be to become a priest. He had such small delicate hands. I didn't let him work, but he worked. I was leaving the world, and he was just entering it. He helped me coil the wire; he followed me carrying the detonators. One time, as usual, I was setting the charges, and he was standing beside me. I said to him, it would be better for you to become a priest, and he just smiled.

One of Wojtyla's friends at the quarry, Wojciech Zukrowski, was part of the combat wing of an underground resistance movement called Unia, which had been formed in the early days of the Nazi occupation. The two of them worked together on the blasting team, and Zukrowski took the opportunity to steal small amounts of dynamite, hiding them first in his mouth and then in his shoe or back-pack. He never let his companion know what he was doing. 'In a conspiracy it is better not to inform anyone,' he said later. 'And I enjoyed being in risky situations. Lolek wasn't that way.' Carl Bernstein and Marco Politi report the following conversation between the two young men, sitting on a bench by the river together one afternoon and watching a coal barge passing on the Vistula.

'Tonight we are going to rob some coal,' Zukrowski told him . . .
'How can you hope to pull it off?' Wojtyla asked.
'I've got a revolver.'
'But they have more weapons, tanks, planes.'
'It doesn't matter,' Zukrowski insisted.
'Prayer is the only weapon that works,' Wojtyla replied.

This is a frustrating period of Karol Wojtyla's life for a biographer because although there are plenty of vivid anecdotes relating to his time as a quarry worker – that he arrived at work one day freezing cold after giving his coat to a stranger he had met on the road, for example, and that he would stop whatever he was doing and sink to his knees every day at noon, when the Angelus bell rang across the fields from Krakow – it is quite difficult to assess how many of them are coloured by his subsequent fame. We do, however, have his own reflections on the experience in his poem 'The Quarry', which was published fourteen years later. It begins:

> Listen to the even pounding of the hammers
> So very familiar. It takes us within ourselves
> To reflect on the power of the blows.
> Listen now as an electric current
> Cuts across a river of stone
> A thought is born within me,
> Slowly day by day, that the greatness of
> Work lies within a man

Once again the would-be academic was internalising his experience and seeking to make sense of it on his own terms. Later the poem paints a picture of the Worker as a sort of intellectual comic-book superhero:

> It is not just his hands overwhelmed by the weight
> of the hammer
> It is not just his torso rising
> And his muscles flexing.
> As he works deep thoughts trouble his forehead
> And his shoulders and veins are arched high over his head.
> He stands for a moment like a Gothic building
> Made vertical stone by an idea.

The poem is one of his more successful excursions into verse, and he seems to have thought highly of it himself; quoting it over half a century later, he remarks, 'I still find that it expresses very well that extraordinary experience.'

In addition to the long days in the quarry, his reading and his continuing passion for the theatre, Karol Wojtyla's energies were becoming more and more concentrated on the welfare of his father. Karol senior still did odd tasks that were helpful to his son – repairing his shoes, for example – but he seems to have had less and less enthusiasm for life, even though he was only in his early sixties, and household duties like the food shopping fell increasingly to the younger man. The theatre again provided Karol junior with a source of support; he first met Julius Kydrynski when the two acted together in a university production during that first year at the Jagiellonian, and as they became close friends the Kydrynski family began to offer him the kind of surrogate family life that he had found with the Kotlarczyks in Wadowice. Karols senior and junior spent Christmas with the Kydrynskis in 1940.

It became Karol's habit during that bitterly cold winter to take a couple of tin dishes round to the Kydrynskis to be filled with food for his father. On 18 February 1941 he left the dishes at the Kydrynski home while he went out to a pharmacy to buy some medicine. Julius's sister Maria accompanied him back to the basement flat in the Debniki area so that she could heat up the meal for Karol senior, but the two found the old man dead in his bed. Maria reported later that the future pope broke down – none of the accounts of the way he reacted to his earlier bereavements suggest that he cried when he heard the news – and hugged her. 'I was not at my mother's death, I was not at my brother's death, I was not at my father's death,' he said. 'At twenty,' he reflected nearly four decades later, 'I had already lost all the people I loved.'

Karol called a priest to administer the last rites and watched the night away by his father's body with Julius Kydrynski. As pope he would pay tribute to the 'kindness, affection and concern' the Kydrynskis showed him after his father's death, and he immediately moved in with the family. Their daughter noted that 'He went to mass every day, he prayed a lot in his room, and he lay prostrate.' The ritual of lying face down to converse with God became something of a habit with Karol Wojtyla; the nuns at the Ursuline Convent in Warsaw, where he used to stay on visits to the Polish capital when he was Archbishop of Krakow, were most insistent that I should take note of the long hours he spent prone before the altar of their chapel on his last night there before he flew to Rome for the conclave which elected him pope. It is something that can only convincingly be done by someone who is quite unselfconscious about displaying their own piety – it is also, like Pope John Paul's later habit of kissing the soil of each country he visited, a highly theatrical gesture.

Karol senior's headstone in the military cemetery states: 'Karol Wojtyla, retired military, lived 62 years. After a short illness, having received the Holy Sacraments, fell asleep in the Lord.' Since he died suddenly and alone we must take this account of his passing as a consoling white lie.

In June that year Hitler launched Operation Barbarossa, his surprise – and ultimately disastrous – invasion of the Soviet Union. The Russians were driven out of Poland, and the area which had been under their control was added to Dr Frank's fiefdom as part of the General-Gouvernement. Life in Krakow was as tough as ever – the month before the Nazis' attack on their former ally, all the Salesian priests of the parish church where Karol Wojtyla and his 'Master' Jan Tyranowski usually worshipped were arrested by the SS. Half an hour's drive away at Auschwitz, new arrivals were being marched through the famous gates bearing the slogan *Arbeit Macht Frei* ('work makes you free'); their life expectancy once they were inside was three months. It was not yet operating as a fully fledged extermination camp, but as military success in the east delivered a whole new source of disposable humanity into German hands they began to make plans for the expansion of Auschwitz, and in the autumn they added enough land at nearby Birkenau to provide room for an extra 100,000 inmates.

Against this unrelentingly bleak backdrop of personal grief and public horror Karol Wojtyla was able to celebrate a small success; he persuaded his old mentor Mieczyslaw Kotlarczyk and his wife to come and join him in Krakow, and because the basement flat he had shared with his father was now vacant he was able to offer them somewhere to live. With the arrival of the distinguished director from Wadowice, Karol Wojtyla's focus on theatre as a means of passive resistance to the occupation became more intense. He was already a member of the 'cultural wing' Unia, the underground movement for which his friend Wojciech Zukrowski operated as a resistance fighter. Now, together with Kotlarczyk, he became involved in putting together a small group of like-minded thespian enthusiasts to stage clandestine perform-ances of Polish classics. It became known as the Rhapsodic Theatre (from the 'rhapsodic songs of knightly troubadours') and Kotlarczyk had very definite ideas of who could and could not be part of the company. One of those involved remembers him whittling down the numbers 'on the pretext of making necessary cuts in the selected texts'; Karol and his long-standing theatrical partner Halina Krolikiewicz were in, his new friend Julius Kydrynski was out, and it seems he left the group in acrimonious circumstances.

The Rhapsodic Theatre met for rehearsals twice a week – they were 'Never to be forgotten Wednesdays and Saturdays', according to Kotlarczyk, when 'regardless of the terror and the arrests, regardless of the posters all over the city announcing more and more executions by firing squad, we held rehearsals of Slowacki, Kasprowicz, Wyspianski, Norwid and Mickiewicz. And often these rehearsals were in the cold, dark kitchen of our "catacomb" in Debniki, sometimes by candlelight with the power turned off.' Kotlarczyk's account of this period is full of echoes of the kind of soulful intellectualism that marks Karol Wojtyla's writing at the time; the director talks about 'Romantic rehearsals, deepening our Polish consciousness, our resolution to survive and reach the shores of freedom, faithful to our ideal of the theatre', and describes their work as 'a theatre that, on an improvised stage, presented the utterance of a tormented Polish soul, an utterance that was brutally banished by a ruthless enemy'.

The Rhapsodic Theatre's performances were put on in the apartments of sympathetic friends, and Karol Wojtyla became something of a star turn. Looking back on the experience as pope, he wrote, 'The recitations took place before a small group of people that we knew, and before guests who because they had a particular interest in literature, belonged in a sense to the "initiated". It was essential to keep these theatrical get-togethers secret; otherwise we risked serious punishment from the occupying forces, even deportation to the concentration camps.' The evenings were intense experiences; there was no scenery, and the actors wore neither costume nor make-up. Lighting was provided by a candelabrum. For the Rhapsodic Theatre's inaugural performance the set was dressed with a black cloth and a death mask of the poet Slowacki, while the actors, all wearing black, 'recited the text with almost no gestures'. There is a story that on a later occasion the future pope was declaiming the dying words of Pan Tadeusz, the hero of Mickiewicz's patriotic poem of the same name, when a German loudspeaker truck passed in the street blaring out news of a great victory over the Soviets on the Eastern Front – witnesses say our man completed his oration *con brio* without missing a beat.

By 1942 Karol's work for Solvay had taken a turn for the better; he had been transferred from the quarry to the company's water purification plant, which meant a longer walk from home (as much as two hours, according to some accounts) but an easier life. His job was to carry lime milk from the kilns up to the tanks where the water was softened – it was done with wooden buckets hung from a shoulder-yoke, and one pictures him looking a little like an old-fashioned milkmaid in a story book. He worked fast, usually on the night shift, and during any spare time he could create he took refuge in the plant's boiler room with a book. One of the other workers in the purification plant was a fellow student from the Jagiellonian, a chemist and geologist, and Karol quizzed him on the natural sciences, a subject about which he knew very little indeed. He told him he 'needed to have these talks', because 'he had decided to become a priest'.

Karol Wojtyla's sense of vocation to the priesthood took final shape over the summer of 1942. Although many of his friends and teachers had remarked on his piety, it does seem that until this point he had genuinely been more interested in the idea of a life dedicated to academia or the theatre; he has said that he began to think seriously about the priesthood after his father's death, and that his vocation gradually became 'an inner fact of unquestionable and absolute clarity'. In his book to mark the fiftieth anniversary of his ordination he wrote of 'a progressive detachment from my earlier plans' during this period. Looking back from the throne of St Peter at his much younger self, he posed the question of whether it was 'mere coincidence' that his vocation was formed during the Nazi occupation: 'Certainly, in God's plan nothing happens by chance. It helped me to under-stand in a new way the *value and importance of a vocation*. In the face of the spread of evil and the atrocities of war, the meaning of the priesthood and its mission in the world became much clearer to me.' Like the writing of *Job,* the ideal of priesthood offered a means for making sense of what he was seeing around him.

In October 1942, accompanied by his friend and fellow member of the Living Rosary Mieczyslaw Malinski, Karol Wojtyla knocked on the door of the Archbishop's Palace just off Krakow's magnifi-cent main square and declared that he wished to be trained for the priesthood. He was entering yet another level of the many clandestine worlds which crisscrossed one another during the occupation, and he was stepping into the orbit of perhaps the most significant of all the hero-figures who influenced his mind as a young man.

Archbishop Adam Sapieha was a prince twice over – by birth and, as the holder of the ancient title of Prince Metropolitan of

Krakow, by office. His style of leadership – grand, holy, national-istic and stubborn – provided Karol Wojtyla with a valuable model when he succeeded to the Metropolitan throne himself under communism. Whether Cardinal Sapieha – as he became after the war – would have felt at ease in today's Church is, of course, altogether another matter; like Karol Wojtyla's father, he was one of those influential figures in the present pope's life whose roots were very firmly in the nineteenth century. He had spent his childhood in aristocratic pursuits – learning to fence and ride – and took pride in an ancestry which included a father and grandfather who had rebelled against the tsar during the years of Polish partition. There have been suggestions that his connections with the Italian aristocracy gave him a measure of protection from the Nazis, who were anxious to avoid alienating Mussolini. When the Polish primate, Cardinal Hlond, scuttled out of the country dragging his unpleasant anti-Semitic views with him, Archbishop Sapieha became the focus for Polish Catholic resist-ance to the Nazis. He maintained links with the resistance movements and the Polish government-in-exile in London, supported the underground group Unia, and used his influence to hide escaped prisoners and resistance fighters on the run. There is a very good story told about his relationship with the Nazi governor-general, Hans Frank, whose residence in Wawel Castle made the two men relatively near neighbours. It seems that Dr Frank repeatedly hinted that he would like to be received for dinner in Prince Adam's palace; when the cherished invitation was finally forthcoming, Dr Frank was served black bread made from acorns, beet jam and ersatz coffee, the archbishop explaining that that was the ration available on the Nazi food coupons, and that he would of course not allow any of his servants to deal on the black market.

Much of the debate over the Catholic Church's response to the Holocaust revolves round the question of how much the Vatican actually knew about what was happening. Archbishop Sapieha, with the Jewish ghetto a relatively short walk from his front door and Auschwitz not far away, made some significant efforts to get the truth out. In February 1940 he took the opportunity offered by a visit from a Dominican theologian who was travelling on a Swiss passport; the archbishop provided him with 'an immensity of shocking detail', and asked him to commit it to memory so that he could repeat it at the Vatican – which the reverend professor apparently did. At the beginning of 1942 the Prince Metropolitan wrote directly to the pope about conditions in the concentration camps, which he described as 'camps from which few emerge alive' where people were 'deprived of all human rights, handed over to the cruelty of men who have no feeling of humanity'. However, it seems he may have become nervous about the risk of the letter falling into the hands of the Germans who would as a consequence 'shoot all the bishops and then many others', and again his 'postman' – in this case a passing Italian chaplain – was required to memorise its contents. The first gas chamber began operating at Auschwitz in May 1942; in October that year the Archbishop of Krakow did manage to get a letter out to Rome, and there are accounts of him smuggling out much more correspondence via his chaplain and the papal nuncio in Berlin.

The average capacity of the crematoria at Auschwitz rose to 20,000 a day at the height of 'the final solution'. Archbishop Sapieha authorised his priests to issue baptismal certificates to Jews who were being hidden in monasteries and private homes; they would trawl through old parish records and give the refugees plausible Christian names and baptismal dates. There has been considerable debate about whether Karol Wojtyla himself directly took part in such activities. My instinct is that he probably did not; we have a wealth of reliable evidence of his friendship with individual Jews and his protective attitude towards Jews in general, and if he had performed any specific act of heroism or generosity we would surely know about it. John Cornwell, author of one of the last papal biographies published during John Paul's lifetime, reported that at the end of the war he is said to have looked after a teenager who had just been released from one of the labour camps, feeding her and carrying her for two miles on his back. Mr Cornwell also pointed out that when Pope John Paul talked about a 'culture of death' in the context of modern debates about abortion and euthanasia, he knew whereof he spoke.

Although the Jagiellonian University had been officially suppressed by the Nazis it continued to operate underground in an informal way, with seminars and lectures in private homes, often at night. By 1942 it had, according to one account of the period, more than a hundred teachers and 800 students, and all the departments which had been in operation before the war were working again in some shape or form. Archbishop Sapieha's secret seminary was attached to the Theology Department, but studying at the Jagiellonian in the years 1942–4 was a very different experience from those carefree days when Karol Wojtyla and his literary friends would spill out of lectures to argue the toss in the corridors. The seminarians continued to live outwardly ordinary lives; most of Karol's academic work was done alone, much of it at night in the boiler room of the purification plant of the Solvay Chemical Company. There are many contemporary accounts of this earnest young man, dressed in denims and wooden clogs without socks, trying to make sense of some volume of metaphysics in this unlikely setting. He would sometimes confess to his friend Malinski that he found it intellectually tough going.

The Warsaw Rising is one of the great stories of wasted heroism of the Second World War; on 1 August 1944 some 150,000 poorly armed Polish resistance fighters took on the full might of the German army. They held out for sixty-three days, but by the time the rebellion had been crushed nearly a quarter of a million civilians had been killed and the city itself had been reduced to ashes. On 6 August, in Krakow, the Germans embarked on a mass round-up of young men to forestall any similar challenge to their authority there. Karol Wojtyla, who by now had moved back to the flat he had shared with his father, hid in his basement while German troops searched his uncle and aunt's house upstairs. His friend Zukrowski said he was still shaking when they met some hours later. More than 8,000 men and boys were taken into custody in the course of that day.

Archbishop Sapieha decided to bring his precious young charges into the palace; the following morning Mieczyslaw Malinski, who had been out playing football during the round-up and had managed to escape being taken into custody, opened the door to a priest who told him to expect 'someone [who] will come to make sure you get to us safely'. When his guide arrived she led him through deserted streets, signalling when the coast was clear. 'I was scared by the Debnicki Bridge,' he remembered, where soldiers stood on guard by the anti-tank barriers, but they paid no attention to us. Then came Zwierzyniecka Street, too long for my taste, after which we crossed the Planty Gardens and entered Franciszkanska Street. Opposite the palace was a high-walled building containing police stores, with a sentry outside; then another gate, an annexe to the residence, also occupied by the police, and another sentry. We passed these in fear and trembling, and finally got to the main door of the palace, where I almost fell into the arms of a tall young man who I had not met before.

'Is Karol Wojtyla here?' I asked.

'Yes, he is.'

At that moment Karol came running out of the cloister, and we embraced each other like survivors from a shipwreck.

Their fellow seminarians, whom they had of course never met, arrived in similar fashion as the day wore on. Seven in all, they were housed in a large communal dormitory and given cassocks and false identity cards so that they appeared to be fully fledged priests. Adam Sapieha despatched another of his priests to the Solvay Company so that Karol Wojtyla could be 'disappeared' from the relevant employment lists, and on 11 September 1944 the future pope 'received the tonsure from the Prince Archbishop' – a curious and old-fashioned ceremony, now abolished, in which an aspiring priest's hair was shaved to symbolise his renunciation of the world. Those last few months of German occupation would have confirmed Karol Wojtyla's sense that the Church offered a kind of alternative reality: Jan Tyranowski had taught him that the Catholic faith could be held safe in the mind and the soul in defiance of external reality; now Prince Adam Sapieha showed him that the institution of the Church had a practical power which could endure the most determined persecution.

On 17 January 1945 Soviet forces advanced into Krakow. As the sound of gunfire grew louder in the early evening Prince Sapieha gathered his seminarians in the chapel, and while he said mass a huge explosion blew out every window in the building; the rest of the night was spent in the cellars of the Archbishop's Palace. Soviet control of the city was secured the following day, and Krakow was spared the wholesale destruction visited upon Warsaw.

Once the fighting was over Karol Wojtyla and Mieczyslaw Malinski decided to revisit their old neighbourhood, the first time they had been able to do so for five months. Malinski recalled the journey vividly in his biography of his friend:

> The streets were crammed and it was hard to get through the crowd. Masses of military vehicles, great Studebakers, Dodges and Fords, machine-gun carriages, peasant carts drawn by two ponies or one, and streams of soldiers on foot wearing fur caps and felt boots carrying submachine guns. At the end of Zwierzyniecka Street we turned into the embankment by what had been the Debnicki Bridge and were able to realize the force of the explosion that had destroyed a whole section of it. We climbed down and walked across the frozen surface of the Vistula, whence we had a full view of the contorted steel girders pointing up at the sky. Soldiers' bodies were scattered on the ice, and there were a few broken down tanks.

The seminarians spent the first days of liberation cleaning up the damage done to the Archbishop's Palace by the final battle for the city and re-opening the pre-war seminar which had been used by the Germans during the occupation. Karol Wojtyla recorded the following incident during that period – the meticulous author of the *Kalendarium* says it is taken from 'the recollections of Karol Cardinal Wojtyla. In the Polish edition, a typewritten note inserted in the printed copy on p. 19':

> I will never forget the impression that a conversation with a Soviet soldier made on me in 1945. It was shortly after the cessation of combat activities in the West. The soldier knocked on the gate of the seminary. I spent several hours talking to him. Although he didn't enter the seminary (besides, he had a very strange idea of what one might learn in a seminary), I learned a lot during our long talk about how God impresses Himself on human minds even in conditions that are significantly negative – as the truth cannot be erased. This man had

never in his life been in an Orthodox Church (although he mentioned that as a small child he was taken there by his mother, but not since), and he heard at school that there was no God. 'But anyway, I always knew,' he repeated many times, 'and now I want to find out more about Him.'

The Nazi occupation gave Karol Wojtyla an experience of living under moral anarchy which few of us can imagine. The capriciousness with which Nazi terror erupted into people's lives – the way, for example, that anyone might be picked up and shot as part of a reprisal operation – reflected a more general sense of living in a world cut loose from its moral anchors. The pursuit of objective moral truth was one of the hallmarks of Karol Wojtyla the thinker and John Paul the Pope – it culminated in perhaps his greatest and certainly his most controversial encyclical, *Veritatis Splendor* – and it is tempting to look for its roots in this period. The factors which decided whether someone lived or died – whether it was the accident of birth that had classified you as Jew or Gentile or something as inconsequential as being on a particular street corner at the wrong time – must have seemed as random as the numbers on a lottery ticket. Karol Wojtyla sought to make sense of this state of affairs by turning to the traditional Catholic idea of Providence: 'I was spared much of the immense and horrible drama of the Second World War,' he wrote as pope in 1994.

> I could have been arrested any day, at home, in the stone quarry, in the plant, and taken to the concentration camp. Sometimes I asked myself: so many young people of my own age are losing their lives, why not me? Today I know it was not mere chance. Amid the overwhelming evil of war, everything in my personal life was tending towards the good of my vocation.

Many of us would have been forced to the opposite conclusion – that our lives are driven by a fate that operates without meaning or logic. That was certainly the lesson drawn by the late Czeslaw Milosz, the Nobel Prize-winning author who was one of Karol Wojtyla's fellow Krakowians and became close to the pope in later

69

years. Not long before he died I asked him whether he shared John Paul's faith in Divine Providence. 'I would like to,' he replied, 'but it is very difficult because I have seen and heard of such horrors in the history of the twentieth century. My problem is to combine providential lines of history with the millions of people who died. That's a permanent problem of history which may work towards good – but what about the suffering, the hell created by history on its way?'

The kind of faith Karol Wojtyla displayed amid the uniquely dreadful circumstances of life in wartime Krakow is immensely impressive, but perhaps there is something a little frightening about it too. The idea that the whole of the Second World War was part of a divine plan to form one man's vocation would of course be repugnant to him if put in such blunt terms, but there is a hint of it in the passage from his reflections on his priesthood which I have quoted above.

The experience of Nazi rule also taught him for the first time that the fact that a set of ideas is laid down by the established order does not make them right. Indeed, in this instance they were very wrong indeed, and one clear lesson Karol Wojtyla drew in wartime Krakow was that the possession of power does not confer moral legitimacy. He learnt that truth can lie within the mind and the soul rather than in the 'reality' outside. These lessons served him well in his struggle against communism, which, like National Socialism, represented a system of power based on a false set of ideas. But it was a habit of mind much less well suited to dealing with modern liberal democracies which are not monolithic power structures, and which by and large do not try to impose a vision of the world on their citizens or to advance an agenda through the use of force and terror.

3

A Student in Rome

The war's memories did not easily slip away. Karol Wojtyla was ordained a priest on All Saints' Day – 1 November – 1946 in the private chapel of the Archbishops of Krakow. 'I remember,' he wrote in *Gift and Mystery*, the book which commemorates the fiftieth anniversary of that day,

> that during the occupation I would often go there in the morning, to serve mass for the Prince Metropolitan. I also remember that for a time another clandestine seminarian, Jerzy Zachuta, would come with me. One day he did not appear. After mass I stopped by his house in Ludwinow [near Debniki] and learned that he had been taken by the Gestapo during the night. Immediately afterwards, his name appeared on the list of Poles who were to be shot. Being ordained in that very chapel which had seen us together so many times, I could not help but remember this brother in the priestly vocation, whom Christ had united in a different way to the mystery of his Death and Resurrection.

The same book includes a more general reflection on the sacrifice of the Polish priests who died during the Second World War, and again it is characterised by that powerful sense of an intimate providential connection between the life of Karol Wojtyla and the great tides of world history which swept through the twentieth century. 'What I have written about the concentration camps represents only a part, albeit dramatic, of this "apocalypse" of our century,' he declares.

I have brought it up to emphasise that *my priesthood, even at its beginning, was in some way marked by the great sacrifice of countless men and women of my generation* [original italics]. Providence spared me the most difficult experiences; and so my sense of indebtedness is all the greater, both to people whom I knew and to many more whom I did not know; all of them, regardless of nationality or language, by their sacrifice on the great altar of history, helped make my priestly vocation a reality.

As pope, John Paul would face frequent liberal criticism for the intransigence he showed towards priests who wished to be released from their vows; to someone who saw his vocation in terms of the suffering of those who gave up their lives on 'the great altar of history', the 'lifestyle' choices made by late twentieth-century priests who wanted to escape from celibacy must have seemed intolerably frivolous.

The way Karol Wojtyla writes about the experience of his ordination provides a striking example of one of his salient intellectual peculiarities: his tendency to view the world as a sort of permanently unfolding symbolist poem, in which everything stands for something else. *Gift and Mystery* includes this reflection on the meaning of the gesture of prostration during the ceremony of ordination:

> I can still remember myself in that chapel during the singing of the *Veni, Creator spiritus* and the Litany of the Saints, lying prostrate on the floor with arms outstretched in the form of a cross, awaiting the moment of the imposition of hands. It was a very moving experience! . . . There is something very impressive about the prostration of the ordinands, symbolising as it does their total submission before the majesty of God and their complete openness to the action of the Holy Spirit who will descend upon them and consecrate them.

Wawel Cathedral, where he celebrated his first mass the following day, is full of evocative symbols of Poland's Catholic past, and John Paul has written at length about his 'special bond' with the building and all that it stands for. 'I remember and recall every corner of this shrine and all of its monuments,' he reminisced in his frail eighties. 'As you walk through the main nave and the side aisles, you see the sarcophagi of the Polish kings. And when you descend to the crypt of the poets, you come upon the graves of Mickiewicz, Slowacki, and finally Norwid.' The crypt chapel of St Leonard had been chosen for Fr Wojtyla's first mass, so at this moment of great emotional intensity he was surrounded by the shades of both the great Polish poets whose works he performed during the Nazi occupation and the national heroes whose exploits had provided the stuff of the stories spun by his father in Wadowice.

As pope he had a somewhat unnerving habit of tossing these characters into his discourse as if everyone should instantly recognise their resonance. Two monuments in Wawel held a particular enchantment for him: the tombs of St Stanislaw and Queen St Hedwig. St Stanislaw was Poland's Thomas à Beckett, murdered at the altar in 1079 after challenging the authority of his monarch, King Boleslaw the Bold, and Pope John Paul called him the 'Father of our Homeland'. Queen Hedwig played a crucial role in the conversion of the Slavs, and her memory is associated with 'the famous Wawel Crucifix' – famous because 'It was at the feet of this crucifix that the twelve-year-old Hedwig made the decision to marry the Lithuanian prince Wladyslaw Jagiello. This decision of 1386 brought Lithuania into the family of Christian nations.' These no doubt great figures of the Slavic past – and others with a similarly venerable if quasi-mythological place in history – featured frequently in the speeches of John Paul II, and his practice of using them as a kind of shorthand sometimes gave his utterances the crossword-puzzle complexity of the more obscure passages of Ezra Pound or T. S. Eliot.

Most of the cohort from the wartime secret seminary were not ordained until Palm Sunday 1947, but Cardinal Sapieha had sound practical reasons for fast-tracking Karol Wojtyla's elevation to the priesthood. The Prince Metropolitan had marked him down as a future leader and he believed that his protégé would benefit from some time in Rome. He wanted to despatch him there in time to begin his doctoral studies in the autumn term of 1946. A week after his ordination Karol Wojtyla performed a ceremony that must have seemed like a sort of valediction to his youth; he administered the sacrament of baptism for the first time, and the child was the daughter of Halina Krolikiewicz, the muse of his thespian days. If he felt the loss of the possibilities she might have offered him or the theatrical world which had inspired them both, there is no evidence of that in his writing; Fr Karol believed that by becoming a priest he had joined a higher caste of men who are 'constantly in contact with the holiness of God', stewards 'of the invisible and priceless treasures belonging to the spiritual and supernatural order', with 'mysterious, awesome power over the Eucharistic Body of Christ'.

And almost immediately he was off to Rome – very much the young man eager for adventure. 'I boarded the train with great excitement,' he wrote later.

> With me was Stanislaw Starowieyski, a younger colleague who had been sent to take his whole course of theological studies in Rome. For the first time I was leaving the borders of my homeland. From the window of the moving train I looked towards cities known only from geography books. For the first time I saw Prague, Nuremberg, Strasbourg, and Paris, where we stopped as guests of the Polish Seminary on the Rue des Irlandais. We stayed only briefly, since time was pressing, and reached Rome in the last days of November.

The world's most indefatigable spiritual tourist was on his first grand tour.

Fr Wojtyla and his companion had been found rooms not at the Polish College, which was full, but at the Belgian College on the Via Quirinale. The accommodation was uncomfortable – there were no showers in the building until 1947 – but the address would have been difficult to better. The Via Quirinale runs along the *manica lunga* (long sleeve) of the sixteenth-century Quirinale Palace, now the residence of Italy's president but once the summer home of the popes, and both Rome's medieval heart – around the Pantheon and the Piazza Navone – and the Vatican itself are an easy walk away. Just across a small park from the College stood the church of Sant' Andrea al Quirinale, a baroque masterpiece by Gian Lorenzo Bernini which contained the tomb of St Stanislaw Kosta, the patron of Fr Wojtyla's parish in Living Rosary days; it was just the kind of coincidence (or providential connection) he relished and he used to stop in the church on his way to the Angelicum University every morning.

Rome had been bombed by the Americans during the German occupation, but the damage to its ancient glories was relatively modest and the two young Poles were eager sightseers. One of the teachers who had trained Fr Wojtyla in Krakow had told him that 'it was more important to *learn Rome itself* than to study' because 'after all, a doctorate in theology can be got elsewhere'. The young priest wrote to a friend in Krakow (a Mrs Szkocka, one of those surrogate mothers he had a flair for attracting), enthusiastically, if somewhat incoherently, about the experience of 'immersing oneself in Rome': 'this is a chapter which absolutely cannot be described in a few statements. This subject contains so many levels, so many aspects. One continually associates them with some detail or another and feels constantly enriched, although I am a long way from having systemised my impressions.' Remembering this period years later, when he was living in the city as pope, he made the intriguing observation that when he first arrived there, 'I carried in me the image of Rome from history, from literature and from the entire Christian tradition. For many days, I criss-crossed the city . . . and I couldn't fully find the image of Rome I had brought with me.' The remark is characteristically Krakowian. Krakow lies on the extreme edge of the 'Roman' world, hard by the fault line where the Catholic West meets the Orthodox East and Latin script gives way to Cyrillic; there is something almost anxious and defiant about the way the neo-classical façades of its wonderful Market Square declare their debt to the Western tradition, and like some far-flung outpost of a great empire the city nurtures an exaggerated and idealised vision of the cultural capital to which it owes allegiance.

Fr Wojtyla's sightseeing tastes definitely ran to the spiritual rather than the aesthetic; he began with the catacombs where the first Roman Christians gathered to pray and bury their dead, and his description of the Eternal City as 'the Rome of the beginnings of Christianity, the Rome of the Apostles, the Rome of Martyrs, the Rome that exists at the beginnings of the Church, and, at the same time, of the great culture that we inherit' gives a pretty clear indication of which of its many faces pleased him most. The city's Catholic character would have been even more obvious then than it is now. In *Gift and Mystery* John Paul remarks on the 'characteristic red cassocks' of the German seminarians he often encountered on his daily visits to Sant' Andrea al Quirinale; in the days before the Second Vatican Council dictated that some of the more flamboyant flourishes of ecclesiastical dress codes should be toned down, the streets around the Vatican would have been a kaleidoscope of sartorial variety and exotic headgear. In Krakow he had experienced the Church working in secrecy under persecution, but in Rome he saw it in its full and self-confident Petrine majesty.

Presiding over it all – and providing the future John Paul with his first master-class in papal style – was the enormously influential figure of Eugenio Pacelli, who as Pius XII occupied the throne of St Peter through the Second World War and for many years thereafter. Today he is a controversial figure because of the grave accusation that he failed to speak out about the Holocaust – *Hitler's Pope*, the title of John Cornwell's successful book on the subject, neatly encapsulates the modern liberal verdict on his record – but to many Romans in the 1940s he was a national hero as well as a spiritual leader. He had remained in the Vatican throughout the German occupation and the Allied bombing campaign, at one stage protesting to Roosevelt about the air attacks; he insisted on a bomb-shelter being built for some of the Vatican's rare books but refused one for himself, and immediately visited the wounded when American planes struck a target near his cathedral church of St John Lateran. Pius XII was Italy's Queen Mother. During the winter he banned all forms of central heating or fires from the Vatican as a gesture of solidarity with ordinary Romans, and the grounds of the papal villa at Castel Gandolfo became a tented refugee camp for hundreds of refugees from political and religious persecution.

In the summer of 1946 Italians voted to abolish their monarchy, leaving Pius an even more dominant figure on the Italian landscape. His understanding of his office could not have been grander or more autocratic. When his secretary of state died in 1944 he simply took on the job himself, effectively ruling the Vatican as both head of state and head of government. In meetings with his senior officials he almost never asked for their advice, and after studying the ecclesiastical equivalent of his red boxes in the evening he would sometimes send documents back to them for redrafting without explanation of why he was dissatisfied. 'I don't want advisers,' he told one of his most senior cardinals, 'I want people who do as I say.' His gardeners were instructed that when he walked through the grounds in the Vatican or at Castel Gandolfo they should hide in the bushes so as not to disturb his solitude. The Vatican bureaucracy over which he presided would have confirmed the worst prejudices of Catholicism's enemies; the British Ambassador to the Holy See, d'Arcy Osborne, complained that a Vatican official would usually deliver his views in a style 'so prolix and obscure that it was difficult to extract his meaning from its extraneous verbal envelope', and described an other-worldly atmosphere in the tiny statelet that was 'fourth-dimensional and, so to speak, outside of time . . . they reckon in centuries and plan for eternity'.

Fr Wojtyla met Pius XII only once – at a private audience organised by the rector of the Belgian College for his students. There is no record of what was said, but the chilly and aloof Pacelli is unlikely to have spent very much time on a young Polish PhD student. Like John Paul, Pius reigned as pope into his eighties, and the accounts of his last years have eerie echoes of the final stages of the John Paul era. Just as bishops in the 1990s and the first years of the new millennium complained about the way access to the pontiff was controlled by his Polish secretary, Stanislaw Dziwisz, so their predecessors whispered their resentment about the influence of Pius's housekeeper, the German Sister Pasqualina. Known as 'the Virgo Potens', or powerful virgin, and sometimes as 'La Papessa' (this sobriquet carried no implication of sexual impropriety; as one writer has put it, 'few suspected the ascetic and sickly pope of any carnality'), she laid down his daily agenda and was said to advise him even on such sensitive church matters as the selection of cardinals.

Karol Wojtyla and Stanislaw Starowieyski did not confine their tourism to Rome – Fr Stanislaw has listed trips to Naples, Capri, Subiaco ('the cradle of the Benedictine Order'), Venice, Milan, Assisi, Florence, Sienna and Monte Cassino. At the time the great monastery on the Cassino mountainside would still have shown the scars of the epic battle fought there in 1944; one of the 300,000 Poles in the Allied vanguard was Karol Wojtyla's childhood Jewish friend Jerzy Kluger. Jerzy, an artillery officer by then, won the Polish Cross of Valour for his part in the assault on what he later remembered as 'a stark, bombed out jumble of broken walls and parapets', which was all that remained of 'a thousand years of beauty'.

Just after Easter 1947 the pious and energetic Polish duo made a trip which especially impressed the future pope: they visited another celebrated mountain-bound monastery at San Giovanni Rotondo, just outside Foggia, the home of Padre Pio. Francesco Forgione – as he was called before he acquired the name by which he was familiarly known to his millions of followers – was sixty at the time (he would live into his eighties) and had joined the Capuchin Order of monks when he was in his early thirties. For most of his life he was said to be afflicted with the stigmata, the wounds of the crucifixion replicated on his hands, feet and side. St Francis of Assisi had the first recorded case of stigmata, and around a hundred such cases have been reported since he died in the early thirteenth century.

The cult of Padre Pio was already well established in the 1930s, and in the winter of 1943–4 William Carrigan, an American Red Cross worker attached to the 5th United States Air Force, drove up the twisting roads to his mountain eyrie in a snowstorm to attend mass together with a couple of soldiers.

> We knelt on the cold marble floor on the side not ten feet from Padre where we could see his every movement. As he began the consecration he seemed to be in great pain, shifting his weight from side to side, hesitating to begin the words of consecration which he would state and repeat – biting them off with a clicking of his teeth as if in great pain. His cheek muscles twitched and tears were visible on his cheeks. He reached for the chalice and

jerked back his hand because of the pain in the wound which was fully visible to me.

Padre Pio's 5.00 a.m. masses – while he celebrated the sacrament he concealed his holy wounds by wearing a pair of fingerless mittens, like shooting gloves – drew thousands of people to San Giovanni Rotondo, and all sorts of remarkable stories began to circulate about his powers. It was claimed that he had appeared to American pilots on bombing missions – sometimes a 'towering apparition' in the clouds – to guide them away from his monastic home. 'There are fliers who swore that they had sighted a figure in the sky, sometimes normal size, sometimes gigantic, usually in the form of a monk or a priest,' wrote Bernard Ruffin, an initially sceptical Protestant minister who became an enthusiastic Padre Pio biographer. 'Several people from Foggia, where thousands were killed in the air raids, said that a bomb, falling into a room where they had huddled, landed near a photograph of Padre Pio. They claim that when it exploded, it burst like a soap bubble.' Mr Ruffin recorded that the stigmatic monk's room often looked like 'the scene of a drunken brawl' in the mornings, and Pio spoke of being attacked by demons in the night who stripped him naked and 'in the most abominable form . . . hurled themselves upon me' and 'struck me most violently'. The Padre was said to enjoy the gift of bilocation (being in two places at once), on one occasion popping up in the Vatican while he was known to be living in his monastery in southern Italy. After his death he is reported to have materialised at the altar to give communion to a woman who was praying in the monastic chapel. Those who confessed to him said that he could see into their souls, knowing their sins before they spoke them.

The young priest brought up on the story of the Black Madonna of Czestochowa appears to have had no problem with any of this. He queued up to make his confession to the Padre, and there is a story – unverified by any reliable evidence that I can find – that the monk predicted his elevation to the papacy. In later years Karol Wojtyla spoke frequently to his friends in Krakow of his admiration for Padre Pio, and when he wrote to him in 1962 requesting his intercession on behalf of a woman suffering from cancer her subsequent recovery was deemed a miracle. Ignoring any theological questions raised by such issues as the somewhat capricious manner in which the Padre appears to have intervened in Allied bombing operations, John Paul canonised him in the Jubilee Year of 2000. Other church leaders have been less convinced about his sanctity; the Vatican twice banned Catholics from visiting him (in 1926 and 1931) and he was investigated by a church court under Pope John XXIII in the late 1950s.

There was another important journey to be made that summer; 'It is the Prince's will,' Fr Wojtyla wrote to Mrs Szkocka, 'that I spend these holidays visiting France, Belgium and perhaps Holland, observing methods of pastoral work.' There is something endearingly fogeyish about this habit of referring to his patron Cardinal Sapieha in the kind of terms an eighteenth-century artist or musician like Mozart might have done. But there were moments of what sound suspiciously like youthful priggishness too; Fr Stanislaw recalls the pair's stay in Paris:

> We often used the Metro system for getting about that huge city. Most often it was crowded and the behaviour of the French often left a lot to be desired. After a few days of such trips Father Karol says to me, 'You know, during these Metro rides one can superbly attend to one's inner life (contemplation).' I must say that I was surprised by this observation on my friend's part.

The rude Parisians on the Metro also helped to give the future pope his first insight into a problem which was to become the focus for one of his crusades in later life – the retreat of Christianity in its historic European heartland. 'From different and complementary angles,' he wrote as pope, 'I was coming to an ever greater appreciation of *Western Europe*: the Europe of the post-war period, the Europe of splendid Gothic cathedrals and yet a Europe threatened by increasing secularisation. I understood the challenge this posed to the Church, and the need to confront this impending danger.' The first article he wrote on his return to Poland – the beginning, as it turned out, of a significant career as a 'Catholic intellectual' – was based on his trip to France; it warned the Polish clergy of the seductive dangers of materialism and left-wing ideology, materialism's dialectic partner, which had undermined the spirit of their French counterparts.

In Rome itself Fr Karol's time as a graduate student afforded him the first chance to enjoy the Church's formidable networking opportunities. The Roman Catholic Church really is a supra-national organisation, different in kind from merely *inter*national bodies like the UN or the European Union, and both its theology and its bureaucratic structure encourage cross-national contacts. A young priest or seminarian lucky enough to be sent to Rome is given a unique experience of the sense of universal brotherhood which the Church can offer – or, if you choose to be more cynical about the matter, a once-in-a-lifetime chance to plug into the incestuous freemasonry which sometimes seems to run the institution. Karol Wojtyla, who was, in the very best sense of the term, clearly an ambitious young man, used his time in the Belgian College to brush up his French and German and to practise his English on the handful of American seminarians who were lodging there too. The rector of the college, Fr Maximilien De Furstenberg, became a cardinal alongside the future pope in 1967, and no fewer than three of Karol Wojtyla's teachers at the Angelicum also received their 'red hats' as princes of the Church. He has recorded that during the conclave which elected him pope in 1978 the former rector of the Belgian College 'came up to me at a certain moment and uttered the significant words "*Dominus adest et vocat te*" ("the Lord is come and he calls you")'. At the time of his election John Paul may have been unknown to most of the outside world, but within the Vatican hierarchy he had friendships that went back decades.

And his Roman stay coincided with a papal reform which laid the groundwork for his own eventual election to the papacy. Pius XII, though himself a member of the so-called 'black nobility', the handful of aristocratic families who had traditionally held the top jobs in the Vatican, was profoundly convinced that the Church's power structures should reflect its supranational character. He lectured his College of Cardinals on the subject in December 1945:

the Catholic Church is by her very essence above nationalism . . . In confused times such as ours, the Church, for her own welfare and for that of humanity, must do her utmost to stress her indivisible and undivided wholeness. Today more than ever she must take up her stand above all nationalism. This spirit must penetrate and pervade her visible head, the Sacred College, and all the action of the Holy See.

In the following year he created thirty-two new cardinals, the largest number ever announced at a single sitting, including the first Chinese cardinal and several others from beyond the shores of Europe. Until then the Italians had twenty-three red hats, the rest of the world fifteen; after Pius's reforms the Italians had twenty-eight and the non-Italians were, for the first time, in the majority, with forty-two red hats among them. In a talk he gave in September 1948 Pius said the change was among the greatest transformations since the fall of the Roman Empire, and thirty years later (almost to the month, as it happens) the young priest who had just completed his studies in Rome proved him spectacularly right by becoming the first non-Italian pope for four and a half centuries.

There was a political battle being fought out in Rome during this period which foreshadowed perhaps the biggest single theme of John Paul's career, both as a bishop and as pope: the battle between Christianity and communism. The Italian resistance movement during the German occupation had laid the foundations for an extremely powerful Italian Communist Party – the most powerful, indeed, in Western Europe. Pius XII, who viewed communism as a mortal threat to the Church (he would later declare that any Catholics who became communist '*ipso facto*, as apostates from the Catholic faith, incur excommunication') saw the Italian general election of 1948 as one of the critical first battles of the Cold War. He threw the Church's weight behind the newly formed Christian Democratic Party, and instructed his deputy secretary of state, Giovanni Batiste Montini (the future Pope Paul VI) to mobilise clerical support for its Catholic leadership. The United States government was channelling money to the anti-communist campaign, and Montini had support from other American sources: cash from the sale of surplus war material which the Americans had helpfully provided and subsidies from the collection plates of the redoubtable Cardinal Francis Spellman of New York. It worked; the militantly Catholic Alcide Gasperi emerged as Italy's prime minister. And Pius was proved right in his instinct that this battle would be decisive; Italy's place at the heart of liberal Western Europe was secured as a result of the outcome.

Things in Poland were of course going the other way – the Communist Party had come to power in Warsaw the previous year in elections which the Americans, the British and most Poles regarded as fraudulent – and in time the struggle with communism would become the overriding preoccupation of Karol Wojtyla's life. But Fr Wojtyla had his head in his books during the decisive electoral battle being fought out around him in the spring of 1948; his doctoral examination was approaching. 'Please believe me that my time flies by,' he wrote to Mrs Szkocka. 'I truly do not know how almost a year and a half has passed. Studies, observations, deliberations – it has all the effect of spurs on a horse. Thus each day is completely filled.'

Karol Wojtyla's doctoral thesis – on St John of the Cross, the mystic he had come to admire under the influence of Jan Tyranowski – was written within the framework of the most orthodox current trends in Catholic theology. It has been said that Prince Sapieha sent him to the Angelicum rather than Rome's more famous and progressive university, the Gregorian, because he admired its conservative ethos. Fr Wojtyla's supervisor was Fr Reginald Garrigou-Lagrange, generally known as 'Reginald the Rigid', who specialised in the works of Thomas Aquinas. Aquinas, a thirteenth-century father of the Church, is perhaps most famous for his association with the idea of debating how many angels could dance on the head of a pin – there is no evidence that he actually did that, but the way the expression has attached itself to his name reflects the somewhat abstruse character of his theology. Even the radical interpretation of 'Thomism' which was beginning to surface in the 1940s sounds pretty *recherché*: Rocco Buttiglione, the controversial Italian politician who has written an account of Karol Wojtyla's philosophical ideas, describes the new currents of Thomist thought he would have encountered like this:

> In the Catholic University of Louvain in Belgium, for example, there was an attempt to bring about reconciliation between Thomism and modern thought (particularly that of Kant). In France, Maritain and Gilson were giving Thomism an existential dimension by maintaining that Thomas' principal philosophical contributions were the distinction between essence and existence and the legitimation of a certain eidetic intuition in the interpretation of the abstract.

Reginald the Rigid was having no truck with such dangerous revolutionary nonsense (whatever it might mean), and nor, it would seem, was his young student: 'One might observe that Wojtyla's works do not, in fact, take a direct position on the intellectual controversies which run through Catholic thought,' writes Buttiglione. 'He limits himself to indications and suggestions within an authentically personal exploration which eventually flow into an original construction.'

Karol Wojtyla's hard work on his dissertation earned him a pass *magna cum laude*, an impressive result but perhaps not quite the ultimate goal of a *summa cum laude* (with highest praise) which he might have hoped for. At this stage of his career he could very happily have picked up a job in the Vatican bureaucracy, but he chose instead to return to his troubled homeland without a second thought, and from the glory that was Rome he was despatched to a country parish outside Krakow.

Like an ecclesiastical version of some eighteenth-century English dandy returning from the Grand Tour with stylish continental manners, Fr Karol had picked up some elegant spiritual flourishes during his time abroad. He had been especially impressed by what he learnt during his pilgrimage to the home of St John Maria Vianney (better known as the Curé d'Ars), the humble nineteenth-century parish priest who became a by-word for simple spirituality, and put the experience to good use when he took up residence in the village of Niegowic.

I went from Krakow to Gdow by bus, and from there a local man gave me a ride in his cart to the village of Marszowice; from there he advised me to take a shortcut on foot. I could already see the church in Niegowic in the distance. It was harvest time. I walked through the fields of grain with crops in part already reaped, and in part still waving in the wind. When I reached the territory of the Niegowic parish, I knelt down and kissed the ground. It was a gesture I had learned from St John Maria Vianney.

The image of a young priest's delight in the beauty of God's creation and his excitement as he arrives in his first parish is authentic and arresting; the gesture seems irredeemably self-dramatising.

4

Priest, Philosopher and Bishop

In the introduction to *Love and Responsibility*, his book about sex and marriage, Karol Wojtyla wrote, 'It [the book] is not an exposition of doctrine. It is, rather, the result above all of an incessant confrontation of doctrine with life (which is just what the work of a spiritual adviser consists of).' *Love and Responsibility* was his first book, and a Catholic who read it when it came out would have been impressed by the frankness of its approach. By and large Catholic clergymen in those days did not publish works which included clinical descriptions of the female orgasm. The tone of Catholic teaching on sex in the 1950s had been set very firmly indeed by Pius XII: 'Unhappily, incessant waves of the pleasure principle are invading the world and threaten to submerge in the growing tide of its thoughts, desires and acts the whole of married life,' he told a group of newly-weds in 1951. 'To this one must say "No". The gravity and sanctity of the Christian moral law do not permit an unrestrained satisfaction of the sexual instinct, which tends only to pleasure and enjoyment; they do not allow rational man to let himself be dominated up to that point, as to either the substance or the circumstances of the act.'

But *Love and Responsibility* opens with the altogether fresher voice of a priest who has actually talked to his parishioners about what was happening in their lives. 'Although it is easy to draw up a set of rules for Catholics in the sector of "sexual" morality,' writes the young prelate,

> the need to validate these rules makes itself felt at every step. For the rules often run up against greater difficulties in practice

than in theory, and the spiritual adviser, who is concerned above all with the practical, must seek ways of justifying them. For his task is not only to command or forbid but to justify, to interpret, to explain.

The evidence suggests that at this stage of his life Karol Wojtyla took the idea of a dialogue with the faithful in his care very seriously – even when the circumstances made it difficult. The tension between 'doctrine' and 'life', between the top-down theology he learnt as a Catholic academic and the practical experience of Catholic life in the world, is one of the enduring themes of his story.

To the much-travelled intellectual just back from Rome, life in a rural parish outside Krakow in the 1940s must have come as something of a shock; Niegowic was 'a small parish at the end of the world'. There was no electricity or running water in the priests' house, and when Mieczyslaw Malinski paid a visit to his friend he found an 'old church surrounded by linden trees . . . a well, a kitchen garden and orchard, a cowshed and chickens'. A horse and cart was the main means of transport to the outlying villages in the parish; Karol Wojtyla taught in four village schools, and according to the school principal in Niegowic he would – true to form – usually read a book while he was being bounced along in the buggy between them. He complained to Malinski – who was now a priest himself – about the ordeal of visiting parishioners during the winter months:

The snow sticks to the hem of your cassock and melts when you are indoors. Then in the open air it freezes so that the cassock is stiff and heavy and interferes with walking. By evening, you feel you can hardly go a step further, but you have to because you know people have been waiting for this visit all year. You go in and say 'Blessed be Jesus Christ', you greet the whole family, you pray with them and sprinkle the cottage with holy water, and the stables too, so that the cattle will prosper during the coming year. Then you go back into the house and you can't escape sitting and talking to everyone for a bit.

This was not his natural milieu.

Yet he seems to have gone about his duties more than conscientiously – he married thirteen couples and baptised forty-eight children during his eight months in Niegowic, and was particularly diligent about hearing confessions. Just after his arrival there – in August 1948 – the parish held its *Odpust,* the annual celebration of its patron saint, and the new arrival was chosen to address the parish dinner about his experiences in France and Belgium. Rather to the irritation of his fellow priests, he turned up late for the meal because he had been kept on in the confessional by penitents.

His escape from snow-encrusted cassocks, livestock blessing and peasant chat came remarkably swiftly. In the spring of 1949 he was recalled to Krakow to take charge of the church of St Florian; just outside the walls of the city's Old Town, it served a prosperous and intellectually curious congregation – it was something of a favourite among both the students and professors of the Jagiellonian University. Fr Karol was now very much in his element, and his talent for working formidably hard – sixteen- to eighteen-hour days were his usual pattern – paid dividends. He started visiting the university boarding houses and dormitories – 'making contacts and drumming up trade', as the papal biographer George Weigel has put it – and put together a programme of events that quickly made St Florian's one of the most popular parishes in the city. A choir was formed to sing Gregorian chant, there were regular Thursday evening conferences on theology, retreats to nearby monasteries and convents in the countryside and days of contemplation. During Lent Fr Karol drew on his theatrical experience to direct some of his student parishioners in performances of the medieval mystery plays, and his sermons drew a good class of worshipper to the pews on Sunday mornings. The confessional seems to have occupied a good deal of his time and energy, as it had done in Niegowic; if you confessed to Fr Karol you could be fairly sure you would not escape with a quick 'Hail Mary' by way of penance. He was said to be a 'demanding confessor' who could keep a penitent in the confessional box for an hour or more. As a result of these spiritual marathons his reputation for a chronic lack of punctuality became settled. One of Cardinal Sapieha's nieces asked him to teach her daughter the catechism; she said later that he was 'never' on time for the lessons at the little girl's home and an eight o'clock appointment would often begin at ten thirty at night. The *Kalendarium* has given us a helpful yardstick for judging the productivity of this prodigious output of priestly effort – the number of altar servers at St Florian's rose from ten in 1946 to nearly a hundred in 1952.

While Karol Wojtyla was busying himself so assiduously with the spiritual welfare of the growing number of souls in his care, Josef Stalin was tightening his control over the world in which the future pope was working.

The Soviet leader had made his intentions towards Poland plain enough during the Warsaw Rising in the late summer of 1944, when for those glorious but savage sixty-three days the Polish Home Army took and held their capital from the Nazis. The British and American governments called on their Russian ally to provide assistance to the Poles, but he dismissed their heroism as 'a reckless adventure causing useless victims'. Asked at least to offer the use of his airfields so that British and American planes could drop arms to the Poles, he hummed and hawed and dragged his feet until it was too late. By the time of the Rising the Soviets had already established an embryo puppet Polish government of their own, and Churchill commented that 'The Russians wished to have the non-communist Poles destroyed in full, but also keep alive the idea that they were going to their rescue.' Poland was to provide a model for the system of satellite states by which Soviet control over Eastern and Central Europe would be secured.

The election which cemented post-war communist control of Poland took place in 1947, while Karol Wojtyla was studying in Rome. The historian Norman Davies describes it like this:

> The Election was neither 'free' nor 'unfettered'. The list of candidates was vetted in advance by the government. Two million voters had been struck from the register by government-controlled electoral committees. Factory workers were marched to the polls by their foreman, and told to vote for the government on pain of their jobs. The rules of secret balloting were ignored. The result was a foregone conclusion.

The election gave the communist-led Democratic Bloc 80 per cent of the vote. And by the time Karol Wojtyla became the parish priest of St Florian's in 1949 Stalin had completed the task of ensuring that the new communist government in Warsaw would always do Moscow's bidding. The independent-minded Wladyslaw Gomulka was denounced and forced to resign from his position as general secretary of the Polish Workers' Party in the autumn of 1948, and his replacement, Boleslaw Bierut (who was also Poland's president at the time), was a loyal Stalinist.

Poland now entered another cycle of abject misery, which was to last until the political crisis of 1956. One of John Paul's biographers, George Blazynski, has memorably described the country during this period as 'a part of the world where the dawn knock on the door was still expected, where prisons were full and beatings were many, where the secret policeman was still his brother's keeper, and where the Great Teacher was neither Christ nor Buddha but the megalomaniac son of a Georgian shoemaker through whom millions had died'. Anyone with a background thought likely to dispose them towards a challenge to communist control or to Poland's 'friendship' with the Soviet Union faced official harassment or worse. One former officer in the Home Army recalled his time in the tender hands of the secret police like this:

> There were the so-called 'Winter Sports', which was perhaps the most painful. One was interrogated all day and then at night put in a cell, a completely empty cell with the window taken out, and it took place in winter, so it was freezing outside and freezing in the cell as well. The person was made to stand naked in front of that window and one had to stand all night like that, because one couldn't move or there would instantly be further punishment.

Stalinist rule was not quite as random and brutal as Nazi occupation had been, but it followed a similar pattern in its assault on Polish national life. 'With the UB [secret police] snapping at its heels,' wrote Neal Ascherson, 'the whole nation was mobilised into a breakneck drive to create a Soviet model state on the Vistula. All independent opinion was stamped out while a totalitarian party dictatorship set about destroying and rebuilding Polish institutions on the Soviet pattern.' And that, of course, put the Roman Catholic Church squarely back in the firing line.

Under the Nazis the Church's oppressor had been a foreign power; now, for the first time in history, the Polish Catholic Church was attacked by the country's own government. Priests and bishops faced capricious arrest again, Church property was confiscated and anti-Catholic propaganda began to appear in the government-controlled press. In January 1950 the papers alleged that goods given to the international Catholic charity Caritas were being sold on the black market and that priests were living on the high hog with the proceeds; there were 'lurid tales of drunken priests and nuns coercing children into sex at a youth home, while dishing out bad food and no medical care'. But the government's most effective weapon against the Church was more insidious: using the 'divide and rule' principle, it established a pro-government organisation called Pax which was nominally Catholic but in fact worked to undermine the authority of the established hierarchy. It was run by one Boleslaw Piasecki, who had a less than glorious pre-war history as the leader of one of Poland's few genuine fascist movements, the Falanga, but it still managed to attract enough genuine Catholic support to present the hierarchy with a real challenge.

The Polish Church was led during this period by another of those towering ecclesiastical figures who played a decisive role in their country's history. Stefan Wyszynski had been a kind of chaplain to the Polish underground in Warsaw during the war years – rather charmingly code-named by the fighters 'Sister Cecilia'. His background was in academia, and an early Cold War CIA report described him as an 'enlightened and liberal thinker . . . often considered a radical'. He became primate of Poland on the death of Cardinal Hlond in October 1948, and was to be a powerful – if not always easy – presence in Karol Wojtyla's life for the next three decades. An American visitor who called on the Polish primate in the 1950s remembered him thus:

His clean cut features were sharp; his eyes were blue and alive, and I thought he had the longest fingers of anyone I had ever seen. There was strength in his face but also an extraordinary repose, as if years of inner reflection had given him a serenity that no outside element could break. This man does not struggle any more, I thought, he won the battle with himself a long time ago. His road lies clear before him and he *knows* that God is with him.

It is an evocation of quiet strength that is oddly reminiscent of later accounts of what it was like to meet John Paul in his prime. The sometimes difficult relationship between these two giants of the Polish Church, Wyszynski and Wojtyla, finally ended in a most poignant way in 1981, when Pope John Paul, himself in a hospital bed in Rome recovering from the attempt on his life, telephoned the dying cardinal in a hospital in Warsaw to bid him farewell.

Wyszynski was prepared to stand up to the authorities when he thought it essential. He banned his priests from attending meetings at which the Church was attacked – a way of striking at Pax, which some priests had joined – and in February 1950 he declared in a pastoral letter, 'The Episcopate has done much and is willing to do more to maintain peace . . . There are, however, limits we bishops cannot cross if we wish to remain faithful to the commandments of God.' But his instinct was to reach an accommodation with the authorities if at all possible, and later that year he signed a kind of concordat with the Polish government, by which the Church accepted that it must act in conformity with the '*raison d'état* of the Polish government', and the government in return accepted papal authority in 'matters of faith, the moral order and ecclesiastical jurisdiction'. 'I want my priests at the altar, at the pulpit, and in the confessional – not in prison,' he said.

Not everyone in the church hierarchy saw it quite like that. Karol Wojtyla's mentor, Prince Sapieha, an old man now, was in Rome when the deal was done – indeed, it rather looked as if the younger but more senior Cardinal Wyszynski had deliberately waited until he was out of the country before going ahead.

Virulently anti-communist, he exploded with rage when he heard the news. And his views were shared by Pius XII, who had just published a denunciation of communists as the enemies of the Church in Central and Eastern Europe. Sapieha returned to Poland with a frosty papal letter criticising the Polish hierarchy for 'capitulating to the state'. However, Wyszynski was soon to prove that he was anything but a soft touch. Three years later the communists tried to go back on the concordat by insisting that the state should be able to appoint and dismiss all priests and bishops. Cardinal Wyszynski responded with a sermon in which he declared, 'We teach that it is proper to render unto Caesar the things that are Caesar's and to God what is God's. But when Caesar seats himself on the altar we respond curtly: he must not.' He was promptly arrested and interned in a monastery.

Throughout this period of political drama and high ecclesiastical intrigue Karol Wojtyla kept his energies firmly fixed on the practical needs of his parishioners – and later, when he became a university teacher, his students – and his mind focused on the great existential questions; it was a mirror of the way he had shut out some of the horrors of the Nazi occupation by devoting himself to his vocation, and of the way he had spent the pivotal 1948 election in Italy with his head buried in the works of Saints Thomas Aquinas and John of the Cross. One of the most striking characteristics of the man who would one day become the most political of popes was that he never seems to have read newspapers and as a young man appears to have had no interest whatever in the small change of political life. Instead, he spent much of the 1950s developing his taste for two passions which would stay with him for as long as he was able to enjoy them: philosophy and the great outdoors.

In the first days of 1953 – as Cardinal Wyszynski and the Polish government were squaring up for their confrontation – Fr Karol's interest in skiing was rekindled by an invitation to spend a few days in a resort in the Tatra Mountains. A group of university science teachers who had come to know him through his work with students provided him with a pair of skis and adapted the bindings to fit the 'plain black shoes usually worn by clergy. The fitting was done by one of us at the Institute of Physics of the

Jagiellonian University on Golebia Street.' He turned out to be rather handy on skis and the outings became a regular feature of his winters. He did, however, insist on saying mass every day; he would either stop at village churches along the ski route or celebrate the sacrament in the open air if necessary; 'Wojtyla, who wore normal skiing attire, carried his cassock in his backpack, donning it at the celebrations. He had a collapsible chalice. Sometimes he said Mass at a peasant's home, other times in a barn, where Wojtyla and his companions erected an altar from straw, or on a mountainside with backpacks and tree branches made into altars.'

One can imagine these occasions having something of the romance and intensity of the clandestine masses said by the 'whisky priest' of Graham Greene's novel *The Power and the Glory*, on the run from the authorities in the hills of Mexico; it is difficult to overstate the preciousness of the celebration of the Eucharist to Catholics at this period, especially those living under regimes which persecuted the Church, and Karol Wojtyla's taste for combining religion with outdoor activity carried a degree of risk. 'You could,' as one of his skiing companions put it, 'go to jail for celebrating Mass in a forest.' It was also illegal for a priest to lead any kind of youth group on an outing, but the future pope began to use his forays into the countryside for pastoral purposes too; he added hiking and kayaking to his list of sporting accomplishments and would often take groups of students with him on expeditions in the summer, using the evenings to talk to them about the life choices and moral questions they faced.

Fr Wojtyla's Christianity was nothing if not muscular during this period; in 1954 he was awarded the Bronze Medal for Hiking Tourism, Category D, after completing 'lowland excursions on foot totalling 166 km'. And in the summer of that year there was a two-week kayaking trip through the canals and lakes of northern Poland, up near the border with what is now Lithuania but was then part of the Soviet Union. It was a party of ten – in five kayaks – and the young priest's companions remembered it thus: 'Daily Mass. Father Wojtyla gladly intones Marian hymns. Discussion at the campfires. During travel, he intones secular songs. Individual conversations, very intimate, very retreat like. The style and form worked out during this excursion endured for many years.' Some members of this group went on taking trips like this together right up until the time of Karol Wojtyla's election as pope, and there does seem to have been something remarkable about the dynamics of the relationships he managed to establish. Fr Malinski would sometimes join the expeditions. 'Karol's young companions called him *Wujek* [uncle],' he wrote.

> There was no vestige of formality, and the whole atmosphere was one of comradeship . . . For all the frankness and simplicity of the young people's behaviour, they genuinely respected their 'uncle' – even, for instance, when they laughed at his attempts to ride a bicycle: one of them usually had to ride in front of him, because if he relapsed into meditation, or 'turned off', he was liable to run into a tree.

The 'intimate' conversations in the great outdoors seem to have provided a good deal of the material which formed the basis for that claim in *Love and Responsibility*, his book on sexual ethics, that priests are qualified to talk about this area because 'in their pastoral work they encounter these particular problems so often, and in such a variety of circumstances and situations, that a different type of experience is created'. Fr Wojtyla had shown his interest in the moral issues thrown up by sex and marriage very early in his career; in 1950 he set up a class at St Florian's to prepare young couples for marriage. And he was anything but coy about addressing head on issues which many priests of his generation might have felt awkward about. 'The sexual drive is a gift from God,' he told a group of students at a Lenten retreat in 1954.

> Man may offer this drive to God exclusively through a vow of virginity. He may offer it to another human being with the awareness that he is offering it to a person. It must not be a matter of chance. On the other side there is another human being who must not be hurt, whom one must love . . . Love is not a fantasy, if it is tied to sexual drive, it guarantees through

95

that drive an extension of love in a new, aroused life of a new person. If we respect the sexual drive within love, we will not violate love, we will not bring love to ruination.

There was nothing revolutionary in the central message under-lying this kind of preaching – certainly, in terms of laying down what Catholics could and could not do in the bedroom Karol Wojtyla was very conventional indeed – but the language was new, and it may have reflected a realisation that the Church needed to rethink the way it presented its teachings about sex. The long hours in the confessional and the fireside chats paid dividends; Karol Wojtyla spotted the sexual revolution of the 1960s well in advance. He was also working in an environment created by an aggressively secular government; Poland introduced extremely liberal laws on abortion in the 1950s, and young people going on state-sponsored summer trips were actively encouraged to experiment sexually, apparently as a direct challenge to the Church's hold on moral standards. On his own summer trips, meanwhile, Karol Wojtyla began handing out drafts of some of the chapters of *Love and Responsibility*, to be read and discussed in camp-site seminars.

The book is not the kind of thing most of us would naturally turn to for relaxation after a hard day's kayaking or hiking, and one cannot help feeling a little sorry for the serious-minded young men and women who were required to wrestle with it over their *al fresco* evening meals. It is dense with philosophical jargon and thick with nice distinctions, many of them rather tiresomely expressed in Latin: 'There is, however, a profound difference between love expressed as desire (*amor concupiscentia*) and desire itself (*concupiscentia*), especially sensual desire. Desire presupposes awareness of some lack, an unpleasant sensation which can be eliminated by means of a particular good . . .' and so on. The style reflects the fact that Karol Wojtyla was spending more and more of his time as a professional philosopher. He was given a sabbatical from St Florian's to write a post-doctoral work in the autumn of 1953 – although he maintained his connection with the parish and his role as a kind of informal chaplain to Krakow's students right up until his ordination as a bishop in 1958 – and he was appointed to teach in the philosophy department of the Catholic University of Lublin in 1954.

The focus for Karol Wojtyla's philosophical efforts during this period was the branch of philosophy known as phenomenology, defined in its broadest terms as 'a descriptive philosophy of experience'. The acknowledged father of the school, Edmund Husserl, summed up its essence in the slogan 'Back to the things themselves', and the American Catholic academic Michael Novak has called it an effort to 'bring back into philosophy everyday things, concrete wholes, the basic experiences of life as they come to us'. Karol Wojtyla chose to approach the subject through a study of Husserl's disciple Max Scheler.

It was daunting stuff. Fr Mieczyslaw Malinski called round at his old friend's lodgings one evening to find him wrestling with a Scheler text. 'Look at what I have got to cope with,' complained Karol Wojtyla. 'I can hardly make it out at all, my German is poor, and there are a lot of technical terms I don't know how to translate. Do you know what I am doing? I've started to make a translation of the whole book – there's nothing else for it.'

The title of the future pope's dissertation – 'An Evaluation of the Possibility of Constructing a Christian Ethic on the Basis of the System of Max Scheler' – is less than encouraging to the philosophically faint-hearted. But it is really an attempt to resolve – in an intellectually rather grand way – that 'confrontation between doctrine and life' which he referred to in the introduction to *Love and Responsibility*. George Weigel describes the Scheler study as 'Karol Wojtyla's first sustained attempt to link the realist *objectivity* embedded in the philosophy he had learned in the seminary and at the Angelicum to modern philosophy's emphasis on human experience and human *subjectivity*'. The future pope concluded very firmly that it was *not* possible to use Max Scheler's teaching as the basis for Christian ethics, but it is remarkable that he tried. Apart from anything else, Scheler was a rake. Born to Protestant Jewish parents he converted to Catholicism at the age of fourteen – because he liked the smells and bells – but as a student he plunged into the pleasures of sex and drink and behaved so badly that he was banned from the University of Munich for moral turpitude. He spent the First World War writing public relations tracts for the kaiser, later renounced his Catholicism, and was married three times; it was not the sort of *curriculum vitae* that naturally recommended itself to the future Pope John Paul II.

The autumn of 1956 was academically productive and successful. Karol Wojtyla began a series of lectures on the 'Propaedeutics of Theology' and on Economic Ethics at the seminary in Krakow. At the same time he was teaching Moral Theology and – his favourite subject – Marital Ethics at Lublin University. In late November he was nominated as an assistant professor; the university's rector recommended 'Rev Dr Karol Wojtyla' as 'one of the most talented lecturers in the department of Theology' and praised his 'good preparation, deep scholarly interests, moral qualities and, finally his loyalty to authority'. On 1 December his appointment was confirmed, giving him a full-time job on the university's staff.

Reading the account of this smooth upward trajectory into full-time academic life in the *Kalendarium* you find nothing to reflect the fact that Poland was going through a terrifying political confrontation that autumn. There had been signs of anti-Soviet unrest in Eastern Europe ever since Stalin's death in 1953. In Poland things remained calm at first, but the political temperature rose steadily over the next three years. In 1954 a colonel in the secret police defected and broadcast his story of torture, blackmail and Soviet meddling in Poland's affairs over Radio Free Europe. The following year World Youth Day was held in Warsaw, bringing thousands of young people into the Polish capital with their tales of what life was like out there in the free world. Intellectuals began testing the limits of censorship, and even within the Communist Party itself there was pressure for change.

The spark was provided by Nikita Khrushchev's famous speech to the Twentieth Congress of the Soviet Communist Party in February 1956, in which he denounced Stalin's crimes. The so-called 'secret speech' proved to be anything but that in Warsaw, where reform-minded communists cheerfully circulated the text among Western journalists, and it ignited a full-blown crisis which dominated the rest of that year. Encouraged by the breath of change in the air, workers at the Zipso Locomotive Factory in

Poznan staged protests about their working conditions in June. On the 28th of that month a workers' march turned into a political demonstration with much broader ambitions; banners reading 'Russians Go Home' were raised alongside those calling for 'Bread and Freedom', and 100,000 people came onto the streets. The communist authorities reacted – with predictable brutality – by shooting at the crowd. A British businessman who was in the city for a trade fair described the moment things turned nasty; he was driving through 'good-humoured' demonstrators who cheered and clapped when they saw the Union Jack fluttering from his car, but 'within minutes of the police opening fire the mood changed. When they heard that a child was one of those shot down the demonstrators, roaring with rage, converged on the secret police headquarters. It soon became a regular battle. Ferocious street-fighting broke out.' Dozens of people were killed in two days of fighting before order was restored, including several Communist Party officials who had the misfortune to be caught on the wrong side of the line.

Things came to a head in October. As Karol Wojtyla was leading a bicycle pilgrimage to Czestochowa, presenting a thesis on 'The Foundation of Perfectionism in Ethics' and receiving his teaching assignments for the next academic year, the Polish Communist Party was locked in a bitter internal struggle between its Stalinist and reformist wings. The reformists won, and Wladsylaw Gomulka, disgraced eight years earlier because of his determination to remain independent of Moscow, was elected general secretary. Nikita Khrushchev immediately flew to Warsaw to protest against this act of gross insubordination by one of the Kremlin's client states, and Soviet forces stationed in Poland were mobilised to strike against Warsaw if it was judged necessary. For the next twenty-four hours the threat of a new Polish–Soviet war looked very real indeed. Khrushchev – 'in an apoplectic mood of undisguised rage' – and Gomulka confronted one another across a table late into the night until the Soviet leader finally backed down, apparently convinced by Gomulka's assurances that, whatever he thought of the Kremlin, he was and would remain a true communist. Khrushchev went home and the Soviet tanks went back to their bases.

Khrushchev accepted Gomulka's position at 2.00 a.m. on Saturday 20 October. The following Wednesday the new Polish leader despatched a cabinet minister and one of his closest advisers to the remote monastery in the Carpathian Mountains where Cardinal Wyszynski had spent the last of the three years during which he had been cooped up under house arrest (he had passed the time studying the works of Marx and Lenin, on the principle that it pays to know your enemy). They were authorised to offer him unconditional freedom, and he was back in his primate's palace in Warsaw a couple of days later. It was an eloquent testimony to the way the Church had kept its place in the nation's life despite Stalinist repression – and, as it turned out, an extremely smart move by Gomulka.

The revolutionary mood in Poland remained strong and the risk of armed confrontation with the Soviets was still acute; the Soviet military campaign to crush the Hungarian Uprising had begun a few days after Gomulka's agreement with Khrushchev, and it provided a salutary reminder of what all-out war with Moscow would mean. The Church's voice could be decisive.

On the first Sunday of November Cardinal Wyszynski rewarded the new Polish leadership for his freedom. As the venue for his first sermon after his release he chose the church where he had been due to preach on the day after his arrest three years earlier; then, a sign had been plastered over the doors of the Holy Cross Church in Warsaw declaring simply, 'The Cardinal will not preach here today', and Wyszynski was now able to begin his homily with a theatrical flourish. 'I am a little late in coming to you,' he declared from the pulpit, 'a little more than three years. Forgive me. This is the first time I have been so tardy.' The American ambassador was there and reported home: 'atmosphere emotionally charged, congregation in tears'. But the cardinal's message was very carefully calculated and exactly what the new Polish leadership needed to calm the revolutionary spirit abroad in the land. 'A man dies once and is quickly covered with glory, but he lives in difficulty, in hardship, pain and suffering for long years – and that is a greater heroism,' the primate said. 'The call is to work and to order, application to daily tasks, rather than to martyrdom and resistance.'

After the archbishop's intervention the crisis cooled, and for about a year Poland enjoyed life under a more liberal regime with a significant degree of independence from Moscow. When the Soviet action in Hungary was debated at the United Nations the Polish representative failed to vote on Moscow's side for the first time since 1945. At home a free press flourished for a brief period. An American visitor to Poland in February 1957 reported that 'All papers, including official government publications, wrote what they pleased. Many attacked Russia bitterly, questioning some of the basic tenets of communism. They blamed the years of Stalinist rule for the acute poverty the country found itself in.' Christine Hotchkiss, a Polish exile in New York, made a pilgrimage to the land of her birth in the immediate aftermath of the October crisis and recorded her impressions and conversations in a book called *Home to Poland*: 'Do you know the story of the two dogs who met crossing the Polish–Czech frontier?' a young student asked her. 'The Polish dog said, "I am going to Prague to buy my wife a pair of your fine Czech shoes" . . . The Czech dog looked over his shoulder and said, "I am crossing into Poland in order to bark."'

The Church benefited from the new political climate too. Cardinal Wyszynski was able to use the leverage he had in the early days after the crisis of 1956 to negotiate a new agreement with the state. Priests and bishops who had been arrested were freed. The Church was allowed to regain something of its place in the nation's institutional life – prisons and hospitals got their chaplains back, and religion reappeared on the syllabus in state schools. And the state relaxed its control over church appointments and agreed to permit genuine Catholic lay organisations to operate alongside Pax. Pius XII – who was very old and very sick by this stage – remained suspicious of any kind of accommodation with a communist regime, but Wyszynski's compact endured and provided the framework for Church–state relations right up until the collapse of communism more than three decades later.

The new concordat meant that when Karol Wojtyla took his first step on the ladder of the hierarchy he was doing so in a church with a new sense of self-confidence. Quite why his name was sent to Rome as a suitable candidate to be an auxiliary bishop remains something of a mystery; he had no real administrative experience beyond the two years he had spent at St Florian's, he was very young, and he seemed increasingly settled in academic life. There has been speculation that Cardinal Sapieha had passed on some kind of master plan for his protégé to his successor on his deathbed; that seems pretty far-fetched, although it is certainly true that the new Archbishop of Krakow, Eugeniusz Baziak, was responsible for putting the name of Wojtyla forward.

Karol Wojtyla was on holiday in the lakes region of northern Poland when he got the call to the purple – it was an area traditionally associated with the cult of the Virgin, so he was able to combine Marian veneration with his kayaking. To complete the conditions for a perfect Wojtyla vacation he had dished out chapters of *Love and Responsibility* to his group so that they could discuss it 'sitting on the grass, on the lakeshore and on the edge of the forest'. But a call to the local church summoned him to an audience with Cardinal Wyszynski in Warsaw. He has given us a rather romantic account of his journey to the capital:

> I set off first in the canoe over the waves of the river, and then in a truck laden with sacks of flour, until I got to Olsztynek. The train for Warsaw left late at night. I had brought my sleeping bag with me, thinking that I might be able to catch a few winks in the station and ask someone to wake me when it was time to board the train. There was no need for that in any event, because I didn't sleep.

As catholic (with a small 'c') as he was Catholic in his reading tastes, he was carrying a copy of Hemingway's *Old Man and the Sea*.

It was a pivotal moment in his life – a decisive change from the academic career which had seemed his destiny – and a number of stories have circulated about the future pope's interview with his primate on that August day in 1958. The most frequently told includes a strong suggestion of ambition. This is the version of events reported by Carl Bernstein and Marco Politi in *His Holiness*:

The primate paused to study Wojtyla's reaction [to the news of his appointment] . . . Sometimes an intimidated candidate for apostolic office in Wojtyla's situation would babble 'I have to consult with my spiritual director about this decision.' Then the primate would say 'If you are a mature person, you should know what you want to do.'

Other priests might try to gain a little time by saying, 'I have to ask Jesus about it in my prayers.' At which the primate would point to the door. 'There's a chapel right behind that door there. Please say your prayer. But please don't take any more than fifteen minutes, because I don't have the time, and neither does Jesus.'

Wyszynski asked Wojtyla, 'Do you accept the appointment?'

'Where do I sign?' the priest replied without hesitation.

John Paul's own recollection of the occasion – in *Rise, Let Us Be On Our Way* – is slightly different but certainly suggests that the exchange was businesslike.

Upon hearing the words of the Primate informing me of the decision of the Holy See, I said, 'Your Eminence, I am too young; I am only thirty eight.'

But the Primate said 'That is a weakness which can soon be remedied. Please do not oppose the will of the Holy Father.'

So I said 'I accept.'

'Then let's have lunch,' the Primate concluded.

Poland's youngest bishop-elect insisted on finishing his canoeing holiday before his consecration – a decision regarded as somewhat eccentric by his superiors. The book he published to mark forty-five years as a bishop includes the intriguing aside, 'When I took up my paddle, I again felt somewhat strange. The coincidence of dates struck me: the date of my nomination was July fourth, the anniversary of the blessing of Wawel Cathedral. It is an anniversary that I have always cherished in my heart. I thought this coincidence must have some special meaning' – the future pope was ever vigilant for the hand of Providence in his life. He was consecrated at the end of September in Wawel Cathedral – close to the chapel where he had been ordained a priest a mere twelve years earlier – and his account of the day reflects the way the richness of Catholic ritual and tradition had taken full possession of his imaginative landscape. He remembers the Litany of the Saints being sung, and the invocation to the 'Holy Angels of God' prompts him to reflection:

> I have a special devotion to my Guardian Angel. Probably like all children, during my childhood I would often pray: '*Angel of God, my guardian, be always with me . . . always stand ready to help me, guard my soul and my body.*' My Guardian Angel knows what I am doing. My faith in him, in his protective presence, continues to grow deeper and deeper.

So for all the outward signs of modernity and openness in his pastoral style the new bishop was attached to a very old-fashioned kind of personal piety – and he can have had no inkling of the dramatic challenge that brand of Catholicism was about to face. A fortnight after the consecration service in Wawel Cathedral Pius XII finally died. After three days in conclave and ten deadlocked ballots, the College of Cardinals elected a successor they believed would serve as a stop-gap pope, Angelo Roncalli, the Patriarch of Venice. Pope John XXIII was seventy-seven and came of peasant stock, and no one expected him to do very much – indeed, that was rather the point of electing him as the *papa di passagio*, the transitional pope; the Church faced some big decisions after Pius XII's long reign but their eminences apparently thought it best to put them off for a while. As it turned out, John XXIII launched one of the biggest revolutions in the history of the Church, and his reign laid the contours of the intellectual battlefield on which the great confrontations of John Paul's pontificate would be fought twenty years later.

The new bishop set about his work in characteristically energetic style. He kept on some of his teaching duties at Lublin University, but most of his work involved diocesan administration and the sort of duties that were part of an auxiliary bishop's routine. The *Kalendarium* lists a characteristic appointments diary in the autumn after his consecration: 'November 16th; 7 a.m. Kozy,

Holy Mass and sermon . . . 10 a.m. Krakow, Pontifical Mass and sermon at St Stanislaw Kostka parish, 6 p.m. service and sermon for male youth at the parish of the Blessed Virgin Mary, 7 p.m. Sermon for lawyers at the parish of the Virgin Mary . . .' It was more stimulating than the usual 'births, deaths and marriages' diet of a parish priest's life, but a pretty punishing schedule for a man who was still writing poetry, plays and articles on top of everything else. He accepted only three 'perks' as a result of his elevation to the episcopacy: a reading light and a folding desk in the back of his car, his own canoe and tent for his trips, and the removal of his mother's and brother's bodies from the graveyard in Wadowice to lie beside that of his father in Krakow.

His new position brought him into reasonably frequent contact with Cardinal Wyszynski and it soon became apparent that the lunch the two men had shared that day in Warsaw had not established a foundation for friendship between them – rather the reverse, in fact. When a visiting American bishop asked the Polish primate about Bishop Wojtyla shortly after his appointment, Wyszynski replied, 'Oh, he's an opportunist.' In his book *Man of the Century* Jonathan Kwitny reports a meeting of the Polish episcopate at which the tension between these two strong-willed men came into the open:

> Wyszynski was lecturing in his usual style. Wojtyla, also as usual, was in the back row, reading. Noting the new bishop's apparent inattentiveness, Wyszynski grew ever more irritated. At last he said 'Now Bishop Wojtyla is going to tell us what we are talking about.' Whereupon Wojtyla looked up and recounted everything Wyszynski had just been saying. It was the first of many times this would happen; Wojtyla's capacity to concentrate on two things at once amazed bystanders and infuriated people like Wyszynski.

Part of the problem was simply generational; Wyszynski was nineteen years older than Karol Wojtyla, and while the young bishop was musing about the proper place of sexual pleasure in Christian marriage in *Love and Responsibility*, the older cardinal was sounding off about loose morals in fire-and-brimstone sermons. 'How much filth there is among us! We protest against the filth in books and in the press and against increasing pornography,' Poland's primate fulminated from his pulpit. 'In the press we can see fashionable dolls and frivolous ladies whose costly dresses are . . . awakening unnecessary desire among peacefully working people . . .' Karol Wojtyla's self-conscious intellectualism probably did not help the relationship; despite his own academic background the primate was suspicious of priests who dabbled in poetry and plays as Wojtyla continued to do, and according to an MP who knew Wyszynski the older man 'considered rural people are the salt of the earth in Poland, and . . . wanted an Episcopate along those lines'. Part of the problem may have been the straightforward rivalry between two powerful figures that can be found in the office politics of any big organisation.

But the two men shared a joint enemy – communism. The hopes of a new and more liberal communist future which were born in the October crisis of 1956 soon foundered, and Gomulka proved that he had been sincere in his promises to Khrushchev – he really was first and foremost a good communist. In a sad irony the first anniversary of the crisis was marked by a scaled-down version of the events of a year earlier: in October 1957 *Po Prostu* (the title means 'Speaking Truthfully'), the newspaper which had become the main voice of the reformers, was closed down by the authorities. When students at Warsaw Polytechnic came onto the streets in protest the police met them with batons, and there were four days of rioting in the capital. Gomulka set in motion a purge of the ruling Communist Party (properly known as the Polish United Workers' Party, or PZPR to give it its Polish acronym) and about a fifth of its members were removed. It culminated in the party congress of 1959 when all the main reformers were expelled from the party leadership. The Church felt the new chill too. In the summer of 1959 the police raided the monastery of Jasna Gora, the national shrine which had played such a prominent part of the future pope's childhood, and removed unlicensed printing equipment. Cardinal Wyszynski's microphone was seized while he was addressing a holiday crowd, and religion was removed from the school curriculum again.

It was a campaign to roll back the influence of the Church and replace it with the power of the state and the ideology of the Party – and Karol Wojtyla's new position inevitably propelled him into the front line of the confrontation. On 22 March 1959 he preached at the beginning of a retreat for lawyers at the Dominican Church in Krakow, and over the following three days he gave a retreat for doctors. The biographer Tad Sculz has turned up a letter written to Archbishop Baziak of Krakow on 23 March by one Wiktor Boniecki, the chairman of the local praesidium of the National Council, accusing the new auxiliary bishop of using his meetings with groups of professional people for seditious purposes. Bishop Wojtyla, the party man alleges, has been encouraging the clergy to 'violate the law', and in evidence against him he cites 'meditation days organised by him for lawyers, physicians, teachers and the youth. Organising such occasions introduces an artificial division between believers and non-believers, violating at the same time the social and political unity of local society.' The document provides an intriguing insight into what it was like to operate in a society where life at every level was scoured by the raw edges of confrontation between two big institutions driven by irreconcilable belief systems. 'Such activity,' it continues,

> deepens the divisions of citizens employed by state institutions into believers and non-believers . . . It distorts society's views, urging people to value more the opinion of a physician who is a practising Catholic combating enlightened motherhood, or of a teacher who omits certain 'sensitive' questions from government-approved textbooks, than the opinions of their non-believer colleagues.

Bishop Wojtyla's response, in a note to his archbishop, was robust: 'I must state that this charge is baseless because there is no law forbidding bishops and priests to conduct normal pastoral work. My activity, or activities that are supported by me, that are mentioned in the letter, are strictly and exclusively part of pastoral work.' Nothing seems to have come of the incident, but Karol Wojtyla had clearly made his mark in the minds of the authorities:

'From the moment Bishop Wojtyla assumed his post in the Curia,' writes the praesidium chairman, 'activities contrary to regulations on the part of a certain segment of the Krakow clergy have grown, for which the Praesidium holds Bishop Wojtyla responsible.'

Karol Wojtyla's life was lived against the backdrop of so much history that it is tempting to see it as a series of dramatic tableaux – a story told in vast action-packed snapshots almost like a gallery of some of the great Old Masters by which he was surrounded in the Vatican. Until this point he has been a peripheral if busy figure – Bruegel's ploughman dutifully attending to his furrow while Icarus falls from the sky. From now on he will move steadily towards the centre of things, driving the action as an increasingly dynamic presence.

As the 1950s gave way to a new decade he fired the first really serious shot in the struggle which would become his greatest achievement. The battleground for this opening skirmish was the industrial suburb of Nowa Huta, which was part of the Krakow archdiocese. Nowa Huta (or 'New Works') had grown up around the Lenin Steelworks which the communist government had begun building in a village a few miles outside Krakow's city centre in 1949. There were no raw materials for steel nearby, nor was there a pool of labour needing work; the decision was taken with the express intention of creating a new industrial conurbation and with it a grateful proletariat who would eclipse the city of Krakow and all that it stood for. It is a hideous place, 'a grey concrete sea of Stalinist architecture' in the words of one guide book. Some of the high-rise blocks contained as many as 450 apartments, and they were designed so that it was impossible to move laterally between them – if you wanted to visit a near neighbour you had to take a lift down to the ground floor and another one up again. Quite how anyone could believe that Nowa Huta would win some kind of culture war with its graceful neighbour is difficult to understand – but that was the plan, and as part of the strategy of social engineering a decision was taken that no church should be built in the new development.

To the extent that large numbers of people flooded into Nowa Huta looking for employment at the Lenin Steelworks the plan worked – the population of the 'suburb' would eventually grow to some 200,000. Unfortunately for the communist authorities most of them came from the countryside, and they brought their rural Catholic piety with them. Far from becoming the proletarian vanguard of the revolution the communist planners had predicted, they became a source of increasingly active Catholic resistance. Their discontent was focused on the official refusal to allow them a church of their own – the old village that had disappeared under the tons of concrete of Nowa Huta had a small parish church which still stood, but it was nothing like adequate to the needs of the new population. At about the time of Karol Wojtyla's appointment there was a formal petition to the government for permission to build a church in Nowa Huta, and the campaign became a running sore that would poison relations between the Church and the state for nearly two decades.

Bishop Wojtyla made the campaign his own. On Christmas Eve 1959 he said his midnight mass in an open field in the Bienczyce area on the edge of Nowa Huta. It was a brilliant stroke of theatre – an early illustration of his instinctive understanding of how effectively Catholic ritual can be used to make a political point. By choosing such a bleak place for such a solemn celebration he brought all the most powerful imaginative elements of the Christmas story alive. The congregation felt excluded and marginalised because the authorities would not give them a church, and on a cold night, in a setting that evoked the first Christmas two thousand years earlier, their bishop offered them the consolation of a Christ-child born in a manger because there was no room at the inn. These open-air Christmas masses in Nowa Huta became an annual event with a symbolic significance that went well beyond the campaign for a parish church, and thousands of people turned out every year despite the rigours of a Polish winter.

5

A Voice in the Worldwide Church

There is a rare piece of film footage of the Polish bishops travelling to Rome on the train from Vienna to attend the Second Vatican Council. You can glimpse the young Bishop Karol Wojtyla for a second or two, and his face is alive with the infectious smile of an excited child. The Council, which opened in October 1962, gave him the first opportunity to leave Poland for fourteen years, and one can scarcely begrudge him the holiday spirit.

His native land had not changed very much in the decade and a half he had spent as a parish priest, university teacher and bishop. The account written by the Polish-born New Yorker Christine Hotchkiss of what it was like to revisit her homeland at the end of the 1950s recreates the flavour of a country still haunted by the effects of the war; on her first morning in Warsaw she is struck by the façade of a building 'still pocked with shell marks' and notes that 'the impact of the war was visible all around'. And Poles were still enduring many of the privations of a wartime economy because of the failure of socialism. Hotchkiss sketches a sad and oddly unsettling scene of people on the streets of Warsaw in winter: 'Bundled up in fleece-lined overcoats, they walked swiftly ahead without looking about. Almost everyone carried some heavy paper-wrapped package. All looked busy and intent on a purpose. I soon learned that the struggle to survive was their worry.' She falls into conversation with a young girl who announces that she has come out to queue at the grocery store because of a rumour that a shipment of Krakow sausage has reached the shop, and she looks in at 'dingy' window displays of 'artificial, sickly pink underwear, dull coloured woollens, kitchenware made of cheap, greyish enamel – all products of the State-owned co-operatives'.

Karol Wojtyla was making the journey in the opposite direction, from communist East to capitalist West, and must have been every bit as struck by the fat plenty which the post-war recovery had delivered. In contrast to the grim state-supplied stores along Warsaw's Nowy Swiat, Rome offered the glamorous designer shops of the Via Condotti and the smart cafés and hotels of the Via Vittorio Veneto. Since he had left the Eternal City after completing his PhD thesis it had added yet another layer to its reputation, identified now as the home of *la dolce vita* (Fellini's film came out in 1959) as much as the ancient capital of popes. Karol Wojtyla stayed at the Polish Institute in an affluent middle-class area near the Ponte Cavour on the west bank of the Tiber, and as he walked to St Peter's past the monumental Palazzo Justicia and the Castel Sant' Angelo each morning to attend the Council sessions, he would have found the Roman streets much busier than he remembered them; the population of the city had blossomed from 1.6 million to 2.1 during the 1950s and European prosperity had brought the tourists back in droves. It would have been much noisier too; the Roman traffic jam was enjoying its heyday. This was a new Rome benefiting from the impact of an extraordinary international economic boom: figures drawn from twelve Western European economies for the years 1950–72 show an average rate of economic growth of 4.6 per cent (by way of context it is worth noting that the figure for the years 1913–50 was just 1.4 per cent).

The Second Vatican Council was the defining event of modern Catholicism – although forty years after it ended people were still arguing vigorously about exactly what it defined. Councils of the Church are very rare; Vatican I began in 1869 and the Council before that, Trent, took place in the late sixteenth century. They involve bringing all the bishops of the world together in one place, and they have traditionally been the means of settling great theological debates and deciding big questions about the Church's direction. Vatican II certainly settled many debates, some of them in a most dramatic and unexpected fashion, but it also opened new ones. The ideological battles fought out during John Paul II's papacy were in many ways simply a continuation of the

Council's disputes by other means – and most of the figures who would emerge as the central players in those battles, including his main theological policeman Cardinal Ratzinger, the future Pope Benedict XVI, attended the Council as theologians.

The Council also marks the moment when the difficulty of describing Karol Wojtyla in terms of the usual left/right labels first becomes apparent. At one level he was very obviously 'the Conciliar Pope'; he took an active part in the Council's deliberations, he wrote a book about it (*Sources of Renewal; The Implementation of Vatican II*) and his decision to take a name honouring the two popes who presided over it (John XXIII and Paul VI) seemed a clear sign of his commitment to its spirit. In his Last Testament – a document that shines with sincerity in every sentence – he thanks the Holy Spirit for 'the great gift of the Council' and says he is 'convinced that for a long time to come the new generations will draw on the riches that this Council of the 20th century gave us'. And yet today the Council's greatest champions tend also to be the sharpest critics of the way John Paul ran the Church. The key to understanding that paradox may have fallen into the gap between the view of the world Karol Wojtyla brought to Rome that autumn and the perceptions of his fellow bishops from Western Europe, and it is worth spending a moment or two rummaging around for it.

The way East and West had diverged in material and economic terms since the end of the war would have been all too obvious to Karol Wojtyla from the moment he arrived in Rome – he and his fellow Polish bishops had been allowed to travel with just five dollars in spending money, which must have brought the point home with some urgency. The social and political developments which had taken place in Western Europe in the years since his time as a student in Rome were even more significant; they had created a climate for the relationship between the Church and secular society which was entirely alien to him.

In Poland, Church and state were locked in constant conflict, and the war was waged at every level of society – from what happened in classrooms right up to the way the country was governed. It made for a very intense moral experience of life because everyone, especially priests and bishops, faced choices almost every day about which side of the line they stood on. The Church was much more than an 'optional extra' providing Sunday services; it offered an alternative social space governed by a value system which completely rejected the ideology of the state. And as a result it was, of course, a persecuted Church, a fact of life which encouraged its leaders to keep their differences to themselves in the interest of presenting a united front to a hostile political establishment. What is more, there was not much evidence that any of this was likely to change; Poland's experience during Karol Wojtyla's adult life had been of a cycle of misery; each new dawn – whether it was the liberation from the Nazis or Gomulka's successful facing down of Khrushchev in 1956 – had proved to be false, and the idea of 'social progress' was little more than a propaganda slogan.

Progress in Western Europe, by contrast, had been real, indeed little short of miraculous. In retrospect it is remarkable how quickly pluralism re-established itself in so much of the continent in the aftermath of the Second World War – Italy, France and West Germany were all well established as solid democracies by the time the Council opened. Catholic politicians – perhaps most notably Konrad Adenauer, a Christian Democrat and the first Chancellor of the new Federal Republic of Germany – had played a prominent part in creating this new order, so secular politics did not represent the Church's enemy in the way it did in Poland. And in the 'free West' political progress seemed to be a trajectory that would endure – in contrast to the pattern of swiftly reversed revolutions that Poland had seen.

J. M. Roberts, in his history of Europe, describes 'historical acceleration' as something 'subjective, inexpressible in numbers or measurement, a reality in the minds of men and women who more and more experience . . . a startling awareness that the world is not as it used to be', and he argues that in this sense 'It is impossible to exaggerate the acceleration of change since 1945.' In the week the Second Vatican Council opened there were a couple of straws in the wind of the wider political and social revolutions afoot: Britain said goodbye to another colony (Uganda) and got its first female high court judge. The process of decolonisation redefined the way the old European powers thought of

113

their role on the world stage and fed into the revolution in social attitudes at home. Deference began to die and the cult of youth began to rise. Across the Atlantic the Civil Rights Movement was taking off in the United States. It was a period pregnant with a sense of new possibilities, and Western societies quivered with the optimism, self-confidence and utopianism that were to become the hallmarks of the 1960s. While Karol Wojtyla's pews were filled with congregations in mulish and resentful revolt against the social order that had been imposed upon them, many Catholics in Western Europe were embracing what they saw happening around them with enthusiasm. The problem for the leaders of the Western Church was not persecution by the state but competition from societies which were being transformed with bewildering speed.

So Karol Wojtyla came to the Council with a very different perspective from that of a bishop from Brussels, Utrecht or Vienna (to name three of the archdioceses which produced the Council's leading liberals), and that perspective coloured his understanding of the Council's purpose and, critically, the history behind it. The Church of the West – Europe and North America – was so dominant during this period that its version of the background to the Council became orthodox. It tended to be a 'Whig' version of history, and this liberal Catholic narrative of the great changes which Catholicism went through in the 1960s begins a century earlier, with the pontificate of Pius IX, the only pope to have reigned for longer than Pope John Paul II (some Catholics hold that St Peter was the longest reigning pope, but his dates have always seemed to me to be, putting it at its mildest, uncertain). In debates about the modern Church the names of past popes tend to be chucked around as a kind of ideological shorthand, and in the liberal narrative Pius IX, or Pio Nono as he is more generally known, is definitely the villain of the piece.

Something of a dandy in his youth, he was forced to give up his early ideas of military glory because of his epilepsy – he had a fit on the street in Rome while he was applying to join the Noble Papal Guard – and after briefly contemplating suicide in his disappointment he decided to become a priest instead. He was charming, handsome and blessed with 'a powerful and musical speaking voice and a natural fluency of speech'. His melodramatic style of preaching – he would sometimes place a skull with a lighted candle in it next to him in the pulpit – won him admirers and he was elected pope in 1846 at the age of fifty-four.

The pope was still a temporal monarch at that stage – governing the Papal States in what is now central Italy – and his sponsors in the conclave saw him as a moderate liberal who would take the sting out of the growing clamour for a less autocratic form of rule. For two years he was an enthusiastic reformer, and the darling of the Roman crowds, but in 1848, the Year of Revolutions when the established order was challenged across much of Europe, mob rule erupted on the streets of Rome. The pope's secretary of state, his senior political official, was stabbed on the steps of the Quirinale Palace, and Pius himself was forced to escape disguised as a servant (Toad of Toad Hall comes irresistibly to mind) before being spirited away to Naples by a Bavarian countess.

When the French restored him to his throne in 1849 it was, in the words of the papal historian Valerie Pirie, 'a very sober and disgruntled Pope who returned to the Quirinale'. Chastened by his experience of revolution he became the most reactionary of conservatives. In 1854 he proclaimed the Dogma of the Immaculate Conception, the belief that Mary was free from original sin from the moment of her conception, which has been a source of tension with Protestant churches ever since. He then set about building a metaphorical wall between the Church and 'modern civilisation', which he regarded as a source of 'vandalous aggression' against true religion. The Syllabus of Errors, which he published in 1864, condemned pretty much every aspect of a liberal culture you can imagine and a few more besides, including 'pantheism, naturalism, materialism, absolute as well as moderate rationalism, indifferentism, and false toleration in religious matters'. Secret societies, Bible societies and liberal clerical societies were condemned along with socialism and communism, and in the eightieth and final article of the Syllabus the suggestion that a Roman pontiff might reconcile himself with progress and liberalism was itself declared to be an Error. For good measure, any books which criticised the Syllabus were put on the Index of books which Catholics were forbidden to read. Pio Nono topped

off the battlements of his Fortress Church by calling the First
Vatican Council, which approved the Dogma of Papal Infallibility
in 1870 (around a tenth of the bishops at the Council left Rome
altogether rather than vote for this new article of their faith). In
thirty-two years on the throne of St Peter, Pio Nono managed to
ensure that the Church looked rather more 'medieval' at the end
of the nineteenth century than it had done at the beginning.

The 'hero' of the liberal story of Vatican II is John XXIII, the
pope who called the Council in defiance of all the expectations
that he would quietly serve out his time as a *papa di passagio*. He
gave the news of his decision to a group of his cardinals after a
service in the basilica of St Paul's-Without-the-Walls in January
1959, and it was greeted with stunned silence; according to the
official account they were 'too moved and happy to utter a word',
but it seems much more likely they were simply horrified by what
he was proposing. John's ambition was *'aggiornamento'*, an
updating of Catholic teaching to bring it more closely into line
with the realities of the twentieth century. There is a story – like
some John Paul stories, this Pope John story has been told so
often and in so many different ways that it is difficult to know
when or indeed whether it actually happened – that when
someone asked him what the Council should aim to achieve John
walked across the room and threw open the window, a symbolic
way of suggesting that it was time for the Church to emerge from
the walls of her fortress and let in the fresh air of the modern
world. And he had to fight hard to keep his vision alive, because
his Curia, the Vatican civil service, were thoroughly opposed to it
and did all they could to frustrate it.

But that is only one version of the narrative, and a 'conservative'
telling of the history behind the Council presents a very different
account of the same story. George Weigel quotes the reaction of
Cardinal Montini, then Archbishop of Milan but in due course to
be pope himself, on hearing the news that John XXIII had called
a Council: 'This holy old boy doesn't realise what a hornet's nest
he is stirring up.' In Weigel's view the whole thing was a huge
gamble. 'In many of its leading intellectual and scientific centres,'
he writes,

the modern world to which the Church proposed to open itself was closing its own windows on any idea of transcendence. Catholicism had been largely cut off from the pan-Christian ecumenical movement . . . An aggressively atheistic opponent [communism] with its own ultra-mundane theory of redemption controlled the destinies of billions of human beings. The Church itself was deeply divided about the possibility of a serious dialogue with modernity.

And according to the conservative view of history, Pio Nono was an altogether more significant figure than the easily caricatured old buffer I have described above. His champions point out that he reigned at a time when the Church's position was under serious assault on almost every front. Most particularly his temporal authority over the Papal States was constantly being challenged – militarily by the Italian nationalist Garibaldi and politically by the Piedmontese – and disappeared altogether when King Victor Emmanuel's forces took Rome in 1870 and the city became the capital of the new Italian state. Much of Pius's energetic proclaiming of new dogmas and hunting down of errors was directed towards securing a space for Catholicism in the new order of things, and it is perfectly possible to argue that he had to build an ideological fortress for the Church to replace the physical security it had lost. Critically, his experience of the relationship between the Church and the world around it was much closer to that of Karol Wojtyla and the Polish bishops living under communism, than it was to that of the Western European bishops living in their easy-going pluralist democracies. Pope John XXIII died in 1964, before his Council had ended, and there was soon a clamour to reward him with canonisation; John Paul II beatified Pope John in the autumn of the millennium year, but, in a move that provoked a chorus of liberal catcalls, he also beatified Pio Nono on the same day.

Some 600 bishops assembled in Rome for Pio Nono's Council in 1869, the vast majority of them European. There were 2,381 at the opening of the Second Vatican Council in 1962, and they came from every corner of the globe. Robert Blair Kaiser, who covered the Council for *Time* magazine, gave me a vivid description of the scene in St Peter's Square as they came piling out of the basilica at the end of the service.

> I saw black faces and brown faces and yellow faces, and ruddy red faces from Ireland and Scotland ... I saw an immense panoply of colour. These bishops and patriarchs were from all over the world and when they came out, they tumbled down the front steps of St Peter's, so that from a distance it looked like a waterfall, a waterfall of red and purple and black and every colour of the rainbow.

The inside of St Peter's had been turned into a sort of parliament building, with banks of seats constructed on either side of the nave like the stands at a football ground, and despite the awe-inspiring character of the setting and the fact that the debates were conducted entirely in Latin, the bishops soon picked up the habits of parliamentary politicians. Groups with a particular line to push began 'caucusing' in the afternoons after the day's formal sessions were over. Bishops from some of the 'new churches' of Africa and Asia formed alliances to ensure that their voices would be heard. Powerful cardinals plotted over dinner in the evenings and successors of the Apostles gossiped during smoking breaks in the bar which had been opened just off St Peter's. And, like all politicians, they began to fight their battles by leaking to the press. 'Covering Vatican II was much like covering Capitol Hill in Washington DC,' Robert Kaiser remembers.

> It was a political event. It was a parliament of the world's bishops and therefore it was a very human event. The Holy Spirit may have been there, but the Holy Spirit normally works through human beings. And I could see the human beings busily at work, and there was a huge argument going on. That was what was fun about it.

This kind of behaviour was entirely alien to the way the Polish bishops were used to operating. As John Cornwell writes in his biography,

Wojtyla was stunned by the apparent anarchy and disarray which marked the early sessions of the Council. What was this? Bishops quarrelling, lobbying, criticising and even attacking each other verbally! Wojtyla would by no means emulate them. He especially deplored leaks to the press, the tittle-tattle and back-biting, the distortions and the spin. This was not how the Church had survived in Poland as it grappled with its totalitarian enemy.

Cardinal König, the Archbishop of Vienna and one of the dominant players at the Council, believes that the Polish primate Cardinal Wyszynski saw the whole thing as something of a distraction: 'he just didn't care very much about the Council, he said, to him it had only to do with the western world, and he was thinking "well, far more important is the other side of Europe . . . Eastern Europe"'. More than that, the Polish primate saw the hand of his favourite enemy at work in the disagreements taking place among the bishops; the communist technique, he wrote in a memo to the Vatican, 'is to form . . . cells of disunity among the faithful, to split the bishops into two blocs . . . by cleverly contrived distinctions between "reactionaries" and "progressives".'

Whatever Bishop Wojtyla's reservations about the way his *confrères* conducted themselves at the Council, he certainly did not treat it with the indifference or open hostility of Cardinal Wyszynski. He gave earnest thought to the Vatican's advance questionnaire on the agenda, and as he left for the first session declared that 'I set out on this road with the deepest emotion, with a great tremor in my heart.' He supported one of the Council's earliest and most radical reforms, the idea of mass in the vernacular rather than in Latin (unlike Wyszynski, who rather oddly remarked that his congregations would 'never understand it in Polish'. His reasoning was that 'The mystery should be in a mysterious language'). Karol Wojtyla gave his first speech in St Peter's (it was technically known as an 'intervention') in the debate on the new constitution for the Church, *Lumen Gentium*, or 'Light of the Nations', and came down firmly on the side of the 'Reformers'; he stressed the importance of an active role for lay people, referring to the Church as 'the People of God' (very much a reformer's phrase), and warning of the danger that the hierarchy might appear 'authoritarian'.

But in retrospect it is clear that his perception of what the Council was doing was quite distinct from that of many of his Western colleagues; when he became pope and his understanding of Vatican II's message gained greater prominence it almost seemed as if he and many of the other bishops had been attending different meetings. The way he deals with the modernising spirit of the Council – that idea of an opening to the world of the late twentieth century – illustrates the point well. The 'manifesto' for a forward-looking Church was officially called *De Ecclesia in Mundo Huius Temporis* ('The Church in the Modern World'), but it was better known by the Latin title which summed up its tone, *Gaudium et Spes*, or 'Hope and Joy'. The document was a direct assault on the Fortress Church built by Pius IX because it accepted the possibility of a benign and creative relationship between Catholicism and modernity. 'In face of the flat rejection of the "modern world" by Pius IX in the Syllabus of Errors just a century before and its continuing influence to the very eve of the Council,' wrote the Irish theologian Enda McDonagh, 'the Council's shift in perspective may well be described as revolutionary.' For the West European bishops the modern world meant new ideas about social justice, war and sex, and those were the areas where *Gaudium et Spes* made headlines; it is economically and politically radical (endorsing trade unionism and the pursuit of civil rights), almost stridently pacifistic (the arms race is condemned as an 'utterly treacherous trap for humanity'), and although the bishops were forbidden to discuss contraception in their debates there were enough hints about a new approach in the final text to give hope to those who were looking for a change in the ban on artificial birth control.

But when the Polish bishops looked beyond the battlements of their Fortress Church they saw the hostile world of communism, and during the debate on *Gaudium et Spes* Bishop Wojtyla pointedly reminded the Council that 'The situations in which the Church finds itself in various countries of the world are diverse and contrasting. In some of them the Church can freely speak the truth. In others, however it is blocked and persecuted.' Looking back four decades later in *Memory and Identity*, the collection of 'personal reflections' he published shortly before his death, Karol Wojtyla explains his distinctive 'take' on the document. He quotes *Gaudium et Spes* on the relationship between the Church and temporal politics and gives it the following gloss:

> The way the Council understands the term 'separation' of Church and State is far removed from the way totalitarian systems interpret it. It came as a surprise and, in a certain sense, also a challenge for several countries, particularly those under Communist rule . . . they realised that it was at odds with their notion of separation between Church and State. According to their vision, the world belongs exclusively to the State; the Church has its own sphere, which lies beyond the 'boundaries', so to speak, of the world. The Conciliar vision of the Church 'in' the world conflicts with that interpretation.

So while the bishops of the West saw the document as a way of staying in touch with the hip and hopeful politics of the swinging sixties, for Karol Wojtyla it was another weapon to be deployed in the war with communism; *Gaudium et Spes* places the Church firmly at the heart of society and not at the margins to which the communist authorities constantly sought to push it. In the same passage Karol Wojtyla reveals the thinking behind his support for a greater role for the laity:

> For the Church, the world is both a task and a challenge. It is so for all Christians, but particularly for the lay faithful. The Council gave prominence to the question of the lay apostolate, that is, the active presence of Christians in the life of society. Yet according to Marxist ideology, this was precisely the area where it was necessary to establish exclusive control by the State and the party.

In other words, the point of the concept of 'the People of God' was not so much to create a new and democratic structure within the Church, it was to empower an army of foot soldiers who would fight those everyday battles on the frontline of the war with a hostile ideology.

There is a similar ambiguity about the significance of Karol Wojtyla's role in the debate on religious liberty at the Council. It is a slightly embarrassing fact for a Catholic to have to admit, but until the 1960s the Vatican did not really approve of the idea that people should be free to worship as they wish. Until Pio Nono lost the Papal States the papacy was of course an absolute monarchy, and it was not known for its tolerance; popes thought nothing of suppressing dissent and clamping down on free speech, and the legal rights of individual citizens who ran foul of the authorities were seriously compromised by the fact that all court cases in the Papal States were heard in Latin. The Jews of Rome were confined to a ghetto, and in 1858 Pio Nono caused scandal throughout Europe by sending a posse of his police to abduct a six-year-old Jewish boy in Bologna because he had been secretly baptised by one of the family servants (the law stated that Jews could not bring up a Christian). Until the end of the eighteenth century, close connections between state power and church power had been the norm in Catholic Europe, and the idea that at the very least Catholicism deserved a privileged position in society ran deep.

The pressure for change came from American liberals and East European anti-communists, each group reflecting the inheritance of their political traditions. For the Americans it was a question of reconciling the teachings of the Church with the Enlightenment ideas – like human rights – that provided the intellectual foundations of the American revolution. East Europeans like Karol Wojtyla saw the principle of religious freedom as an essential line of defence against the encroachment of aggressive, state-sponsored atheism. This slightly odd alliance between Old and New World bishops – with very different instincts on other issues – faced ferocious opposition from the die-hard conservatives who did not want to see any change at all – mainly the bishops and cardinals of the Curia, the Vatican civil service, who had an entrenched interest in the status quo. At one point the pope was forced to intervene personally to stop the issue being buried by a procedural putsch, but after much debate *Dignitatis Humanae,* the 'Declaration on Religious Liberty', was finally delivered from the dark womb of St Peter's Basilica, and the Roman Catholic Church could claim with some honesty to be the defender of the rights of the oppressed.

It is impossible to overstate the importance of this battle: the idea that the Church owed its legitimacy to a source of power that was quite separate from – and often in conflict with – temporal authority had enormous consequences, especially in Eastern Europe and Latin America. Karol Wojtyla had of course learnt the value of that lesson at first hand as a young man under the Nazi occupation in Krakow. His 'intervention' in the debate on *Dignitatis Humanae* is instructive. His support for the principle is, as one would expect, unambiguous; 'This principle [of religious liberty] constitutes a fundamental right of religious man in society, which ought to be observed by all most strictly and especially by those who govern states', he told the Council on 25 September 1964. But it is equally apparent that he believes strongly that religious liberty does not mean a free-for-all; addressing the way freedom of religion should work in relation to the other Christian churches, he says:

> It is necessary that the nexus between liberty and truth be further underlined in the Document. For on the one hand liberty is on account of truth, and nevertheless, on the other hand it is unable to be perfected without the help of truth . . . The relation of Truth to Liberty is of the greatest moment in ecumenical activity. For the end of this action is none other than the liberation of the whole of Christianity from schisms, which surely cannot be fully accomplished unless union be made perfect with the truth. Thus it does not suffice if the principle of religious liberty towards the Separated Brethren should appear as only a principle of toleration. For toleration does not so much have a positive sense as in some way a negative one.

The language is painfully opaque but the message is clear: freedom of expression for other religious traditions is fine as long as all concerned recognise that it takes place within the context of a hierarchy of truth – and truth, of course, is most perfectly expressed in the teachings of the Roman Catholic Church. At a later session of the Council he opened the debate on the Declaration on Religious Liberty with a speech representing the considered views of the Polish bishops as a group:

> It is not enough to say in this matter 'I am free', but rather 'I am accountable'. This is the doctrine grounded in the living tradition of the Church of the confessors and martyrs. Responsibility is the summit and necessary complement of liberty. This ought to be underlined so that our Declaration will be intimately personalistic in the Christian sense, but not derived from *liberalism or indifferentism*. [my italics]

Many of the critics of John Paul's pontificate complained that, while he insisted on human rights when he was fighting a totalitarian state, he seemed unwilling to grant them to dissenting members of the Church. That position is perfectly consistent with what the future pope actually said at the Council.

The fact that Karol Wojtyla was chosen to speak formally on behalf of the Polish episcopate reflected a significant change in his status. Eugeniusz Baziak, the Archbishop of Krakow who originally put the Wojtyla name forward as a potential bishop, died of a heart attack in the summer of 1962 during preparations for the Council. The news was greeted with particular dismay because the Polish Church had only just completed a tortuous negotiation with the communist authorities to have Baziak's position in Krakow officially recognised, and it was generally accepted that someone would have to run the archdiocese on a temporary basis while things settled down. The city's Cathedral and Chapter voted for Karol Wojtyla.

The process of finding a permanent replacement for Baziak was complicated by the unique position of the Polish Church. By convention Cardinal Wyszynski would submit names for major appointments to the Department for Religious Denominations in Warsaw before passing them on to the Vatican – it was in fact an arrangement that rather suited the Polish primate, who feared that direct contact between his government and the Vatican might diminish his influence. There are differing accounts of exactly what took place in the negotiations to find a new Archbishop of Krakow, but all of them agree that Wyszynski tried several names before accepting the idea that the temporary incumbent deserved a place on the list. Karol Wojtyla was not formally appointed until the end of 1963, a year and a half after his predecessor's death.

Scruffiness, like lateness, is a *leitmotiv* of the reminiscences of those who knew Karol Wojtyla during his years as a priest and bishop. But like all actors he knew the value of a good costume, and as the Metropolitan Archbishop of Krakow he had access to one of the most spectacular ecclesiastical dressing-up boxes in the world. At his inauguration in Wawel Cathedral he wore a chasuble donated by Queen Anna Jagiello in the sixteenth century and a pallium given to the archdiocese even earlier – by the fourteenth-century Queen Jadwiga. His crozier was made in the reign of King Jan Sobiesko, the Polish king who stopped the advance of Islam into Europe at the battle of Vienna in 1683, his mitre was early seventeenth century and his episcopal ring dated from the twelfth century. He had certainly not tricked himself out like this out of pleasure in possession; one of the most touching revelations in his Last Testament was that he died without any personal property at all, leaving only 'the everyday objects that were of use to me' to be 'distributed as seems appropriate'. His dazzling appearance at his inaugural mass was, rather, another illustration of his tendency to treat life like a permanently unfolding symbolist poem, a way of saying that he understood the history of the position he was taking up and that he had every intention of making that history live again in his ministry.

He moved into Krakow's archiepiscopal palace – though he slept in a small back bedroom rather than the grand one used by his predecessors – and set about transforming it into a living expression of the role he felt the Church should play; it became an administrative headquarters, a drop-in social work centre and an intellectual salon rolled into one. The residence of the Metropolitan Archbishops of Krakow is right in the heart of the city, just off Grodzka Street, the oldest street in Krakow, which links the Market Place and the Wawel complex with its castle and cathedral. It is a handsome building, and stands immediately opposite the imposing plain bulk of the thirteenth-century Franciscan Church with its frescoed monastic cloisters. The new archbishop loved living and working in a place heavy with a sense of the past, but there was no question of allowing that fusty, museum-like smell which haunts many ecclesiastical buildings to penetrate the doors of 3 Franciszkanska Street – history was there to be used. 'All kinds of meetings and scholarly gatherings took place there,' he wrote as pope in a reflection on his Krakow days,

> including the 'Studium for the Family'. There was a special family consulting room. Those were times when the authorities looked upon any large gathering of laity as an antigovernment activity. The bishop's residence became a place of refuge. I invited all sorts of people; scholars, philosophers, humanists. I also held regular meetings with priests, and the parlour was frequently used for lectures . . . You might say that the residence was throbbing with life.

The archbishop's day would generally begin at 5.30 a.m. He said mass at 7.00 a.m., followed by a brief breakfast, but most of the morning was spent in his private chapel praying and working; he saw the chapel as 'a place of special inspiration' and used to write his books there – *The Acting Person,* his big philosophical offering during this period, was produced during these sessions. Public life began at 11.00 a.m. when he received visitors – he operated an 'open door' policy and pretty much anyone could turn up without an appointment. The archdiocese of Krakow was huge, serving some one and a half million Catholics – there were 329 parishes, 1,500 priests, 3,000 nuns and monks and nearly 200 seminarians. So there was an endless round of canonical visitations to be made, special masses to be celebrated, sermons, retreats and reflections to be given, ordinations and professions of vows to be presided over. His pursuit of his personal spiritual life was unrelenting, and he would sometimes ask his driver to take him out to the shrines of Kalwaria which he had known as a child, walking and meditating among them into the night. On top of all that there were academic commitments – he had an apparently limitless appetite for participating in seminars and colloquiums – and the trips to Rome for sessions of the Vatican Council.

The last week of March and the beginning of April 1965 provide a snapshot of the way his intellectual interests added to the burden of archiepiscopal duties. He spent almost every afternoon meeting groups of artists and intellectuals:

> March 22 – 3.00 p.m. – at his residence – meeting with the national directors of ministries to the artists. March 23 – 5.00 p.m. – meeting at his residence with artists. March 24 – 5.00 p.m. – meeting at his residence with professors. That same day at 7.00 p.m. A low mass for *Tydodnik Powszechny* (the weekly Catholic magazine). March 25 – meeting at his residence at 5.00 p.m. with writers.

On 26 March he was at the University of Lublin where two PhD students he had supervised were defending their theses (one on Jean-Paul Sartre, the other on Aquinas) and then it was off to Rome for a week's attendance on the working group which was drafting *Gaudium et Spes*, before returning to Krakow to ordain new priests and celebrate Holy Week.

The archbishop continued to enjoy skiing, hiking and kayaking with undiminished zeal. George Blazynski, one of his earliest biographers, has left us an engaging sketch of the sporting prelate:

> He would often set off after midnight once he had celebrated mass on New Year's Eve. Usually he stayed at the Ursuline Convent in Zakopane, the winter resort in the Tatra Mountains, skied from 11 in the morning to 4 in the afternoon, sometimes for as long as two hours at a time non-stop, and then spent the rest of the day working. His favourite ski runs were the Chocholowska and the Kasprowy Wierch [the highest peak in the Tatras]. He often climbed the ski slopes on foot. From the parking lot of the Chocholowska he had himself towed on skis behind a sleigh . . . A friend of Wojtyla's, who describes him as 'one of the dare devil skiers of the Tatras', adds: 'He loved the thrill of it, the sheer danger.' Once, during a midwinter interview with the head of the *Times* office in Bonn, Wojtyla

gazed out of the window of his residence and sighed 'I wish I could be out there now, somewhere in the mountains racing down into a valley. It is an extraordinary sensation.'

It is a yearning every skier would understand, and there is something especially poignant about reading this passage with the fresh memory of his final frailty.

At this distance in time the Karol Wojtyla of the mid 1960s looks an immensely attractive figure. Physically and intellectually he was in his prime, and he was engaged with awe-inspiring energy in two great enterprises – the reshaping of the Catholic Church underway at the Council in Rome and the struggle with communism in Poland – both of which he relished. But it is difficult to avoid the suspicion that he must at times have been extremely irritating to deal with. Every day was stretched to meet the demands of this extraordinarily full life, and he almost invariably took an over-optimistic view of how long his appointments would last and the time it would take to travel between them. His capacity to do two things at once, both apparently with total attention, was a great gift, but it led to incidents which could easily have been interpreted as bad manners; at one dinner in Krakow he spent the entire meal dealing with his mail – and then accurately summed up the debate that had been going on round him for two hours before calling a halt to the party and sending everyone off to bed. This gift of 'divisible attention' was also responsible for some truly dreadful poetry, which he would write while listening to the speeches of his fellow bishops in St Peter's during the meetings of the Second Vatican Council. This offering is a reflection on the Church and St Peter:

It is here that our feet meet the ground –
Where so many walls and columns have been raised.
If you don't lose yourself among them
But walk finding oneness and sense,
It is because the Marble Floor guides you.
It joins not only the space between the Renaissance structures
But it also brings together
Spaces within us.

When we walk, so much aware of our weaknesses and defeats,
It is you, Peter, who wants to serve as the Marble Floor
So we can be guided by you – as we walk ahead without
    knowing where.
So you can take our footsteps to oneness,
And to a vision from which
A thought is born.
It is you, Peter, who supports the feet
Just as a rock supports the hooves of sheep
A rock is also a marble floor of a gigantic temple
And the cross is a pasture.

Perhaps it is better in the original – and it is only fair to record the testimony of one of the priests on his staff in Krakow that he 'never minded being teased or criticised ... when friends who knew about his poetry writing complained that the poems were obscure'.

Shortly after his elevation to the rank of archbishop there was an incident which demonstrated that Karol Wojtyla – so patient in conversation and in his marathon sessions in the confessional – could be provoked into anger when something really got under his skin. The affair of the 'German bishops' letter' is one of those historical curiosities that serve as a reminder of how much has changed in Europe during the past half century. During one of the final sessions of the Vatican Council in 1965, the Polish episcopate sent out fifty-six letters to episcopal conferences from around the world inviting them to participate in the celebration of a millennium of Christianity in Poland the following year. The letter to the German bishops took a good deal of work because of all the obvious historical sensitivities, and since German and Polish bishops were in Rome together the two groups collaborated to try and get the tone exactly right. The letter they finally came up with reviewed Germany's crimes against Poland (notably the occupation during the Second World War) but it also recognised German suffering, and concluded with the words, 'We forgive you and ask your forgiveness.' It was a propaganda gift to Poland's communist government, which accused the Church's leadership of selling out on an issue which remained raw in the Polish national consciousness; the Party launched a campaign against the bishops under the rallying cry 'We will not forget and we will not forgive.'

Karol Wojtyla's name was one of the signatories to the invitation, and he received an 'open letter' from employees at the Solvay plant where he had worked during the war.

> The tragic history of our nation during the Nazi occupation is well known to your Excellency, who as a labourer in the 'Solvay' factory during the occupation felt its tragic results. It is therefore with great indignation, as well as with astonishment, that we received news of your participation, Rev. Archbishop, in the initial discussions with the German bishops, and your participation in drawing up and signing 'the Message', in which authoritarian decisions were made on matters of vital interest to our nation . . . the licence which the bishops took in drawing up 'the Message' where, among other things, mention is made of the alleged guilt of Poles towards the Germans, offends our sense of national identity . . .

And so it goes on, with some colourful language about 'German henchmen' and their 'bestial methods of biological extermination' thrown in for good measure. Karol Wojtyla concluded that the open letter was a put-up job by the communists – probably correctly, as it was published in the government-controlled press – and sent the workers a long forensic defence of his position. The archbishop's response is detailed and clever, but it simply boils with righteous indignation:

> I respond to this letter above all as an individual who has been wronged. Wronged, because I was accused and defamed publicly, without any attempt to look honestly at the facts and the essential motives. When we worked together during the occupation, a lot of things united us – and among these, the first and foremost was a respect for the human being, conscience, individuality, and social dignity. This is what I learned in large measure from the workers at 'Solvay' – but I am unable to find this fundamental principle in your open letter. As I

write and publish this with great pain, I must state that not only do I have the right to my own good name, but all the people whom I represent and for whom I am a Shepherd as the Archbishop of Krakow also have a right to my good name.

Karol Wojtyla's temper would later come as a nasty shock to some of those he dealt with as pope.

At the Council the Archbishop of Krakow did not enjoy the kind of clubbable reputation that some bishops acquired – he tended to slip into a side chapel to pray once the daily sessions were over rather than head out to play politics over a relaxed drink in the Roman evening – but he went about the task of networking with characteristic seriousness of purpose. He was greatly helped by having an old friend well placed at the heart of the Curia. Andrzej Maria Deskur had joined the seminary in Krakow in 1945 and, having chosen the curial career path, was now well established as one of those *éminences grises* that turn the wheels of power in the Vatican. His official position was President of the Pontifical Commission on Social Communication (a grand way of saying that he was head of the Church's press operation) but his real skill was making connections; he said later that 'all my friends wanted to meet this Wojtyla', because 'lots of people knew old Cardinal Sapieha and wanted to meet his successor' – poor Archbishop Baziak having been rather quickly forgotten, it seems. Deskur obliged by setting up meetings with the friends that mattered.

The Sapieha connection proved valuable in establishing a bond with the most important contact of all those he made during the Council. Pope John XXIII died on 3 June 1963 – the cardinals who elected him had been wrong about the impact of his pontificate but right in their conviction that it would be brief. It took only three ballots – one of the shortest conclaves in history – to choose Cardinal Giovanni Battista Montini, the Archbishop of Milan, as his successor. And Paul VI, as he became, had begun his career as a young priest in the Vatican's embassy, or nunciature, in Warsaw in 1923. He had read the works of one of Karol Wojtyla's literary heroes, Adam Mickiewicz, and by an odd quirk of fate had visited the town of Oswiecim near Krakow on church business before it became notorious under its German name of Auschwitz. Karol Wojtyla gave an account of his first audience with the new pope to the Krakow deanery:

> The Holy Father . . . greeted me by expressing his satisfaction at the opportunity to make my acquaintance, although I had the fortune of knowing him when he was still a cardinal, during the first session, but this was the first time we were meeting in the new circumstances. Immediately the Holy Father began reminiscing about the Prince Cardinal [Sapieha]. This is indeed a great thing – wherever one goes in Rome, whomever one speaks with, when that person hears the word 'Krakow', he remembers the Prince Cardinal.

If there is a suggestion there that Montini, who was very much the Italian ecclesiastical grandee, had forgotten his first encounters with a thrusting young bishop from Poland, it did not stop the two men becoming close. Karol Wojtyla's affection for Paul VI was expressed with an intensity unusual in the rather formal and often pompous discourse favoured by senior clerics at the time. After that first audience he told his congregation in a sermon that the pope's face was 'so profound, fatigued with love, this face so deeply moved with the difficult matters of the Church and contemporary humanity' – exactly the kind of observation that commentators would one day make of him – and in his Last Testament he wrote of Paul as 'my great predecessor and Father'. When Paul gave Karol Wojtyla his cardinal's hat in June 1967, at the remarkably young age of forty-seven, it was seen as a clear sign of special papal favour. There are stories suggesting that Paul expressed an explicit preference for Karol Wojtyla as his successor, but they have the feel of anecdotes after the fact.

Karol Wojtyla used the international stature he had secured through the speeches and contacts he had made at the Council to press the concerns of the Polish Church on a wider audience. He established himself as a modest star of Vatican Radio on his visits to Rome and would often be recruited to broadcast his thoughts in the form of what used to be called 'talks' at the BBC. In the final days of Vatican II, with Christmas approaching, he gave his comfortable Western European audience a picture of what Christmas Eve would be like in Nowa Huta:

> For a few years now I have been celebrating [Christmas midnight mass] there, under the open sky, in temperatures twenty degrees below freezing and among ice covered trees; at other times in the snow, and still other times in rain driven by December winds, with wet ground under one's feet, directly in the mud. The people gathered in the thousands, regardless of the weather... Maybe nowhere else but here do Christians give that kind of witness to the mystery of the birth of the Son of God.

Paul was a sympathetic and receptive listener to this new and insistent voice seeking to claim the attention of the wider Church. Like his predecessor, Paul VI was focusing on the plight of the Church in the Soviet bloc with a new energy, and he was beginning to develop the policy known as *Ostpolitik*, the opening to the East. The Council ended on 8 December 1965, and on New Year's Eve Archbishop Wojtyla announced from his pulpit that the 'Holy Father blessed a stone from the grave of St Peter... so that it would be the cornerstone of the church that is supposed to stand in Nowa Huta'.

6

A Campaigning Cardinal

What must surely rank as one of the oddest episodes of the communist era in Eastern Europe took place on 2 September 1966. In the interests of Polish national security, a car was stopped by the Interior Ministry's militia near the town of Bedzin. It was on its way to the Katowice region, the most densely populated and heavily industrialised in the country; with its sixty collieries – including the biggest pit in Europe – and its ironworks, Katowice was the heart of the Polish economy. The threat to its security which provoked the Interior Ministry into action was not some sinister agent of capitalism, secret arms cache or even seditious literature: it was a picture. As part of the celebration of a millennium of Christianity in Poland – it was a thousand years since the baptism of the Piast prince Mieszko I – a copy of the icon of the Black Madonna of Czestochowa was being taken on a pilgrimage around the country. Sunday 4 September was due to be 'the inauguration of the peregrination of the image of Our Lady of Czestochowa around the diocese of Katowice', and the authorities had decided to put a stop to it; the picture was escorted back to the monastery of Jasna Gora, where it was kept under armed guard for the duration of the millennium celebrations. But the inauguration ceremony went ahead anyway, and Karol Wojtyla, whose archdiocese included Katowice, was there to address the congregation in the city's cathedral; speaking of the absent image he told them, 'The reason we have all come here is to look at the sign of our unity; of our Christian unity but also our national unity; this unity, which has been shaped in our Polish souls over the centuries;

this unity, whose shaping has been watched over by the image of Our Lady of Czestochowa.'

The slightly surreal character of this incident – this was the height of the Cold War, when a large part of humanity lived under the shadow of nuclear annihilation – was a backhanded compliment to the way the Polish Church was holding its own in the struggle with communism. The millennium celebrations were always going to be a flashpoint in Church–state relations, and both sides had been squaring up for a battle for some time. Karol Wojtyla and Stefan Wyszynski had both pressed the government to allow Paul VI to come to Poland in the course of the millennium year – whatever the tensions between them the two worked closely together in their dealings with the authorities. Gomulka – who had long since squandered the popular authority he had acquired by standing up to Khrushchev – was far too nervous about the impact of a papal visit and sat on the idea emphatically. His regime did everything possible to detract from this great Catholic celebration; a British Catholic journalist who covered the story reported that 'Football matches were rearranged to coincide with special masses. Children were taken on excursions to prevent them attending. The Polish media pretended that the whole event did not exist. It was confrontation politics with a vengeance.' But Gomulka could not stop the Church marking the millennium moment altogether, and throughout 1966, in a seemingly endless succession of sermons, the leaders of the Polish Church reminded people over and over again of the deep historic links between Catholicism and Polish identity.

The city of Krakow, ancient capital of Poland's kings, had been at the heart of the long romance between faith and nation, and the millennium celebrations inevitably propelled its archbishop onto the national stage. In the course of the year Karol Wojtyla celebrated fifty-four millennium masses across the country, blessed acres of parish banners and walked marathons of processions through towns and villages. And he had found his rhetorical voice, using symbols from the past to address contemporary conditions in the way that would become so distinctive and familiar on his elevation to the papacy. After leading a procession of the relics of St Stanislaw (Krakow's great martyr) and St

Adalbert (Poland's first missionary) from his cathedral at Wawel, for example, he told the crowd, 'When hard blows fall upon us, we always feel that these blows reach back through the past to the head of St Stanislaw and to the heart of St Adalbert'; to an outsider these allusions would have been perplexing in the extreme, but for his listeners they were code for defiance of state power (St Stanislaw) and Polish Catholic identity (St Adalbert). And it went down well; the sermon was 'interrupted repeatedly by applause and outcries', according to an eyewitness.

The new cardinal's campaign for a church at Nowa Huta had finally persuaded the authorities to relent, and after years of bureaucratic resistance work on the building began in earnest during the millennium year. The Catholic writer Peter Hebblethwaite visited the site in 1967 and found an affecting scene:

> a vast crowd had gathered for mass in the open air, unprotected from the drizzle that was falling. They knelt in the mud and spilled across the road. Lorries and buses splashed by, drowning the sound of the reedy harmonium. All one could see above the umbrellas was a chocolate-box painting of Our Lady surrounded by a triangle of fairy lights. If only one could understand – I remember thinking – why these peasants-turned-workers were here, in the rain and the mud, then one would have a clue to Polish Catholicism.

Karol Wojtyla had also become adept at dealing with the kind of (in retrospect) absurdly trivial political gaming strategies employed by the Polish authorities. A 1967 document which emerged from the files of the secret police after the collapse of communism confirmed what many suspected at the time: the government made strenuous attempts to drive a wedge between Poland's two cardinals in the belief that their rivalry could be exploited to weaken the Church as a whole. So when prominent foreigners came to Poland the government would try to arrange a meeting with Wojtyla instead of Wyszynski as a way of snubbing the primate. But Karol Wojtyla was determined not to fall into the trap. When Charles de Gaulle visited Poland in 1967, for example, he abandoned his intention of meeting Cardinal Wyszynski at the insistence of his government hosts and flew to Krakow instead. But when the French president arrived the city's archbishop found himself 'otherwise engaged', and was not there to welcome his distinguished guest to his cathedral. There was a similar display of solidarity later that year when the authorities denied Cardinal Wyszynski a passport to attend a meeting of the Synod of Bishops in Rome; Cardinal Wojtyla refused to go without him, and the Polish Episcopate agreed a joint communiqué accusing the authorities of 'seriously restricting freedom of religion' which was read out from every pulpit in the country the following Sunday.

The would-be actor of Wadowice days was evidently enjoying the theatrical possibilities offered by his position. Krakow, with its largely unspoilt medieval and baroque centre, provides plenty of stagey backdrops, and looking through the record of big church occasions during this period one is struck by the number of them which took place outside, in the streets. It was a strategy of public witness, a way of declaring to the communist authorities that the Church would not shut itself away quietly behind closed doors with its hymn books and its hassocks. When the copy of the Black Madonna arrived in Krakow in May 1966 (this was an early stage in her 'peregrination', before she was arrested), there was a crowd gathered outside the cathedral to welcome her; the archbishop halted his procession in the torrential rain so that they could pay homage to her. He then processed inside and declared triumphantly,

> Now we are about to enter the second millennium and behold, Mary has arrived at the Wawel Cathedral to lead us there . . . This is exactly how she has led the Polish nation, the entire Church of Poland, step by step . . . into the new millennium of faith and Christian life . . . We welcome You to the Wawel Cathedral, O Handmaid of the Lord, Queen of Poland.

It was a similar story when he returned from Rome after being created a cardinal; he was welcomed by 'thousands of jubilant people showering him with flowers', and his street theatre performance on this occasion had a Shakespearean grandeur. Dressed in the scarlet of a prince of the Church he told his 'dear Krakowians' that 'It [the scarlet] is a gift for the Church of St Stanislaw, bishop and martyr – who, through his blood, was the first to identify the colour red with the Bishops of Krakow'. During his sermon inside he warmed to the theme:

> By placing a cardinal's red biretta on my head, the Holy Father wanted to tell me that I should place an even greater value on blood. Above all that I should value the Blood of our Redeemer; that for the price of our Redeemer's Blood I should take a stand in the Church of God even if I have to spill my own blood.

It was spine-tingling stuff, and far from idle rhetoric; it would not be long before Polish blood was being spilt again.

Karol Wojtyla's achievement over the next few years was, in a way, the greatest piece of poetry he created. By tapping so accurately into that curious mixture of religious emotion, romanticism and cultural pride that lay at the centre of Poland's national cortex he managed to create his own, very Catholic narrative for what was in fact a much wider struggle against communist oppression. The roots of Gomulka's difficulties towards the end of the 1960s certainly did not lie exclusively in the challenge he faced from the Catholic Church; there was a much broader crisis of confidence in the communist system in Poland – and indeed in other parts of the Soviet Empire. Gomulka and the party leadership had set out bold economic targets which would make Poland self-sufficient – but completely failed to deliver them. During his first five years in power productivity and real wages actually fell. Agricultural production, which was supposed to rise by 30 per cent by 1965, also dropped. Ordinary people found little or no improvement in their living standards, but the party elite ostentatiously enjoyed their privileges. When Moscow 'fraternally' suggested a tightening of the lid on dissent, Warsaw obliged by locking up academics and closing magazines. And Gomulka himself became increasingly remote, relying heavily on a small circle of cronies.

To complicate things further he faced a threat to his authority from within the government. General Mieczyslaw Moczar, who had been a commander of the communist partisans during the occupation, had become the minister of the interior and was using his wartime credentials to mount a challenge from what one might call the 'patriotic left'; he and his supporters played on anti-Russian resentment, called for the restoration of 'strong leadership' and – bizarrely, since Poland's Jewish population had dwindled to almost nothing in the aftermath of the war – revived anti-Semitism.

The incident which ignited this cocktail of popular discontent and political intrigue illustrated the power of the cultural chords to which Karol Wojtyla's ear was so finely attuned – it was a performance of a play by his literary hero Adam Mickiewicz. The contemporary resonance of *Forefathers' Eve* rang out like a bell in the political circumstances of 1968. 'Written in the early nineteenth century this beloved and mysterious play,' wrote the journalist and historian Neal Ascherson, 'sanctifies the national struggle against the Tsar, a work about morality, religion and nation which no Pole can watch without feeling that he or she is being given a key to the present. In January 1968, all the audience's pent up emotion burst out in passionate applause at passages taunting Russian power.' The Soviet ambassador ordered that the play should be closed and the authorities obliged. Students took to the streets in protest and the police waded in with their clubs.

Across the border in Czechoslovakia the 'Prague Spring' was beginning to bud. In Poland the spring of 1968 was marked by political chaos. General Moczar stirred up trouble on the streets as much as he could in the hope of being seen as the 'strong leader' who would rescue Poland from anarchy; in what Norman Davies has described as 'a classic piece of political provocation so common in the annals of East European dictatorships', he sent the riot police to attack the Jagiellonian University in Krakow even though there had in fact been no student riots in the city. Jews, liberals and intellectuals were singled out by his supporters, who wound up their anti-Semitic campaign to such hysteria that by the end of 1968 two-thirds of Poland's remaining Jews had been driven into exile. Gomulka, whose wife was Jewish, defended

'Jewish cosmopolitans' but joined in the attack on liberals and intellectuals, and seemed anyway incapable of controlling events. The whole episode was thoroughly confusing, and had nothing particular to do with religion – it was a symptom of the sickness of a political system that was flawed at its heart.

During the crisis of 1956 Karol Wojtyla had been an obscure if hardworking priest and theology don; in 1968 he was a cardinal with a national platform and an increasingly well-articulated message that Catholicism offered a frame of reference which made sense of these bewildering events. 'All the hardships and perils to which our living faith is exposed,' he declared in a homily in May that year,

> produce . . . a special opportunity to shape that faith. We must all tell this to ourselves and not be afraid. God is more powerful than people! If someone really wishes to live his faith . . . he will be equal to the task! . . . May the knowledge of who we are accompany us everywhere; let us not lower our heads – let us look everyone in the eye.

He was prepared to make what would have been clearly under-stood as political points from the pulpit; at the celebration of the 150th anniversary of the diocese of Sandomierz in June he used the nineteenth-century partition of Poland in exactly the way that the banned play *Forefathers' Eve* did. 'During that difficult period,' he said, 'the Catholic Church played a significant role in the Polish lands when it came to the preservation of the unity within the nation . . . Bishops and priests never allowed the Church to become Russified . . . The unity of the Church with the nation always had, and still has, a fundamental meaning for both the Polish nation and the Church.' Like Cardinals Sapieha and Wyszynski before him, Karol Wojtyla was becoming one of those church leaders that gave Poles an anchor in turbulent times.

It turned out that Moczar had over-reached himself: the threat of all-out civil war which might have led the nation to turn to him never quite materialised. Gomulka still had the support of the Soviet leader Leonid Brezhnev, who needed Polish help to crush the outbreak of liberalism and independence in Prague. The

Soviet forces which invaded Czechoslovakia in August that year included Polish troops and tanks, and a grateful Brezhnev turned up at the Polish Communist Party's Congress in the autumn to express his solidarity with the leadership. The crisis passed and Gomulka would struggle on for another couple of years. But Neal Ascherson made an acute observation about what had changed in the course of 1968. Until that point, he argued, much of the intellectual opposition to the regime had been 'liberal, in the sense that it sought to find a sceptical, humanist path between the dogmatic blocks of Catholicism and Communism', it had been based on the assumption that the communist system could be reformed from within, and 'Many of its leading lights had been assimilated Jews, often from a Marxist background'. All that died in the confusion and brutality of the events of 1968, and when intellectual opposition revived it was, Ascherson has suggested, in a very different form; 'more conservative, more influenced by history, above all looking to the Catholic Church for moral guidance and protection' – in other words, the kind of intellectual movement that was being given shape in the afternoon salons at the archiepiscopal palace in Krakow.

Gomulka was finally finished off by a combination of economics and sensational insensitivity to Polish religious sensibilities. In the aftermath of the 1968 crisis he tried to introduce a measure of free market reform; it inevitably produced pain before it bore fruit, and in December 1970 he was forced to accept the need for rises in food prices. They were announced on Warsaw Radio in, of all times, the run-up to Christmas, and they were enough to blow a hole in most families' Christmas budget; the cost of flour went up by 16 per cent, sugar was up by 14 per cent and meat was to be 17 per cent more expensive. There were strikes and marches in the shipbuilding cities of Gdynia and Gdansk, and the police responded with guns as well as clubs. This is an eyewitness account of how the shooting began:

> One of the commanders, a lieutenant, just simply shot at the crowd with his pistol. It was about an arm's length from me, and I only realised what had happened when I saw this squirt of blood. One of the lads from the shipyard had been hit straight

in the larynx, in the artery, and the blood – you know – just spouted up about four feet. It was like oil on the flames, as we say in Polish; the people saw it, and they threw themselves at the police cordon. Then there was a massacre.

The dead marcher was carried to hospital: 'A Polish flag was found somewhere, and the flag was soaked in blood; there was so much of it that it was all over the whole flag.'

It was the beginning of several days of fighting. The government was confronted with the threat of a general strike or even a full-scale revolution, and on 20 December Gomulka was removed from office to be replaced by Edward Gierek. Cardinal Wojtyla was on his way to visit a priest who was convalescing from an operation on a tumour at a hospital in Krakow. The patient heard the news on the ward radio and broke it to his visitor when he arrived; 'the Cardinal listened in silence with the utmost attention. At the end, his comment was "Indeed, God works in mysterious ways."' The year ended with midnight mass at the Franciscan Church just across from his residence in Krakow, and he showed his now sure rhetorical touch in the tone of his sermon on the recent events in the Baltic ports:

> Behind us are the hard experiences of the last few weeks, and these just before Christmas. They will be recorded as a bloody page in the annals of our national history – written in Polish blood spilled by Poles . . . This night has a different character than usual, and only very few could spend this time looking for entertainment. Instead we feel the need for expiation, for recollection before God, for an examination of conscience, prayer for the dead, and for those suffering there, far from us, in the cities of the coast.

His message to the new regime of Edward Gierek was explicit, even by the standards of the highly politicised Polish Church; he spoke out for 'the right to food, the right to freedom . . . an atmosphere of genuine freedom untrammelled and not questioned or threatened in any practical sense; an atmosphere of inner freedom, the freedom from the fear of what may befall me if I act in this way or go to that place, or appear somewhere'.

I have made much of Karol Wojtyla's belief in Providence and his tendency to see the hand of God – and indeed the hand of the Virgin – at work in history and in the course of his own life. But it is worth recording as a footnote to this period that he could be quite clear-eyed about the social dynamics that brought people to the Church in a time of turmoil and persecution. 'Religion isn't compulsory any more,' he said.

> On the contrary, it is prohibited. As such it fulfils the need for freedom, but only for a short time. In the long run, you can't treat religion as an occasion to show your own independence . . . A sort of Catholic asylum is being created. People are seeking the Church as a hiding place, for the qualities they cannot live without . . . Meetings at Mass . . . give them a feeling of strength and security . . . Christianity is being made by administrative means.

Poland's two cardinals – both of whom now enjoyed a national profile – could have been forgiven for complaining that they were somewhat neglected by the universal Church during the traumas of the late 1960s. Support reached them in the form of money given by American Catholics – the aid was organised by John Krol, the Archbishop of Philadelphia, who was of Polish descent and had been created cardinal in the same ceremony as Karol Wojtyla – and Archbishop Agostino Casaroli, the Vatican's diminutive but energetic envoy to Eastern Europe (he would later serve as John Paul's secretary of state), would bustle through their lives from time to time in pursuit of Paul's policy of *Ostpolitik*. But a crisis of a different kind had erupted in Rome which convulsed the Church and paralysed Paul – and Cardinal Wojtyla had a walk-on part in the drama which acquired a retrospective significance during his pontificate.

The Pontifical Commission for the Study of Population, Family and Births – the Birth Control Commission as it became more generally known – had a curious genesis. It began life in 1963 as the brainchild of Cardinal Leon Suenens, the Archbishop of Malines-Brussels; a prominent liberal voice at the Second Vatican

Council, he was one of those pastoral Western European bishops who were feeling the pressure for change from a sophisticated laity which no longer accepted the idea of huge families as a Catholic duty. Pope John took up the idea as a way of answering the clamour of anxiety about the world population explosion – the United Nations' first conference on world population problems was being planned, and the pope wanted an intellectually coherent Catholic response. In the autumn of 1963 six men – a Dominican diplomat, two Jesuits, a demographer, a sociologist and a British doctor – met in secret at a hotel called the House in the Woods outside Louvain in Belgium, and began considering the sensitive question of whether the Church could change her position on artificial contraception.

The Commission moved to Rome for its second session, and the British delegate, John Marshall, reminisced to me about the curious atmosphere in which they conducted their discussions. 'Occasionally friends of a member who happened to be in Rome would be asked to dinner,' he said, 'and you would see the look of astonishment on their faces as the pros and cons of *coitus interruptus* were discussed over coffee.' Their deliberations were taking place in an atmosphere of high secular excitement about the possibilities offered by easily available and apparently risk-free contraception, and the Catholic press was caught by the mood like everyone else. Cardinal Suenens even raised the question on the floor of the Vatican Council, taking the book of Genesis as his text; 'Hasn't there been,' he demanded, 'too much emphasis on the passage "increase and multiply", and not enough on another phrase which says ". . . and they shall be one flesh"? . . . I beg you, my brother bishops, let us avoid another "Galileo Affair". One is enough for the Church.' The reference to the Church's attempt to deny science by condemning Galileo's theories in the early seventeenth century prompted prolonged applause in St Peter's. In the summer of 1964 Pope Paul officially admitted that the Commission existed – a huge step in itself, because it amounted to confirmation that the Church was at least open to the possibility of change.

Later that year the Commission took the radical step of expanding its membership to include lay people. 'Those of us who were approaching it from a scientific point of view,' said John Marshall, 'realised that the man and woman in the street – or the man and woman in bed – ought also to have a say in the matter. It wasn't just high theology or science, it was human involvement and feelings and experience as well.' The Crowleys, an American couple who had been invited to join the Commission, were asked to conduct their own survey of grassroots Catholic opinion about the matter, and the letters that poured in painted a picture of the pain being endured by couples struggling to remain faithful to the Church's teaching. 'Following my third pregnancy in two years I almost smothered the baby with a pillow because I couldn't stand its crying,' one woman wrote. 'We have three sick kids at home, another kicking in my stomach, and a husband full of booze,' reported another. 'I have lived on hope, hope in God, hope in taking a long time for the next pregnancy, hope that someone understands my problem.' 'The pain in those letters was heart-rending,' said Patty Crowley, 'and we just couldn't imagine that the Church would expect such sacrifice and obedience from couples.' The survey had a profound impact on the Commission, which was now fifty-five strong; the membership at the final session included fifteen bishops, and in June 1966 they voted to endorse 'Responsible Parenthood', the report approved by the majority of Commission members which recommended a change in the Church's teaching.

The text of the document was subsequently published in full in the American *National Catholic Reporter* and the British magazine *The Tablet,* and there was a widespread assumption throughout the Catholic world that Pope Paul would accept its recommendations. He did not, and when *Humanae Vitae* ('On Human Life') was published in the summer of 1968, it proved to be perhaps the most controversial encyclical in the history of the Church. 'We remind you,' Paul told the faithful, 'that to have recourse to contraceptives is a serious sin that offends God, destroys the life of grace, prevents access to the sacraments, and, even more painfully, wounds the life of the couple.' There was open rebellion throughout the Western Church; 640 American priests and theologians signed a petition against the encyclical, 5,000 Catholic laymen in Germany declared openly that they would refuse to follow its teaching, and the bishops of England and Wales issued a statement that came very close to endorsing a rejection of papal teaching. 'Understandably,' they declared, 'many husbands and wives anticipating the promised statement of the pope, have come to rely on contraception. In this way they have acted conscientiously and often after seeking pastoral advice. They may now be unable to see that, at least in their personal circumstances, the use of contraception is wrong.' Paul was so traumatised by the whole experience that, in the judgement of some of those around him, he never really recovered and spent the remainder of his pontificate in miserable contemplation of the divisions which had split the Church.

Karol Wojtyla's part in the affair remains somewhat opaque, but it is intriguing. As the author of *Love and Responsibility* he was a natural choice for a place on the Commission, and Paul did indeed invite him to join. But he missed the critical final session – it covered three months in early 1966 when he was heavily involved in the millennium celebrations in Poland – and was not there for the final vote. He did, however, set up his own commission in Krakow to study the issue, and its conclusions, 'The Foundations of the Church's Doctrine on the Principles of Conjugal Love', were sent to Rome in February 1968, when Paul would have been putting the final touches to his encyclical. There have been all sorts of claims made about the degree to which the contribution from Krakow influenced the final text of *Humanae Vitae* – it has even been suggested that Karol Wojtyla's influence was so strong that he more or less drafted the whole thing, but this is certainly an exaggeration. The record suggests that Paul had in fact been 'nobbled' by conservatives in what was then called the Holy Office – today's Congregation for the Doctrine of the Faith – who were determined to hold the line on contraception. Most of the work on the document was done in 1967 by yet another commission, a group of four conservative theologians brought together for the express purpose of ensuring that the Church's traditional teaching was maintained. However, it is certainly true that *Humanae Vitae* was welcomed with more enthusiasm by the Archbishop of Krakow than it was by many of the bishops of Western Europe. Shortly after its publication

Cardinal Wojtyla endorsed it in characteristically bracing moral terms in a sermon at the ancient Church of St Mary in Krakow's Market Square: 'If it appears to be difficult, if it creates great demands for man in the realm of morality, it is necessary to answer these demands.' He established '*Humanae Vitae* Marriage Groups' to encourage couples to follow the Vatican's teaching.

Like the Second Vatican Council, *Humanae Vitae* defined the contours of the battles that would be fought during John Paul's pontificate. The pressure for change from liberal Catholics in Western Europe and the United States which originally provoked the crisis more or less evaporated – for the simple reason that in the end the vast majority of them simply decided to ignore the encyclical's conclusions. But in the developing world the Church's attitude to contraception would in due course become a matter of life and death because of the spread of AIDS. And behind the debate about sex there was a deeper one about authority. The conservative argument for holding the line in *Humanae Vitae* was that if the Church changed its mind on a teaching which past popes had promulgated with such certainty, the very idea of papal authority would be undermined; as it has turned out, papal authority has been seriously damaged anyway, because the encyclical produced the first case of mass disobedience to a papal instruction by people who otherwise thought of themselves as loyal Catholics. The *Humanae Vitae* affair also threw up some of the questions about the nature of truth which would become such a salient theme of John Paul's pontificate. The inclusion of lay people on the Birth Control Commission reflected the Vatican II ideas that truth was to be found in the whole Church, not just the hierarchy, and that the experiences of those living as Catholics in the modern world should be part of the process by which the Church comes to its decisions. The rejection of the views of the majority on the Commission was widely seen as a rejection of those ideas too. The Church, the encyclical states, 'no less than her Divine Founder, is destined to be a "sign of contradiction"'.

Finally, *Humanae Vitae* gave rise to another phenomenon which would become familiar in the John Paul years: the high-profile theologian in open conflict with the Vatican. Charles Curran, a prominent professor of theology at the Catholic University of

America, held a press conference in the Mayflower Hotel just down the road from the White House to denounce the encyclical, and soon found himself embroiled in a long battle with the guardians of orthodoxy in Rome. Hans Kung, a hugely influential Swiss theologian who had been one of the intellectual power-houses of Vatican II, argued that the birth control teaching was an example of a 'creeping infallibility' with no basis in theology. His 1970 book *Infallible?*, with its pointed question mark, set him on a collision course with Rome that ended when his licence to teach as an approved Catholic theologian was finally withdrawn under John Paul in 1979.

Karol Wojtyla went through a testing intellectual experience himself in 1970. In mid-December he attended a twenty-four-hour conference at the Catholic University of Lublin devoted exclusively to his latest book, *Person and Act* (or *The Acting Person*, to use the title it was given when it was published in English). The meeting was held at the height of the violence provoked by Gomulka's hike of food prices, and the fact that anyone was able to give any attention at all to this latest Wojtyla excursion into pheno-menology amid the terrible news coming in from Gdansk and Gdynia is a tribute to the powers of concentration of all con-cerned, including the future pope. But the verdict of some of the cardinal's peers in the academic world was less than flattering; one of the nineteen philosophers present said he had read the book twice and was still not sure that he had understood it. Karol Wojtyla may have developed a clear voice as a preacher by this stage of his life, but the same could not be said of his discourse as a philosopher. George Hunston Williams, a Harvard academic who produced a thorough and largely sympathetic study of *The Mind of John Paul II* in 1981, describes *The Acting Person* as 'a very difficult read in any language', and laments the author's failure to learn the lessons of his own education: 'if he could only have remembered how he once wept in the boiler room of the Solvay chemical works during the Occupation trying to master Father Wais on metaphysics, or how he had so much despaired of understanding the *Formalismus* of Scheler that he first translated it into Polish to get a grip on it!' For those of us who have tried to grapple with Karol Wojtyla's philosophical writing and found ourselves wanting, this judgement from a trained philosopher's mind is immensely reassuring. Professor Williams's tone is almost avuncular, and he is at once kindly and merciless in his critique; Wojtyla 'enumerates and defines many faculties', he writes, 'and speaks of such things as the difference between the reflective and the reflexive consciousness, and of such events as the objectification of subjectivity. These complexities need not detain the reader.' Picking through the comments of the philosophers meeting at Lublin, it sounds very much as if they thought the book was simply muddled; it 'mingled without due care to discrimination the intersecting vocabularies of two philosophical languages', and 'with respect to the phenomenological terms [drawn from Scheler], *Erfahrung* and *Erlebris*, it was not always certain that they were being used with exactitude'.

Yet for all that the book, certainly the most significant work of Karol Wojtyla the philosopher before his accession to the papacy, has at its core a fairly straightforward and profoundly Christian message. Its focus is the age-old question of what it means to be human – a question Karol Wojtyla confronted with much more urgency than most of us because of his experience of living under systems of government which routinely acted inhumanely. 'At the heart of Wojtyla's argument,' Professor Williams explains, 'are the concepts of free will and self-determination . . . a normative ethic . . . and a concept of absolute truth, natural or revealed.' He argues that we all see the world through 'ethically tinted glasses', and rejects all forms of determinism – whether drawn from the psychological schools of Freud and Jung or the iron laws of Marxism; 'Freedom, for Wojtyla,' says Professor Williams, 'consists in choosing truth for oneself in one's acts without coercion either from instinctual or subliminal drives from within or from without (socio-political pressures) towards conformism.' *The Acting Person* would give the future pope the foundation for two of his most consistent messages: his stress on the dignity of the individual, and his insistence on our duty to live a moral life.

Although the book presents itself as 'phenomenological investigation' Professor Williams argues that it is in fact no such thing because it is based on good old-fashioned Christian presuppositions like the existence of free will and an absolute truth. It is characteristic of a trait Karol Wojtyla showed in almost every walk of life; he was willing to plunge into all sorts of areas that many more conventional clerics might feel nervous about – whether it was his intimate chats about sex on his kayaking trips, his choice of exotic and *recherché* philosophical disciplines or his unprecedented love affair with the television cameras as pope – while remaining at heart a profoundly old-fashioned, pre-Vatican II style Catholic priest.

The publication of *The Acting Person* had two unexpected consequences: it triggered a chain of events which gave Cardinal Wojtyla a serious profile in the Catholic Church in the United States, and it led him into an intense relationship with a married woman. Dr Anna-Teresa Tymieniecka was born into the landed gentry of pre-war Poland and studied at the Jagiellonian in Krakow in 1945–6 – so she and the cardinal had something of a shared past to draw on. She left Poland after securing her degree and continued in academic life, first in Fribourg and Paris, and later in the United States, teaching and doing research work at Berkeley, Oregon State University, Yale, Pennsylvania State (where she was assistant professor of philosophy) and Bryn Mawr College. Petite, strawberry-blonde, and – by the accounts of those who met her – extremely attractive, she must have cut a dashing figure in the academic world with her aristocratic background and cosmopolitan *curriculum vitae*. She married a distinguished Harvard economist (Professor Hendrik Houthakker, an adviser to the Nixon White House) and established a body rather grandly calling itself 'The World Institute for Advanced Phenomenological Research' at her home in Massachusetts.

As the name of her institute suggests, Dr Tymieniecka shared Karol Wojtyla's philosophical field of interest, and in the autumn of 1972 a visiting Polish scholar gave her a copy of the cardinal's book. Unlike his colleagues at Lublin she was bowled over by the work – indeed, so great was her enthusiasm that she flew to Krakow to meet the author. Talking to the future pope for the first time in one of the drawing rooms of the residence on Franciszkanska Street she found him 'surprised to find such admiration for his philosophical thinking, since his work had been severely criticised on all points by a number of Catholic philosophers' at Lublin. He would not have been human if he were not a little flattered too, and when Dr Tymieniecka invited him to deliver a paper at a Thomas Aquinas conference she was organising in Naples he agreed. Cardinal Wojtyla's contribution to the conference was enthusiastically received, and the two philosophers began to talk about the possibility of collaborating on an English-language edition of *The Acting Person.*

It was not just a question of translating in the literal sense; Dr Tymieniecka's enthusiasm for the book could not disguise the fact that the text was something of a mess, full of those imprecisions noted by the Lublin seminar, half-developed ideas and, indeed, grammatical lapses. In view of the number of careers Cardinal Wojtyla seemed determined to cram into his life it is scarcely surprising that he wrote in a hurry and seldom revised what he had set down. For the next three years the task of turning the cardinal's thoughts into a form fit for publication in the United States became Dr Tymieniecka's passion – and it consumed vast amounts of her time and energy. She would travel to Europe half a dozen times a year, visiting Krakow, Warsaw and Rome as the cardinal's diary dictated, staying for several weeks on each trip and making herself available whenever the cardinal could squeeze a moment into his absurdly crowded schedule; sometimes it would be no more than a snatched breakfast or dinner together, sometimes she would accompany him on a long car journey so that she could secure his undivided attention for a while. During her trips to Krakow they would usually manage to steal a day away together so that they could focus more fully on their joint enterprise. 'There were these walks in the woods,' she later remembered: 'he was a dedicated walker.' 'These would be with Dziwisz [the cardinal's personal assistant],' she added very firmly, 'the three of us . . .'

Anna-Teresa Tymieniecka's own account of her relationship with Karol Wojtyla is recorded at some length in the biography written by Carl Bernstein and Marco Politi, and the way she describes it does make it sound a little like the story of a high-powered executive snatching what time he can to spend with his star-struck mistress. She called the cardinal 'the most elegant man', and praised his gift for making 'a person feel there is

151

nothing else on his mind' when he talked to them. She talked of his 'innate personal charm', 'poetical nature' and 'captivating way of dealing with people', and remarked that 'he had a way of smiling, a way of looking around that was different and exceedingly personal. It had a beauty about it.' But she denied any suggestion of a romantic attachment: 'How could I fall in love with a middle-aged clergyman?' she said in her interview for the book. 'Besides I am a married woman.'

No one has seriously suggested that anything improper took place between the two of them, but Dr George Hunston Williams, the author of *The Mind of John Paul II*, knew Dr Tymieniecka well during this period and has no doubt that there was a sexual charge at work in the relationship – on her side at least. 'Yes, of course there was that,' he said. 'Eros is the basis of philosophy in a way. You have to love. She is a passionate human being. Hers was a Catholic passion towards Wojtyla, that is to say it was restrained by his ecclesiastical dignity and her own understanding of what restraints there would be.' Those who look to the relationship in the hope of finding a skeleton in the future pope's cupboard – and I have been startled by the number of people whose reaction to the news that I was writing this book has been to ask whether John Paul ever had sex – will be disappointed. But his consuming friendship with Anna-Teresa Tymieniecka – like his teenage relationships with girls – suggests he was very far from being the sexually indifferent cleric of caricature.

In 1976 Dr Tymieniecka organised a trip to the United States for the cardinal with Father Stanislaw Dziwisz, his private secretary. He was leading the Polish delegation to the Eucharistic Congress in Philadelphia that summer, and she built a three-week programme on the back of it in the hope of introducing him as 'a great personality, a great statesman'. She 'got him a dinner at the Harvard president's house' for 250 people, and hosted another evening in Washington. He delivered a well-received lecture at Harvard, met leaders of the American Catholic Church in Washington and was discussed as a possible future pope in the pages of the *New York Times*. There was some 'down-time' during his American sojourn, and he spent it with Dr Tymieniecka at her house in the woods of Vermont. There was early morning mass on a picnic table in the back garden – with Fr Dziwisz and Dr Tymieniecka's son serving and occasional attendance by the family horse, donkey and goat. There was a daily swim in the neighbour's lake, and there was the kitchen table for more determined intellectual pounding on *The Acting Person.*

Karol Wojtyla's collaboration with Dr Tymieniecka came to a somewhat sour conclusion. When he was elected pope she rushed into print with the English translation of *The Acting Person*, giving rise to a prolonged dispute with the Vatican about whether her version of the book was an accurate representation of his thinking. One of those commissions which the Vatican so often has recourse to was set up to study the matter, and years of argument between the Vatican's publishing house and the Dutch company that brought out the Tymieniecka version followed. Dr Williams notes rather dryly that 'Dr Tymieniecka introduced substantial changes so that what the author regards as the "definitive version" is considerably more phenomenological in technical vocabulary than was the original Polish version, wherein the Thomist substructure and vocabulary are much in evidence.' George Weigel takes a more polemical view of the matter, and states that Dr Tymieniecka's insistence that her version is definitive is 'a claim no serious student of Wojtyla's work accepts'. It is striking that in the thousand-odd pages of his biography of John Paul Dr Tymieniecka features in no more than an extended but rather aggrieved-sounding footnote about the copyright row over the text. The relationship is unlikely to feature largely in the cause for John Paul's canonisation which was begun after his death in the spring of 2005.

But Anna-Teresa Tymieniecka's reflections on Karol Wojtyla as a man are extremely illuminating; she knew him well in the fullness of his life, just before he disappeared behind the veil of deference and good form which shroud the personality of a pope. 'People around him see the sweetest, [most] modest person,' she said. 'They never see this iron will behind it . . . His usual attitude is suavity. His iron will is exercised with suavity and enormous discretion.' She described him as 'by no means as humble as he appears. Neither is he modest. He thinks about himself very highly, very adequately.' Asked whether he was someone who changed his mind, Dr Tymieniecka suggested that while he was interested in new ideas, he was only really open to them when they were consistent with his own.

Cardinal Wojtyla was in fact establishing a growing international reputation independently of Dr Tymieniecka's campaign to promote his cause. The slightly ramshackle and ad hoc way in which the Roman Catholic Church is governed allows individual cardinals considerable latitude in deciding how prominent a role they wish to play in the affairs of the universal Church. The Vatican's government departments ('dicasteries' is the technical term, and they are divided, for no particularly good administrative reason, into congregations and councils) are run on a day-to-day basis by civil service staffs based in Rome under the direction of a resident prefect or president (usually a cardinal, sometimes, in the case of councils, an archbishop). But they operate under the direction of a kind of board of management or 'members' appointed by the pope, and an enthusiastic and energetic cardinal can exert considerable influence over the way they work. Cardinal Wojtyla was a member of the Congregations for the Liturgy (one of the most sensitive of all the Vatican departments at this period because of the ruckus over Vatican II reforms in the mass), for the Eastern Churches, for the Clergy, and for Divine Service and Catholic Education (an issue about which he felt especially passionate because of the communist attempts to restrict Catholic teaching in Poland).

He was also an active participant in four out of the five Synods of Bishops which followed the Vatican Council – the 1967 meeting which he stayed away from in solidarity with the passportless Cardinal Wyszynski was the only one he missed; his enthusiastic endorsement of papal primacy at the 1969 Synod cannot have done him any harm in the eyes of Paul VI, and in the 1971 Synod on the priesthood he gave a clear hint of things to come with his insistence on the value of priestly celibacy. He was appointed 'rapporteur' at the 1974 Synod and was chairman of the Council of the Synod's Secretariat by 1977. His performance on these occasions evidently impressed; the late Archbishop Derek Worlock of Liverpool – who could be waspish when the mood took him – called Cardinal Wojtyla 'one of the best brains of any man I have ever met'.

His position also allowed him to gratify that insatiable appetite for travel which was later to transform the office of the papacy. In the mid 1970s Cardinal Wojtyla visited Australia, New Zealand, the Philippines and New Guinea in addition to his trip to the United States and his regular trips to Western Europe (Italy and West Germany were his most frequent destinations, for obvious reasons). 'Not only did Cardinal Wojtyla travel more than most Catholic prelates ever do,' wrote George Blazynski in 1979, 'but he also established many more world-wide contacts. There is perhaps only a handful of Church dignitaries he has not met in all the countries he visited.' It would be wrong to regard the cardinal's networking as cynical careerism; if he took delight in the opportunities offered by his position, it is equally certain that he fulfilled its responsibilities with an irreproachable seriousness of purpose.

Another of Poland's political cycles was playing itself out during the mid 1970s. Edward Gierek's regime – like that of Gomulka before him – began in hope. A former miner with some experience of working in Western Europe, Gierek combined an apparent willingness to listen to popular opinion with a determination to give Poles some share in the European prosperity they had been denied since the end of the Second World War. For five years from 1971 he delivered economic growth at a level unprecedented in the communist era. But the realities of trying to run a controlled economy finally reasserted themselves and – again like his predecessor – he was forced to order huge price rises in the summer of 1976. Again there were riots, and again the government backed down. Gierek survived the crisis, but his position had been seriously weakened, and opposition groups of various stripes and hues grew in numbers and confidence.

As a result the Church became an even more powerful factor in the political equation. Its popular reach and political influence were approaching their zenith; 93 per cent of Poles (including, of course, many party workers) had been baptised as Catholics, and an astonishing 90 per cent of the population regularly attended church services. The process of 'making Christianity by administrative means' (as the future pope had put it) was proceeding apace. There were so many applications for training to the priesthood that the seminaries were turning people away, and, in sharp contrast to the picture in Western Europe, the overall number of churches, priests and bishops was actually increasing. Poland could boast the only Catholic university in the communist world (Lublin), and religion was being taught outside schools in 18,000 so-called 'catechetic points' (in other words in parish churches, private homes and church-owned buildings).

Catholicism was simply too big a presence in Polish society for Gierek to ignore, and in the aftermath of the 1976 crisis he turned to Cardinal Wyszynski for help. The two men met at a Church–state summit to discuss the challenges to 'the unity of Poland' in October 1977, and it was the First Secretary of the Polish Communist Party rather than the cardinal who was the real supplicant – Gierek badly needed a statement from the hierarchy to calm the increasingly fractious mood of the citizenry. In a sermon a few days later – in yet another echo of earlier dealings between the Polish Church and the Polish state – Wyszynski explicitly acknowledged that the Church must recognise the 'demands of the Polish *raison d'état*', especially in 'difficult situations'. In return Gierek seems to have made a series of promises about the way the Church would be treated. The meeting did not, as many of the Polish bishops hoped, lead to the government giving full recognition to the Church as a legal entity, but the fact that a communist leader had been forced to turn to a Catholic cardinal for help spoke volumes, and Wyszynski was described as 'an eminent Polish patriot' by the authorities. By this time his pragmatic approach also had the support of the Vatican. Paul and his envoy to Eastern Europe, Cardinal Casaroli, were still pursuing their *Ostpolitik* with vigour, and little more than a month after the Gierek–Wyszynski meeting, Gierek travelled to Rome for an unprecedented audience with the pope.

Cardinal Wojtyla, however, increasingly favoured a more robust approach to Church–state relations. Although he remained extremely careful to ensure that there was no open division with the primate – and certainly none with the Vatican – his language focused on principle rather than pragmatism. In view of the sheer scale of Karol Wojtyla's lifetime production of words it comes as no great surprise that the quality of his writing and his addresses was very varied indeed, but at his best he could use words with both precision and power, and some of his most penetrating insights belong to this period of his life. Here, for example, he is talking about education in Poland:

> It should not be required of our teachers, the overwhelming majority of whom are, as children of this nation, themselves believers, that they should by virtue of their position and profession become advocates of a viewpoint they do not share. You cannot expect such an act of harakiri to be inflicted on human conscience and on human personality. You cannot expect a person who teaches and hands down truth himself to live a falsehood. For this goes against the dignity of Man, and does not suit our Polish national interest . . . The future of our country depends on whether the people we are now teaching in our schools will be independent, spiritually mature and socially responsible.

He had learnt to use language like the lens on a camera, sharpening the focus so that the contours of paradox and falsehood of life under communism were as clear as they could be. John Paul's Latinist – the man with the job of translating papal utterances into the Church's official language – once complained to me that his master had a tendency to verbosity and imprecise socio-babble, but the Wojtyla sermons of the late 1970s are marked by luminous clarity and directness. His ethic of Christian human rights was now well developed – this is from a sermon in 1977:

> The rights of Man are an essential part of being human, and God, by becoming man, confirmed the dignity of being human. That is why they cannot be arbitrarily circumscribed. No one can say: you have these rights because you are a member of such and such a nation, race, class or party; and to you they are denied because you do not belong to this race, class or party . . . Every man by virtue of being man has a right to social advancement in the framework of his community. And every man has the duty to shape the life of the whole community by

promoting justice and love, not factional struggles, in the name of a single class. Every man born on Polish soil is by this very token a child of the Polish motherland. It is impermissible to tell anyone that he or she is a lesser kind of Pole than any other Pole.

Even read cold on the page thirty years later it is stirring stuff; when addressed to people with direct experience of a society which rewarded some people and discriminated against others on the basis of ideology and party membership it must have been electrifying.

With the growing confidence about the message came a growing willingness to confront the authorities more directly. On 7 May 1977 a student opposition leader at the Jagiellonian University died in mysterious circumstances not far from the cardinal's Krakow residence; the official account of the cause of death was that he had had a fall, but almost everyone believed he had been beaten to death by the secret police. Thousands of people attended the funeral at Wawel Cathedral; Cardinal Wojtyla presided, and in his sermon he more or less accused the government of murder. It was an extremely bold accusation to make, and it stiffened the courage of others to express their feelings openly; that night crowds of students gathered at Wawel with black banners and candles. The young victim had been a member of KOR, the Workers' Defence Committee, an increasingly influential underground movement formed to help workers who had been arrested, and after the incident Cardinal Wojtyla became more and more open in his support for KOR's agenda. It was, in the judgement of one contemporary commentator, the moment when 'The Church began to appear not merely as an institution committed to defending its own rights, but as the only organised body capable of defending human rights generally.'

A few days later Cardinal Wojtyla was celebrating a more tangible victory: a decade after it had begun, the building work at Nowa Huta was complete, and after all those years of midnight masses in an open field the suburb's distinctive ark-shaped church was ready to be consecrated. On 15 May 50,000 people turned out for the ceremony in pouring rain, and the cardinal rewarded them with another memorable sermon. Reflecting on the aggressively anonymous environment which had been designed for the people of the industrial suburb by the central planners and their socialist realist architects, he told the crowds, 'This city is not a city of people who belong to no one, of people to whom one may do whatever one wants, who may be manipulated according to the laws of production and consumption. This city is a city of the children of God . . .' And he went on – prophetically, as it turned out – 'This was built as a city without God. But the will of God and the people who work here has prevailed. Let this be a lesson.' Peter Hebblethwaite, who attended the service, remembered it with a characteristically acute judgement:

> In the end the Polish experience of Wojtyla helped him grasp not merely something about a never-say-die traditionalism but something more important about what matters and what does not in Christian faith. He was driven back to the essentials, to the survival kit of faith that is needed for the Church on its pilgrim journey. The building of the Nowa Huta church was a summary in concrete of his pastoral ministry in Krakow.

Three weeks later another huge crowd celebrated the Feast of Corpus Christi – an event which was by then well established as an annual occasion for public defiance of the authorities. Traditionally the day had been marked by an extended procession from Wawel Cathedral into the centre of Krakow's Old Town, with stops at a series of altars placed around the Market Square. The practice had been banned under the Nazis, and the communist regime restricted the procession to the cathedral courtyard. But the faithful still turned out in their thousands and Cardinal Wojtyla's four sermons at the four altars along the processional route had become something akin to an annual State of the Union address. The 1977 procession took place in an even more highly charged atmosphere than usual, and the communist authorities intervened in the form of a military jet which circled above the crowds in the apparent hope of drowning out the cardinal's words. There is film footage of this incident, and it shows Karol Wojtyla at his crowd-pleasing best: he looks up and welcomes the 'uninvited guest' with a grin, provoking a wave of laughter and applause. He is enjoying himself hugely, and crowd and cardinal are feeding one another's confidence.

The following year the Corpus Christi crowds were even bigger – tens of thousands turned out to hear Karol Wojtyla speak out for Poland in terms that in another context might have seemed stridently nationalistic; looking up towards the towers of Wawel Castle – the castle and cathedral stand in a similar relationship to that of Westminster Abbey and the Houses of Parliament – he declared:

> Wawel means our past – the past that is still present in our hearts, in our present time, in our reality. We pray for our Homeland, as we look at its entire past. It is a great and difficult past; a past which squeezed out the tears from entire generations. Whole generations shed blood, wore shackles! Our Homeland is much more precious because it was bought at the price of so many generations. We will never tear ourselves away from our past! We will never allow it to be torn from our souls!

The cardinal from Krakow was on a roll – and in Rome, the era of Pope Paul was drawing to a close.

7

Election

Cardinal Wojtyla took his holiday in two chunks in 1978. The last week of July was spent on Lake Krespo with a group including many of those who had been his regular summer companions since the 1950s. On the 31st of the month he had a meeting with Cardinal Wyszynski, and he gave a speech that evening on the occasion of the primate's name day. He was back with his friends in the great outdoors on 2 August.

Four days later Paul VI died at the pope's summer residence of Castel Gandolfo. He was approaching his eighty-first birthday and it was, by the accounts that have come down to us, a 'good' death. The pope had been anointed by his secretary of state, and it was reported that his last words were 'an unfinished "Our Father"'. It was also said that the pope's alarm clock, which he had bought during his youthful tour of duty in Poland in the 1920s, went off at the moment of his passing. Unfortunately what would later emerge about the Vatican approach to the reporting of papal deaths means that all these details need to be regarded with a degree of scepticism. The pope's body lay in state for two days at Castel Gandolfo before being returned to Rome for burial, the members of the Sacred College of Cardinals were summoned to Rome and the curious process by which the Roman Catholic Church chooses its leader began.

Cardinal Wojtyla travelled to Rome with Cardinal Wyszynski and was driven straight from the airport to St Peter's by his old friend Bishop Deskur to pay his respects to the dead pope. He prayed for a while and gazed 'into that face which I had seen so many times in our conversations'. Ten days later he gave a talk on

161

Vatican Radio about 'my meetings with Paul VI', singling out for special attention Paul's interest in the church of Nowa Huta and the talk the two men had had about 'the document which . . . appeared as *Humanae Vitae*'. He confirmed that he had indeed sent Paul his opinion on the birth control question 'in writing', and reflected that after discussing it with the pope directly, 'I understood . . . the gravity of the problem that Paul VI faced as the highest teacher and shepherd of our Church.'

Pope Paul had indeed faced grave problems; during the final decade of his pontificate the divisions opened by *Humanae Vitae* had festered, and by the time of his death the wounds in the Church gaped wider than ever – indeed, it is difficult to avoid the conclusion that, for all his gifts and deep experience, he had left Catholicism in much less robust health than he had found it when he was elected. Conservative resentment about some of the reforms introduced by Vatican II had if anything hardened in the years since the end of the Council. In William Oddie's, *John Paul the Great*, the Australian theologian Tracey Rowland paints an alarming picture of the way the post-Conciliar Church looked from the conservative perspective. It sounds decidedly Maoist:

> as is typical of cultural revolutions, all symbols and idioms of the previous order were subject to suppression. High altars were destroyed and Catholic children in first world countries were no longer taught Latin hymns, but they were taught pigeon English songs such as the theologically facile Kum-by-a. The trend was to deem anything 'third world' or popular as 'relevant', while anything classical or requiring learning was 'irrelevant' and 'pre-Conciliar'.

The symbols of the new Church were 'the American nuns in shorts and T-shirt with a guitar slung over one shoulder and a book on Eastern meditation in the other hand; the "just call me Kevin" sort of priest who was not sure what he believed about key doctrines but was certain that he had to be "with it" wherever "it" was . . .'

And there were some powerful figures on the right of the Church. The traditionalist Archbishop Marcel Lefebvre, who refused to accept the Council or the pope's right to enforce its decisions (despite, of course, being, as a conservative, a strong believer in papal authority) had established a rival power centre at Ecône in Switzerland and threatened the Church with the spectre of schism. Within the Sacred College of Cardinals itself the 'archconservative's archconservative' was Cardinal Guiseppe Siri of Genoa, who was reported to have described Vatican II as 'an attack of insanity of Pope John' and 'the greatest disaster in recent ecclesiastical history'. He proclaimed that 'it will take forty years to undo the harm that John did the Church in a few years', and had argued forcefully for a new Syllabus of Errors which would condemn subjectivism, relativism and, rather surprisingly, Pelagianism, a heresy associated with the English theologian Pelagius, who taught in Rome in the fifth century. Siri had been mentioned as a possible pope after the death of Pius XII, and was a serious candidate in 1978.

Even some progressives recognised that Vatican II had left a testing legacy. Peter Hebblethwaite, a leading liberal commentator and biographer of Paul VI, observed that the spectacle of bishops 'arguing vehemently among themselves' at the Council had bred fractious habits among priests and the laity, and that the figure of a bishop had been 'demythologised'; 'he ceased to be a remote and magical figure in a very special hat, and became instead the man who waited at the bus stop like everybody else. This was a welcome trend in that it made bishops approachable; but it also made them considerably less imposing.' The progressive agenda in the late 1970s was, by today's standards, extraordinarily radical. The pros and cons of married priests, women priests, communion for remarried divorcees (one American Catholic pressure group had even devised a 'liturgy for divorce') and contraception were debated much more widely and openly in the Church then than they are at the time of writing – in fact, all sorts of things that John Paul II spent his pontificate making unthinkable were being thought in those days. There was even a group lobbying for a change in the way the pope himself was elected; CREP (the Committee for the Reform of the Election of the Pope) organised a press conference in Rome shortly after Paul's death at which the prolific American Catholic writer and sociologist Fr Andrew

Greeley said he would be perfectly happy to see a woman pope elected because 'a *papessa* could not make more of a mess of the Church than we men have over the last 1900 years'.

All of this weighed heavily on the shoulders of 111 members of the Sacred College (for the first time cardinals over eighty were excluded) who processed into the Sistine Chapel on the afternoon of 25 August. The idea that their life during the conclave should be made as uncomfortable as possible to encourage swift deliberations really meant something then. John Paul II would in due time build a sort of Vatican *pensione* which would allow those who gathered in 2005 to choose his successor in reasonable comfort, but in 1978 the cardinals were accommodated in temporary 'cells' erected in the Apostolic Palace. I interviewed Cardinal Hume about the conclave not long before his death, and despite being accustomed to the rigours of monastic life in North Yorkshire he described living conditions as 'very rough': 'We were four cardinals sharing one tap, and I was sleeping in an office with a bed which I am sure came from a seminary for very short people,' he said. Journalists had been allowed in to inspect the accommodation in advance, and one described it as like 'the enlisted men's section on an aircraft carrier':

> Each cardinal is issued with one roll of toilet paper, two ballpoint pens . . . maybe ten sheets of writing paper . . . Each also gets a plastic wastebasket out of a dime store, a washbowl and pitcher, a red plastic glass, a tiny bed lamp, one hard-backed chair and an even harder looking kneeler. To make it clear that he ought to be out in a hurry, he gets only one bar of soap and two very tiny towels, which will drive the Americans up the wall.

One or two cardinals were lodged amid the almost more inconvenient grandeur of 'vast Renaissance reception rooms, where the cardinal, after putting out the chandelier for the night, would have to pick his way nimbly around vast tables and capacious sofas'. All the windows were shuttered to prevent any possibility of communication with the outside world, and it was a stifling Roman August.

All of which may go some way to explaining why the first conclave in what became known as 'the year of three popes' was one of the shortest in history; Albino Luciani, the Patriarch of Venice, was elected pope on the fourth ballot on the evening of the following day, 26 August, and took the double-barrelled name which combined those of his two predecessors. It does not, of course, explain how John Paul I went from – as far as the outside world was concerned – rank outsider to unstoppable frontrunner in a matter of hours. Peter Hebblethwaite has observed that 'In Rome everything is a mystery and nothing, in the end, is a secret', but the process of reconstructing what happened in a papal conclave is greatly complicated by the habit of after-the-fact rationalisation. The Holy Spirit is supposed to have a hand in the proceedings, and it is always possible to find a logic for pretty much every outcome – because all the cardinals take a vow of secrecy it is, of course, impossible to check anything on the record.

It is, however, clear that Cardinal Siri was the man to beat, with around a quarter of the votes in the first ballot. And it seems likely that Cardinal Benelli, the Archbishop of Florence who had served Pope Paul in the Curia for years and saw himself as the guardian of Paul's legacy, mobilised a 'stop Siri' campaign and ran Albino Luciani as the man most likely to defeat the archconservative. There is also some merit in the piece of conclave lore which states that the character and style of a dead pope can play a significant role in deciding his successor. The rule has both a positive and a negative application. Thus in 2005 the cardinals felt themselves driven to choose someone who could match the stature of John Paul II, but in 1978 they were looking for someone who could make up for the defects in Paul which had marred the final period of his once promising pontificate. So to replace this highly intellectual, socially grand and slightly distant figure they chose a 'pastoral' leader from a peasant background who liked to travel round Venice on the *vaporetto*, dressed as an ordinary priest. Cardinal Hume, in a statement he would later come to regret, called him 'God's candidate'. On his way back to Krakow from Rome, Cardinal Wojtyla stayed the night at the Ursuline Convent in Warsaw, and the Mother Superior there told me he was in high spirits, declaring, 'We have chosen a good pope.'

Much excitement was generated by some of the new pope's comments. Just before the conclave he had written a newspaper article about the birth of Louise Brown, Britain's first test-tube (or IVF, as we should now say) baby, which had taken place that month. He sent his 'heartfelt congratulations' to her, and added, 'As for the parents, I have no right to condemn them, subjectively, if they acted in good faith and with a right intention, and they may have great merit before the Lord.' Could a revolution in Catholic teaching on bioethics be in the offing? Anything seemed possible, and in the meantime John Paul I's famous smile beguiled the world. But we now know from *Thief in the Night*, John Cornwell's officially sanctioned and devastating investigation into John Paul's brief reign, that the new pope was in fact ill and miserable. He felt bullied by his secretary of state, Cardinal Villot, who delivered a huge suitcase full of paperwork to his desk twice a day ('on every page a problem,' the pope complained). He was 'overwhelmed' by the job according to one Vatican insider, and 'didn't know where to start' according to another. His legs swelled up horribly because of a circulatory problem, and he startled his staff by erratic behaviour such as his insistence on serving as his secretary's altar boy at early morning mass. Above all, he seemed convinced that he had been chosen by mistake, asking his secretary repeatedly at meals, 'Why did they choose me? Why on *earth* did they choose me?' Even more startlingly, he began, according to the testimony of Sister Vincenza, the nun who looked after him, to pray for his own death and to talk of a 'Foreigner' who would replace him. 'Look, sister,' he would apparently say, 'I should not be sitting here in this seat. The Foreign Pope is coming to take my place. I have *begged* the Lord.'

John Paul I's prayer was duly heard. Sister Vincenza found him dead in bed after only thirty-three days in office. The Vatican felt that it was inappropriate that the first person to see a dead pope should be a woman, and invented a story that he had been found by his secretary, Monsignor Magee – thus adding fuel to the fires of conspiracy theory which soon broke out. The cardinals trooped back to Rome, many of them badly shaken. When he heard the news Cardinal Hume said he had trouble believing that 'God's candidate' was dead.

Cardinal Wojtyla was with the Ursuline nuns in Warsaw again on the night of 2 October on his way back to Rome, and they have their story that he spent long hours of this last night as a cardinal on Polish soil prostrate in prayer in the convent chapel; there is no reason to doubt this, since he was much given to marathon prayer sessions, but there has been a great deal of 'mythologising' of these final days before his election, and all sorts of actions which would otherwise have gone unremarked have been endowed with retrospective significance. He was, for example, said to have tidied up his affairs with special care before leaving Krakow. A priest who knew the cardinal well said he 'behaved strangely' at a meeting just before his departure, and 'asked me to pass greetings to friends as if he did not expect to return soon from Rome'. There are also lots of stories circulating of people who had predicted his election.

But if Cardinal Wojtyla did worry about the possibility that he would never see his 'beloved Krakow' again as its archbishop, he had some reason for the anxiety. He had attracted a handful of votes in the later stages of the August conclave, and although his name was absent from most newspaper lists of *papabile*, the logic that drove the August conclave and the lessons of the brief reign of John Paul I did point to a papal profile which he fitted well. Like John Paul I, he had a record as a successful pastor with the common touch, the warmth which Paul had been – rather unfairly – accused of lacking, and an easy rapport with a crowd. But unlike John Paul I he appeared to be in rude health – a few days before the conclave he visited the mountain shrine of Mentorella and left the three Polish priests he was with standing as he climbed to the summit. Similarly his age – fifty-eight – counted very much in his favour after the sudden death of one pope and the doddery final days of another. Like Paul – but unlike John Paul I – he had a formidable appetite for hard work. Finally, there are a number of contrasts with Paul that it is tempting to believe were a factor in the cardinals' collective mind: Paul was an obsessive reader of newspapers, devouring *La Stampa*, *Corriere della Sera* and *Le Monde* every day and making use of a cuttings service which gave him an insight into what the world was thinking and writing about him; Cardinal Wojtyla, as we have seen, never read the papers and was quite confident enough about what he was doing to be careless of his reputation. And while Paul was famous for his Hamlet-like tendency to see so many sides of a question that he never made up his mind, the Archbishop of Krakow was unshakeable in his convictions and simply far too busy to spend time agonising before reaching a decision.

A conclave cannot begin until at least fifteen days after the death of a pope – the rule dates back to the days before air travel when even European cardinals needed time to make their way to Rome. In the interregnum – the period of what is known as the *sede vacante*, or empty throne – the Church is run by the College of Cardinals, who meet daily to deal with arrangements for the dead pope's funeral and any urgent matters of government or administration that arise. It is a breathing space when the cardinals probably get to know one another better than they do on any other occasion, and it is the nearest there is to an election campaign period – there are plenty of telephone calls and discreet dinners, and if a *papabile* gives a sermon he can be assured of a good audience. Cardinal Wojtyla's old friend Bishop Deskur was hard at it organising meetings and making connections during this period in 1978 – it was, as it happens, the last time he was able to enjoy his role as an insider to the full, as he suffered a devastating stroke just before the conclave began. Because it was the second conclave in such a short space of time their eminences felt they already knew one another well, and during the inter-regnum after Paul VI's death Cardinal Wojtyla had impressed a young cardinal who was to play a very significant role in his life. Joseph Ratzinger, the Archbishop of Munich, said later that he and the future pope felt a 'spontaneous sympathy' for one another's views.

Three days before the conclave began, on 11 October, there was a meeting of fifteen heavy hitters in the College of Cardinals, liberals from Western Europe with a smattering of Third World figures too. With the prospect of a Siri papacy once more a real possibility, men like the Dutch Cardinal Willebrands, his country-man Alfrink of Utrecht (a leading figure at the Vatican Council), Hume of London and Marty of France formed the core of the anti-Siri camp. Whether they actively discussed the possibility of a non-Italian pope is a matter of some dispute, but the idea was certainly in the air, and on some points there was already a consensus emerging: it would not, for example, have been possible to choose an American pope with Cold War tension as high as it was, and the memory of Nazism was thought by some to be too fresh to allow for a German pope. Moreover, the shift in the balance of power away from Rome which had been begun by Pius XII had gathered momentum under Paul VI; in the conclave which elected Paul, 65 per cent of the cardinals were from Europe and more than a third were from Italy. By 1978 the Italian contingent was down to less than a quarter, and the West Europeans as a group had fewer than half the votes.

But in the end the decision to look for a pope outside the Italian block was dictated as much as anything else by the conduct of the Italians themselves. Cardinal Siri made the mistake of giving an interview to the *Gazetta del Populo* on the eve of the conclave. He apparently thought he had the journalist's agreement that it would not be published until 15 October, by which time the doors of the conclave would be safely closed and the cardinal electors would be unable to read it, but the paper published the interview a day early, and the views it revealed were fruity. At Vatican II much had been made of 'collegiality', the concept that the Church should be governed more collectively by the pope and the bishops acting together; the cardinal scoffed at the idea, and said he did not even know what the word meant. He berated his interviewer when he did not like the line of questioning ('I don't know how you could ask me such a stupid question,' he said at one point: 'If you really want an answer you will have to sit there and shut up for three hours'). Cardinal Siri then compounded his error of judgement by denying he had given the interview; there was a tape-recording to prove that he had, and the archconservative went into the conclave as badly damaged goods. The incident appears to have made a profound impression on the young Cardinal Ratzinger; when he presided as Dean of the College of Cardinals in the interregnum after John Paul's death their eminences agreed a blanket ban on press interviews between funeral and conclave.

Siri's chief Italian rival in the conclave was Cardinal Benelli himself; after rallying the anti-Siri forces around Albino Luciani in the August conclave he now became a candidate. But Benelli had spent most of his career climbing the greasy pole of Vatican power, and a curial insider with a reputation as a sharp politician was not what most cardinals had in mind as they looked for a new leader – Peter Hebblethwaite observed that Benelli 'seemed more like a manager of Church Inc than a man of God'. The four ballots on Sunday 15 October produced deadlock between the two Italians. Siri's secretary later claimed that his master came within a few votes of the required two-thirds majority, but by the end of the first day of voting it was becoming apparent that neither man was likely to make it over that threshold. Italy lost its hold on the papacy because its two main candidates were tried and tested and failed, and to that extent the first non-Italian pope for 455 years was elected *faut de mieux*. Cardinal Benelli remarked afterwards that 'There was not the convergence of votes an Italian needed to be elected pope. But this did not matter, for in the Church there are no foreigners.'

There is a conclave tradition of what are known as 'great electors', powerful cardinals who do not run for the papacy themselves but deploy their authority to swing the votes of others, and there is strong evidence that it was Cardinal König of Vienna who turned the Italian deadlock into a Wojtyla victory. König was a remarkable figure, combining intellectual brilliance (he had complete mastery of ten languages) with a Wojtyla-like passion for physical fitness (Cardinal Hume remembered him jogging around one of the courtyards of the Apostolic Palace during the 1978 conclaves, by which time he was already in his seventies). He had been appointed head of the Secretariat for Non-Believers by Pope Paul, a curious job which gave him a kind of roving brief to wander around Eastern Europe, and in the course of his travels he had met Karol Wojtyla and been profoundly impressed by him. There is a story that when he first gingerly broached the subject of the possibility of a 'pope from Poland' with Cardinal Wyszynski the Polish primate mistook his intentions: 'I could never leave Poland,' he said, 'too much is expected of me there.' 'But what of Wojtyla?' König gently followed up. 'Too young, he'll never get elected,' came the reply. That at least is the version of the story that König told me in an interview in 1997 – I have also seen versions in which Wyszynski replies that Wojtyla is too 'unknown' for the job, and a well-known critic of the John Paul papacy once assured me that the Polish primate actually offered the view that his colleague wasn't intellectually up to the demands of the papacy. It is certainly true that König, who mellowed into an increasingly liberal view of his faith as he aged, came to regret his enthusiasm for Wojtyla before he died at the great age of ninety-eight.

Quite how König made his case among his *confrères* on the evening of 15 October and during the morning ballots the following day remains unclear. Cardinal Hume, who was himself spoken of as a possible pope, has left an intriguing insight into the way these things work. 'It's a very odd thing to be a member of a conclave,' he said. 'No one says anything to you – but then you suddenly realise your name must be under consideration because no one comes up to you any more.' After lunch Wojtyla's votes began to take off, and on the fourth ballot of the day he secured the necessary two-thirds majority. The *camerlengo* or chamberlain – the cardinal who performs the main rituals of the transition period – asked him whether he was willing to accept, and received an unequivocal yes.

At 6.19 p.m. white smoke informed the crowd gathered in St Peter's Square that a pope had been chosen. The announcement of the new pope's name was made, as tradition dictated, by the senior cardinal-deacon, Pericle Felice. Felice had been the secretary-general of the Vatican Council and was famous for making clever jokes in Latin which very few people understood (and which many people thought were designed to make bishops from the developing world feel small), and he made his announcement with 'his usual relish and faintly ironical smile': '*Annuncio vobis gaudium magnum. Habemus papam, eminentissimum ac reverendissimum Dominum Carolum, sanctae Romanae ecclesiae cardinalem Wojtyla, qui sibi nomen imposuit Joannem Paulum Secundum.*' On television recordings of the event you can hear a kind of collective sigh from St Peter's Square as people turned to one another and asked 'Who?' – those who were in the square that night remember that many Italians were convinced that the new Bishop of Rome was an African. When John Paul himself appeared on the balcony

171

half an hour later he broke with tradition by addressing them directly, and he was at his theatrical best:

> Dear brothers and sisters, we are still saddened at the death of our beloved Pope John Paul I, and so the cardinals have called for a new bishop of Rome. They called him from a faraway land – far and yet always close because of our communion in faith and Christian traditions. I was afraid to accept that responsibility, yet I do so in a spirit of obedience to the Lord and total faithfulness to Mary, our most Holy Mother. I am speaking to you in your – no, our Italian language. If I make a mistake, please correct me . . .

It was a master-class in public seduction, and it worked – the possibility of Roman hostility to a pope from 'a faraway land' evaporated.

John Paul's inaugural mass had many writers reaching for chivalric metaphors. It took nearly an hour for the new pope to greet the cardinals who had elected him – hugging some and helping the more elderly to their feet as they knelt to kiss his ring – and Peter Nichols of *The Times* wrote that 'with no great stretch of the imagination [the cardinals] have been transformed into knights awaiting a kiss from King Arthur before setting off on another legendary venture'. George Weigel takes off in similar rhetorical style, describing the moment when John Paul 'took the great silver papal crosier in both hands and shook it at the cheering throng, as if it were a sword of the spirit wrenched free of the stone in which it had been imprisoned'. And John Paul's address most definitely had something of the Church Militant about it:

> Be not afraid to welcome Christ and accept his power. Help the pope and all those who wish to serve Christ and with Christ's power to serve the human person and the whole world.
>
> Be not afraid. Open wide the doors for Christ. To his saving power open the boundaries of states, economic and political systems, the vast fields of culture, civilisation, and development. Be not afraid.

It was the message that had inspired the thousands of Poles who had come to hear Cardinal Wojtyla's Corpus Christi sermons earlier that summer, and in the context of the oppressed churches of Eastern Europe it made perfect sense. It is impossible to imagine a pope from Western Europe saying anything similar in 1978; for most of the churches in Catholicism's historic homeland the enemies were indifference and materialism, not fear.

And yet the late 1970s were – if it is possible to generalise about the mood of an epoch – a time of anxiety, and the journey from the 1960s optimism of the Vatican Council to the fractiousness of the post-*Humanae Vitae* Catholic Church had been reflected more broadly in the mood of many Western societies. There were riots against the Shah in Teheran as the cardinals gathered for their conclave, and Jimmy Carter's America was heading into the period of doubt and self-questioning that culminated in the long hostage crisis of its embassy in Iran. Britain was limping through the last stages of the Labour government that came to grief in the Winter of Discontent that year. And the only certainty seemed to be the Cold War. The interregnum following the death of John Paul I had provided a colourful reminder of this enduring reality when Georgi Markov, a Bulgarian dissident working for the BBC, was murdered with a poisoned umbrella in London.

John Paul himself, of course, had no doubt why a pope with a mission to fight fear had been chosen at this particular moment in history. He would later cite his inaugural address as an example of the Holy Spirit at work:

> When, on October 22nd 1978, I said the words 'Be not afraid!' in St Peter's Square, I could not fully know how far they would take me and the entire Church. Their meaning came more from the Holy Spirit, the Consoler promised by the Lord Jesus to his disciples, than from the man who spoke them. Nevertheless, with the passing of the years I have recalled these words on many occasions.

And it is hard to believe that he did not find himself reflecting on a poem written by one of those literary heroes he held so dear. In

1848 the Polish poet Julius Slowacki had been inspired by Pio Nono's ignominious flight from Rome to write a prophetic piece about the election of a Polish pope.

> God's bell the conclave's petty strife has stilled;
> Its mighty tone
> The harbinger of Slavic hopes fulfilled –
> The Papal Throne!
> A Pope who'll not – Italian-like – take fright
> At sabre thrust
> But brave as God Himself, advance to fight.

8

Rewriting the Rules

On 24 October 1978, less than a week after the election of Pope John Paul II, Fr Mieczyslaw Malinski telephoned the new papal secretary, Stanislaw Dziwisz, and asked for some time with his old friend from the wartime days of the Living Rosary. The two Krakow priests knew one another well, and Dziwisz decided to slip Malinski into the diary for lunch that same day (after the pope's first meeting with the president of Italy). He told Malinski to present himself to the Swiss Guard at the St Anne's Gate, adding, 'Only don't say you're lunching with him, say it's with me.' The 'Polish mafia' was already settling in, and for the next quarter of a century Dziwisz would maintain basilisk-like vigilance over his master's diary.

After negotiating the Swiss Guards Malinski found himself in a 'small and windowless' waiting room, and decided to look around. Like Karol Wojtyla when he first visited Rome, he seems to have had a provincial's exaggerated expectation of what he would find here at the heart of the Catholic world. 'While exploring,' he recorded when he wrote down his impression later that afternoon,

> I ran into a sister of the Sacred Heart of Jesus whom I had known in Krakow – I already knew that the pope had brought three nuns from his residence there. I asked her where the others were, and she led me to a kitchen, which was small but conveniently arranged. I was struck by the small scale of everything compared with Krakow – a single room in the archbishop's residence would have contained all the rooms I had just seen and the kitchen as well.

George Weigel was similarly struck by the 'simplicity, indeed middle-class conventionality' of the papal apartment 'amid all the splendour of the Apostolic Palace – the Raphael frescoes, the gilding, the rich tapestries, the omnipresent marble'.

Over lunch – with Dziwisz and 'an Italian secretary' in attendance – Fr Malinski explained that he had been asked to write up his reminiscences for publication. His account of the conversation sounds curiously stilted.

'. . . there are a few gaps I'd like to ask you about, your Holiness (please forgive me for not using your title rightly, but it is always hard at the beginning).'

'What do you want to know?'

'First, about the development of your philosophical ideas.'

'Goodness me, that's a big subject! Well, to begin at the beginning, as you know there was St John of the Cross and St Theresa of Avila, and the other St Theresa . . .'

And then a little later,

'Does your Holiness expect to travel anywhere in the near future?'

'Yes, I want to visit the patron saints of Italy, and go to Assisi and Sienna. I want to put down roots in this country.'

These two men had known one another for more than three decades, but the papacy turns an individual into the holder of an office more completely than any other position there is. The triple crown, the ostrich feathers and the mobile throne known as the *sedes gestatoria* may all have gone, but there is still something about being a 'Holiness' that is different in kind from being an 'Excellency', a 'Mr President' or even a 'Your Majesty'. The robing-room where a new pope puts on his white silk soutane for the first time is sometimes known as the Room of Tears, which is perhaps a reflection of the frightening loneliness of the job; from the moment of his election a pope can never have a relationship of equality with anyone, and the sentence is for life. John Paul frequently entertained friends from the Polish past in the Vatican and at Castel Gandolfo, but things could never be quite as they were before he became Bishop of Rome, Vicar of Christ, Successor to St Peter, Prince of the Apostles, Supreme Pontiff of the Universal Church, Patriarch of the West, Primate of Italy, Archbishop Metropolitan of the Roman Province and Sovereign of the Vatican City State. When John Paul's Last Testament was published after his death in 2005 it included only one individual from the long years in office who is remembered in anything like 'personal' terms: Fr Dziwisz is thanked 'for his help and collaboration, so understanding for so many years'.

Andrzej Deskur, the curial insider from Krakow who had shown Karol Wojtyla the Vatican ropes during the Council and the conclaves, once told the Catholic writer and papal biographer John Cornwell that 'the pope lives in a gilded cage', and the way Fr Malinski describes that lunch in October 1978 evokes a sense of the cage doors already closing. Some of John Paul's early off-the-cuff banter suggested he was aware of what was happening to him. A few days after his election he gave a press conference – a remarkable thing in itself. 'Will Your Holiness hold other press conferences like this one?' he was asked. 'If they let me . . .' was the reply. 'Will Your Holiness go skiing?' came as a follow-up question. 'I am afraid I probably won't be allowed to,' he answered. A parting shot he fired at one of his earliest audiences is particularly striking when recalled in the light of the way he subsequently used the Congregation for the Doctrine of the Faith, the Vatican's theological watchdog, to discipline wayward theologians: he had spent far too long shaking hands and when the crowd pressed him to linger yet longer he declared, 'I shan't say any more, or the Congregation for the Faith may be after me.'

Of course, for the rest of the world what was striking about those early days of his pontificate was not the closing of the gilded grill but John Paul's determination to rewrite all the rules and break through old conventions. The day before his meeting with Mieczyslaw Malinski he had hosted a large lunch party for Polish bishops and priests. Fr Malinski heard the news on the radio and his reaction was a reflection of the general air of excitement and optimism which the new pontificate inspired:

Hitherto the custom has always been for the pope to take his meals alone, now suddenly everything is different. But in the last few days novelty has become the norm. The rigid, hierarchical character of the papacy suddenly changed to a simple regime bearing the imprint of a new personality. It has become common knowledge that when the present pope decides that something is artificial he makes no bones about changing or abolishing it. Everything to do with the latest successor of St Peter is natural, genuine, spontaneous.

That same afternoon produced another flourish of innovation in the papal style at an audience for Polish pilgrims, when Cardinal Wyszynski delivered an *adieu* to the new pope from the people of Poland. John Paul II remained standing as the Polish primate, forgetting any reservations he might have had about Karol Wojtyla in the past, told him, 'We know, Holy Father, what a costly decision this was for you. We know how dearly you love your country and your city of Krakow, the Tatra Mountains, the forests and valleys, and the solitary walks that gave you joy and renewed your strength. All these things you have laid on the sacrificial pyre of your loving heart.' When he had finished the Polish primate approached John Paul to kiss his ring, only to find that the pope had himself fallen to his knees to kiss Wyszynski's ring. 'Thus for a few seconds the two greatest men in Poland's recent history remained locked in each other's arms,' wrote a Polish observer of the scene, 'the exaltation of the spectators – weeping, cheering and applauding, knew no bounds.' Later Wyszynski said, 'I wanted to free myself, for it was quite wrong that the pope should kneel to me. But he realised it and clasped me so hard that I couldn't move – I couldn't even breathe.'

It is impossible to overstate what a break with the past that kind of public gesture of humility represented – after all, it was not so very long since Pius XII's gardeners were hiding in the bushes at his approach. It was also quite different in kind from the slightly unsettling manner in which his immediate predecessor had humbled himself by serving mass as an altar boy. Whether these gestures were entirely 'natural' or 'spontaneous' must be open to some doubt; the way John Paul held his former Polish colleague in a bear hug makes the whole thing sound slightly studied. But that did not mean it was any less genuine. For Karol Wojtyla, who had once been as serious-minded about his study of drama as he later was in pursuit of his priestly vocation, the word 'theatricality' carried none of the negative connotations it sometimes does in English; just as he had once used theatre as an authentic means of expressing his opposition to the Nazi occupation, so he now used it as a way of expressing his message as pope.

His sense of how to work a crowd was beyond anything that drama school could teach. Papal audiences take place in a modern building tucked away behind St Peter's. The hall is designed to hold 7,000, but 10,000 were crammed in for John Paul's first 'general' audience on 29 October. It began conventionally enough with a homily on 'the three theological virtues; faith, hope and charity', but at the end, when he had delivered his formal apostolic blessing, he stepped down from the dais which separated him from the crowd and, in the newsroom argot of the period, 'went walkabout'. 'The outburst of joy was indescribable,' according to one report of the event. 'Men were shouting, women weeping, forests of hands were thrust out – everyone wanted to touch the pope and be noticed by him, if only for a second. People held out their children so that the pope could stroke them or lay his hands on their heads.'

Every time he appeared the crowds seemed to get bigger. The following Sunday 150,000 turned out in St Peter's Square to hear his Angelus address, and he teasingly asked the Romans if they could tell him the way to the mountain shrine of Mentorella – teasingly because by then word had got round that it was a favourite shrine of his, one of those 'Polish places' which featured prominently on his idiosyncratic world map because of its associations (his favourite childhood author Sienkiewicz wrote up the legend that St Peter had an encounter with the risen Christ at the spot now marked by the chapel). That afternoon he made a pilgrimage to Mentorella, and an estimated 40,000 people tried to follow him there. Large numbers got stuck on the mountain roads, but John Paul saluted them from his helicopter by circling overhead three times before leaving them. The sense that came through all this was of a pope who actually enjoyed his job, and enthusiasm is an enormously valuable political asset. Paul VI had been reduced to Hamlet-like paralysis by the *Humanae Vitae* debacle and by the end of his life clearly felt his office to be a very heavy burden, but John Paul II relished the challenge he had been given, and that communicated itself to Catholics everywhere.

The routine of his days – when they were routine – reflected the habits of Krakow; he would rise at 5.30 a.m. and spend the time before his daily 7.30 a.m. mass in private prayer. Breakfast was at 8.30 a.m., he would write between 9.30 and 11.00 a.m. – often in his chapel as he had done at Krakow, and no less prolifically than when he was a bishop and philosophy don. There would be two further hours of audiences and appointments before lunch, which was generally followed by a brief snooze and a walk in the Vatican gardens. In the afternoon he met what in secular terms we might call members of his cabinet – his secretary of state and the cardinals who ran the big Vatican dicasteries – dinner was at 7.30 p.m. and bed at 11.30 p.m. Each day – at 3.00 p.m. and after dinner – there were two deliveries of those pouches of documents from the Secretariat of State which had so terrified John Paul I.

John Paul could not quite maintain the 'open house' policy he had run in Krakow, but he did like inviting guests to every meal (including breakfast), and Fr Dziwisz would select some twenty people who would attend the early morning mass. This kind of thing was not especially popular with the veterans of Vatican life as it had formerly been lived: 'These halls were once a place of respect, of good taste,' one insider complained, 'now it has become a great Campo de Fiori.' The reference was to the noisy and vital open-air Roman market where flowers, fruit, vegetables and cheap clothing in questionable taste are sold, and one suspects that the new pope would have regarded the slur as a compliment. I was involved in a 'popular' version of his obituary for Radio 2, and when we were looking for people to interview about him we found all sorts of unlikely names on the list of those who had met him in the socially energetic early period of his pontificate; the actress Patsy Kensit had an audience with him after the premiere of one of her films and described it as 'the most unbelievably beautiful moment'. 'I just couldn't stop looking at his eyes,' she told us, 'and I just knew that I was in the presence of someone great.'

It is perhaps worth pausing for a moment amid the scrap-books of swooning notices and tallies of record-breaking crowds to point out that Karol Wojtyla's health record when he became pope was not quite as clean as the image of a vigorous fifty-eight-year-old suggested; the past held one serious accident and some nasty bouts of illness. The accident took place during the war when he was hit by a German military truck on his way to work at the Solvay plant; the truck drove on without stopping and the young man was taken to hospital unconscious. He appeared to make a full recovery, but the accident was thought to be the cause of his slight stoop in later life. His habit of punishing his body with overwork had taken its toll, too, and in March 1959, during his early days as a bishop, he came down with exhaustion, a high temperature and swollen glands. His doctor diagnosed glandular fever, and just to make sure there were no complications he extracted a sample of bone marrow from his spine. It was an extremely painful operation at that time, and in what must have been a slightly sour joke the bishop said he sympathised with his doctor for having 'to fight so hard trying to penetrate the hard bone with the needle'. The disease knocked him out again for the whole of December 1961, and in the autumn of 1963 he missed the beginning of the second session of the Vatican Council because of another attack. He quite often had to take time off because of illness when he was the Cardinal Archbishop of Krakow, and in the year of his election as pope he had been suffering badly from migraines. It was the kind of health record you might expect from a man who pushed his body too hard.

But no one gave any of that much heed as the tales of new and ever more glamorous papal adventures filled the world's headlines, and three months after his election he made his first papal trip abroad. The occasion was the meeting of Latin America's bishops at Puebla in Mexico in January 1979 (the meeting had been postponed from the previous autumn because of the death of John Paul I). There was no great surprise about his decision to accept an invitation to open the conference; there were – and still are – more Catholics in Latin America than anywhere else in the world, and Paul VI had set a precedent by attending the last great gathering of the region's bishops at Medellin ten years earlier. However, the way John Paul planned his trip to the region was, like so much else he did at this stage, unprecedented. This was to be the first of those foreign tours which, part pilgrimages and part rock-star-style road shows, would become such a hallmark of his pontificate.

The journey from Rome was made on a specially chartered Alitalia jet – with the pope, in presidential style, travelling up front, his aides behind and the press corps in economy. Selected journalists were called up to be granted interviews during the flight, and one of them, Jon Snow, who was then working for Independent Television News, rather eccentrically reflected that 'He seemed strangely heterosexual for such a monastic figure, a man who knew about women; I can't say why I felt it, but we correspondents all discussed it afterwards.' There was a whirlwind stop-over in the Dominican Republic (1.30 p.m. arrival at Santa Domingo, afternoon meeting with bishops and priests, 5.00 p.m. open-air mass, overnight stay, early morning parish mass in the country outside the capital, return to capital for departure), and when he arrived in Mexico he kissed the ground in that flourish he had learnt as a young man. Snow recalls the scene in his autobiography:

> The airport appeared to be under siege; there were tens and tens of thousands of people spilling onto the apron. We stood at the foot of the Alitalia steps as the Pope came out of the plane, and went down on his knees and kissed the tarmac. It was a sublime and unexpected moment that stole a million hearts and more.

There was an open-sided vehicle of the kind that became known as the 'popemobile' waiting to ferry him around, allowing him to acknowledge the vast crowds that gathered wherever he went. The schedule was packed, and the numbers who attended his open-air masses were beyond comparison with any contemporary religious event. There were more moments of pure theatre unthinkable under any previous pope; at Guadalajara hundreds of thousands of people flashed mirrors at the papal plane while it circled for an hour above them, and at one stop during his seven-day pilgrimage he recited prayers through a loudspeaker with 2,500 inmates of a Mexican prison.

But John Paul was not one of those politicians who enjoy the exercise of power for its own sake – he actually wanted to do something with it, and the Latin American trip provided an early indication of his willingness to risk alienating his audience when he felt it necessary. His intervention at the Puebla meeting proved to be the opening salvo in a campaign which would preoccupy him for much of the next decade: the war on the new school known as Liberation Theology which had emerged from the Latin American Church.

The way he fought that battle has often been cited by Catholic liberals as the first item of evidence for the prosecution in the case against John Paul's pontificate; in dealing with the followers of Liberation Theology, runs the charge sheet, he was guilty of shocking double standards, condemning in Latin America precisely the kind of political church activism that he was supporting so enthusiastically in Poland. He was, in the view of many contemporary commentators, blinded to the reality of the region by a Reaganite world view which filtered everything through the lens of the Cold War ('He misread the situation' in Latin America is the blunt judgement of his biographer Jonathan Kwitny) and the severity of the Vatican crackdown on the new movement was presented as proof of his authoritarian instincts. Those were, broadly, the assumptions which came to dominate the view in most secular newsrooms as the clash between the Vatican and the Liberation Theologians developed in the early years of the pontificate, and when I began covering the story as a young television journalist I shared them. With the benefit of two decades' hindsight it is possible to make out a much more complex picture.

There were in fact many characteristics of the Latin American Church which John Paul understood very well – instinctively, indeed, because of his own experience in Poland. To begin with the region had its own variation on the Marian theme which had so inspired him since his childhood visits to Czestochowa. In

1531, not long after the Spanish conquest of Mexico, a peasant called Juan Diego had a vision of the Virgin at a mountain outside Mexico City. She instructed him to tell the local bishop that a church should be built at the spot, and when the bishop refused she provided Juan Diego with a miracle to lend force to his argument – her image materialised miraculously on the inside of the peasant's cloak, and the bishop was suitably impressed. The mountain where the Virgin's new church was built, Tepeyac, had been a place of pilgrimage in the cult of the Aztec earth-mother goddess Tonatzin before the arrival of the *conquistadores*; conveniently, Tonatzin had a Mary-like ability to conceive immaculately, so the Juan Diego story and the shrine helped the recently conquered and Christianised indigenous population to absorb their traditional culture into their new religion. Like the Black Madonna of Czestochowa in Poland, Our Lady of Guadalupe came to have a particular significance for the local church. 'The appearance of the Virgin on Latin American soil,' writes the church historian David Tombs,

> speaking the language of the colonised rather than the coloniser, addressing Diego as a son and taking the side of the peasant against the bishop, has been an icon of popular religion ever since. The poor of Latin America have understood the appearance of Our Lady of Guadalupe as a sign of Mary's adoption of the native peoples and her solidarity with the repressed.

One of the biggest masses of John Paul's first Latin American trip was at the shrine of Our Lady of Guadalupe – journalists travelling with him estimated that in the course of the day he was seen by ten million people, and reported the roads lined by crowds twenty deep the whole way along his seven-mile journey to the shrine. In his subsequent reflections on the apparition story he was every bit as uncritical as he had been as an awe-struck child watching the adoration of the Black Madonna icon in the monastery of Jasna Gora. There is considerable scholarly scepticism about whether Juan Diego actually existed, and many historians treat his story as a myth which, though extremely important for Latin

American culture and religion, may not be based on historical events. A restorer hired to clean up the image on Juan's cloak in the 1940s later said that there was nothing miraculous about it – it was simply painted. But in 2002 John Paul canonised Juan Diego anyway.

The idea that popular piety of the kind expressed in the cult of Our Lady of Guadalupe had a modern political resonance would have made complete sense to the Liberation Theologians. The writings of Gustavo Gutierrez, the theologian who did the most to lay the intellectual foundations for the movement, include a book with the suggestive title *We Drink from Our Own Wells*; the whole Liberation Theology movement in Latin America was built on the premise that the region's Catholic tradition provided a narrative for making sense of the contemporary world – a reality which of course was in perfect harmony with John Paul's experience of the Church in Poland. Both Fr Gutierrez and Pope John Paul came from societies in which the overwhelming majority accepted the Roman Catholic faith, both saw the Church as an institutional mechanism for defeating an unjust social and political order, and both were to some degree impatient of Western European theological ideas which were designed to answer the challenge of secularism. Both believed in the importance of placing men and women – 'the Human Person', in John Paul's rather cumbersome phrase – at the centre of all theological endeavour, and both believed in the idea of social activism as a Christian duty.

There was even a degree of synchronicity about the way John Paul's ideas and those of the Liberation Theologians had developed. The seeds of Liberation Theology were sown in the documents of the Second Vatican Council so dear to John Paul's heart, and specifically in that phrase 'the People of God' which the then Bishop Wojtyla had himself used in the Council's debates. As we have seen, in the Polish context that meant the foot soldiers in the daily struggle against communist oppression; in the Latin American context it meant the poor. *Lumen Gentium,* the so-called church Constitution which emerged from the Council, recognises an especially close relationship between the poor and Christ:

Just as Christ carried out the work of redemption in poverty and oppression, so the Church is called to follow the same path if she is to communicate the fruits of salvation to men. Jesus Christ, 'though he was by nature God ... emptied himself, taking the nature of a slave' (Phil. 2:6–7) and 'being rich, became poor' (2 Cor. 8:9) for our sake ... Christ was sent by the Father 'to bring good news to the poor ... to heal the contrite of heart' (Luke 4:18) ... Similarly the Church encompasses with her love all those who are afflicted by human misery and she recognises in those who are poor and who suffer, the image of her poor and suffering founder.

And the intellectual development of both Karol Wojtyla and Latin America's Liberation Theologians reached decisive moments during the turbulent year of 1968 (it was the year of the Prague Spring and the Paris *événements*, the Tet Offensive in Vietnam and the assassinations of Martin Luther King and Robert Kennedy). In Poland it saw the chaos provoked by the *Forefathers' Eve* crisis and the first serious challenge to Gomulka, and Cardinal Wojtyla responded by articulating his increasingly well-developed idea of a Catholic doctrine of human rights. In Latin America 1968 was the year of the Medellin Conference, which David Tombs calls 'one of the most important landmarks in the first five centuries of the Latin American church'. Until then the Church in the region had been – broadly speaking – a stakeholder in its established power structures, a 'traditionally reactionary institution wedded to the upper classes', as another Latin American church historian has put it. At their meeting in the Colombian city of Medellin the bishops of the region changed sides and declared a 'preferential option for the poor'. They had the documents of Vatican II to inspire them and the presence of Pope Paul VI at their opening session to give official blessing to their revolution, and their decision had far-reaching consequences. It brought on what Penny Lernoux, in her history of the Liberation Theology movement, calls 'decades of martyrdom for the Church in Latin America, including the imprisonment, torture and assassination of more than a thousand bishops, priests and nuns'. The phenomenon of Catholics being killed by fellow Catholics in an overwhelmingly

Catholic region was without precedent in the history of the Church.

The Puebla meeting in 1979 was intended to confirm the direction the Latin American Church had taken at Medellin and to give it new impetus, and many of the Puebla documents do indeed reflect the spirit of the earlier meeting. But in retrospect Puebla looks like the high-water mark of Liberation Theology, and John Paul's addresses and sermons at the conference marked the beginning of the Vatican's ultimately successful campaign to defeat the hold which the Liberation Theologians had established over the Latin American Church. At a closed session of the conference, in a lengthy address which George Weigel has described as 'one of the most important of his pontificate', the new pope told Latin America's bishops they were meeting 'not as a symposium of experts, not as a parliament of politicians, not as a congress of scientists or technologists, but as . . . pastors of the Church'. He reminded them that they were 'teachers of not a human and rational truth, but the truth that comes from God'. 'Some Christians,' he went on, 'portray Jesus as a political activist, a fighter against Roman oppression, even as one involved in the class struggle. This idea of Christ as a political figure, a revolutionary, as the subversive from Nazareth, does not tally with the Church's teaching.' With his visit to Guadalupe fresh in his mind he praised the 'religious practices and popular piety' of the Latin American Church, which, he said, should be the real focus for the bishops' attention. 'You are priests . . .' he told the Latin Americans, 'you are not social or political leaders or officials of a temporal power.' Needless to say, there has been plenty of comment about the irony of a pope from the highly politicised Polish Church lecturing Latin Americans on the need to keep priests out of politics, and it is worth spending a little time trying to unravel what was going on in John Paul's mind as he made these remarks.

It certainly did not reflect a lack of love for the poor and the oppressed, although John Paul would face that accusation in the course of this bruising battle. Even a cursory glance at his sermons and speeches on that first visit to Latin America – leaving aside the huge body of writing he later produced on questions of social justice – is enough to demonstrate that the accusation was absurd. Here he is addressing the hundreds of thousands of Indians who came to hear him in the miserably poor state of Oaxaca:

> The pope wants to be your voice, the voice of those who cannot speak or who are silenced; the defender of the oppressed, who have the right to effective help . . . not the crumbs of justice . . . It is necessary to initiate, without delay, agricultural reforms. The Church defends the legitimate right to private property, but it teaches no less clearly that private property always carries with it a social obligation . . . If the common good requires, there must be no doubt about expropriation itself, carried out in the proper manner.

And a few days later he was telling workers in Monterrey – many of them employed by the American firms who came south in search of low-wage labour – that the Church backed their right to unionisation:

> Those who have the fortune to work wish to do so in more human and secure conditions, to participate more justly in the fruit of the common effort . . . They wanted to be treated as free and responsible men, to take part in the decisions that concern their lives . . . It is their fundamental right to freely create organisations to . . . promote their interests.

This was the voice of the man who had so inspired the crowds in Krakow, using his deep convictions about the inherent dignity of men and women to illuminate the social and political reality he found in Latin America, and speaking about poverty with all the passion he had brought to bear on a different form of oppression in Poland. It is difficult to see how calls for land redistribution and unionisation can be characterised as a wickedly uncaring right-wing economic agenda. It is also too simplistic to argue that John Paul made a crude equation between his own experience of communism in Poland and the communist tendencies he detected in the Liberation Theology movement; clearly, in practical terms communism as the inspiration for an oppressive state and communism as a weapon of resistance *against* an oppressive state are two very different things and require very different responses.

The key to understanding John Paul's quarrel with Liberation Theology is to be found in the fact that the new pope was a genuine intellectual – in the sense that he thought that ideas really mattered. Gustavo Gutierrez was not a Marxist, but in his influential book *A Theology of Liberation* he acknowledged the movement's debt to Marxist analysis: 'Many agree with Sartre,' he wrote

> that 'Marxism, as the formal framework of all contemporary thought, cannot be superseded' . . . contemporary theology does in fact find itself in direct and fruitful confrontation with Marxism, and it is to a large extent due to Marxism's influence that theological thought, searching for its own sources, has begun to reflect on the meaning of the transformation of this world and the action of man in history.

He made free use of that very Marxist concept of *praxis* (action), and he argued that the particular social and political conditions in Latin America gave Marxism a special relevance to Catholic theology: 'On this continent,' reads another passage, 'the oppressed and those who seek to identify with them face ever more resolutely a common adversary, and, therefore, the relationship between Marxists and Christians takes on characteristics different from those in other places.'

Other Liberation Theologians went well beyond Gutierrez's relatively nuanced approach to Marxism. Jose Miranda achieved notoriety with two books called *The Bible and Communism* and *Marx and the Bible*. 'For a Christian to claim to be anti-communist,' was, he declared, 'without doubt the greatest scandal of our century . . . The notion of communism is in the New Testament, right down to the letter – and so well put that in the twenty centuries since no one has come up with a better definition of communism than Luke in Acts 2:44–45 and 4:32–35' (the passages which describe the way the early followers of Jesus 'held everything in common'). Gutierrez had argued that 'justice was a central and essential part of God's character', but Miranda went further and, using texts from the Old Testament, built the case that God and justice were one and the same; it was only a step beyond that to the conclusion that God 'should not be thought of as a being, nor did God have any existence except in the ethical imperative to justice'.

There was plenty here to convince John Paul that Liberation Theology was fundamentally wrong-headed – corrupted, as it were, in its theological genes – and the experience of living under Nazism and communism had taught him that when ideas go wrong the consequences can be terrible. The distinction he made between the political activism of priests in Poland and the political activism of priests in Latin America was not so much about what they did, it was about the ideas which inspired them; and once we recognise that, the apparent hypocrisy of John Paul's Latin American lectures on mixing politics and religion becomes easier to understand. And he did also see evidence that the flawed ideas at the heart of Liberation Theology were taking some priests down an avenue he would never have tolerated in the Polish Church – the road of violent resistance to the state.

Camillo Torres was perhaps the best-known example of the 'guerrilla priest' phenomenon that emerged as part of the Liberation Theology movement. A scion of a rich Colombian family, he studied at the Catholic University of Louvain in Belgium after being ordained and returned to Colombia as the chaplain and professor of sociology at the National University in Bogota. He became increasingly radical in his politics, and in 1965 he left the priesthood to set up his own political movement. That autumn he joined the guerrillas of the National Liberation Army group, and in February 1966 he was shot and killed in the mountains by the Colombian army. His example inspired others, and a decade later young novices were giving up on their vocations to fight with the rebels in El Salvador and priests were supporting the Sandinista revolution in Nicaragua.

Although the defenders of Liberation Theology argue that 'in fact very few priests went as far as to follow Torres's example or encourage others to do so', there was sometimes an uncomfortable lack of clarity on the question of violence from some really very senior members of the Latin American Church. Dom Helder

Camara, the Archbishop of Olinde and Recife in Brazil, was one of the towering figures driving change in the Latin American Church throughout the 1950s, 1960s and 1970s; he more or less invented the modern concept of a regional 'bishops' conference' which bore such dramatic fruit at the Medellin meeting, and when I visited his archdiocese during the last years of his life I found a deep well of affection and admiration for him among the priests who had served there. So it is especially shocking to read this passage in his book *Honesty and Hope*:

> I respect those who feel obliged in conscience to opt for violence – not the facile violence of the armchair guerrilla, but that of a man who has proved his sincerity by sacrificing his life. It seems to me that the memory of Che Guevara deserves as much respect as that of Dr Martin Luther King. I point an accusing finger at the real instigators of violence, at all those, on the left and the right who wrong justice and block peace.

Dom Helder sought to focus attention on the 'institutional violence' of Latin American political and social structures – those so-called 'structures of sin' the Liberation Theologians were so fond of talking about. He insisted that he himself was committed to peaceful change – 'My own personal vocation is to be a pilgrim of peace, following in the Footsteps of Paul VI. Personally I would prefer a thousand times more to be killed than to kill anyone' – but the implication of the sort of arguments he advanced was that actual violence against people was justified by the rather more abstract violence said to be inherent in the way the region's governments conducted themselves. John Paul, who chose the non-violent path as a young man during the Nazi occupation, would have no truck with any of this.

It was instructive reading the Liberation Theologians on violence in the aftermath of the suicide bombings on public transport in London in July 2005. The fact that the attacks were carried out by British-born Muslims forced everyone – especially Britain's Islamic leaders – to face up to some very tough questions about Islam in British society. Those Muslim leaders who, in the immediate aftermath, offered somewhat ritual condemnations while arguing that the attacks could in some way be 'explained' by British foreign policy and the alienation of young British Muslims came in for a good deal of criticism. The 'of-course-I-wouldn't-do-it-myself-and-yes-it's-wrong-but-I-can-understand-why-they-did-it' position is weasely and dangerous, and it is very easily read as tacit religious endorsement of violent acts. It is pretty much what Helder Camara is saying in the passage quoted above.

If John Paul deserves more credit than he is usually given for the intellectual coherence of his assault on Liberation Theology, it nevertheless remains true that the battle was fought in a shabby and bullying way, and there was a sub-plot at the Puebla meeting which sheds light on his willingness to keep rum company if he believed it served his vision for the Church. In 1972 the conservative Colombian bishop Alfonso Lopez Trujillo had secured the post of secretary-general to the Latin American bishops' conference (known by its Spanish and Portuguese acronym CELAM), and in the run-up to the Puebla meeting he did what he could to frustrate the progressive agenda. Sympathetic conservative bishops were manoeuvred into the chairmanships of the committees which would draft the documents to be placed before the conference, and Lopez Trujillo himself took charge of decisions about which theological advisers were to be invited. Gutierrez and some of the other Liberation Theologians who had played such a significant role at Medellin were pointedly omitted from the list – although a group of them travelled to Puebla anyway and set up an unofficial office in the town – and press access to the meeting was severely restricted.

Lopez Trujillo managed to neutralise much of the impact of his own scheming by inadvertently giving a journalist a tape-recording of a discussion in which he outlined what he hoped his plotting would achieve. The contents of the tape were duly published, and they were also found to include some extremely disobliging comments from the good bishop about his more progressive *confrères*. Nevertheless, the Colombian conservative prospered mightily under the new regime – Lopez Trujillo was elected president of CELAM a couple of months after Puebla, and created cardinal four years later. In 1990 he was summoned to serve in the Curia in Rome as the President of the Pontifical Council on the Family, in which post he steadfastly opposed any relaxation of the ban on married couples using artificial birth control. When I interviewed him in 1997 he informed me – as I understand he informed almost everyone he met – that he was one of John Paul's regular lunching companions, and we shall meet him again when he manages to embroil the Vatican in a disastrous spat with the BBC's *Panorama* programme over condoms.

The methods John Paul used in his battle with Liberation Theology reflected one facet of his Polish experience which certainly influenced his view of the Latin American Church – and indeed of the Church as a whole. In his book *Latin American Liberation Theology*, David Tombs makes the acute observation that

> the strength of the Polish Church that he had led was based on a tight-knit unity under a hierarchical leadership. A firm chain of command and strict obedience to authority were the military-style values that helped the Polish Church defend itself against a hostile state. John Paul sought to transfer this to the worldwide Catholic Church. His policy has been called a restoration because it sought to vigorously reassert Catholic influence in society.

It took a bit of time for most commentators to realise what this meant, and to appreciate the scale of John Paul's ambition for his pontificate. But we should have spotted what was coming, because within a couple of months of his return from Mexico John Paul had laid it all out for us.

Most modern popes are remembered by their encyclicals. The word means something that is 'sent around the world to many persons and places', and in a Catholic context it refers to a document which the pope addresses to all the world's bishops, and through them to the universal Church. Encyclicals are not infallible papal statements, but they do represent the considered thought of the pontiff on matters of great moment, and as such they are supposed to weigh especially heavily with the faithful. Paul VI's encyclical on birth control had produced not obedience and reflection but contempt and rebellion, and after *Humanae*

193

Vitae he simply gave up writing them. When John Paul II published *Redemptor Hominis* in March 1979 it was the first encyclical for more than a decade.

It was a manifesto for his pontificate, although few realised its significance at the time. The Dominican Aidan Nichols, in his contribution to a book of essays published under the title *John Paul the Great*, writes that *Redemptor Hominis* 'sets out an entire programme for dealing with the doctrinal and spiritual weaknesses of contemporary Catholicism, as well as the wounds in the secular world, and, by implication, pledges the pope to do what he can about them'. Michael Walsh, whose biography of John Paul is written from a somewhat different perspective, says the importance of *Redemptor Hominis* was missed at the time because 'Popes were not expected to make "state of the pontificate addresses". They were not expected to spell out a policy for the Church.' But with the benefit of hindsight it is possible to see the encyclical as exactly that, and more or less everything John Paul did for the next quarter of a century can be traced back to the ideas he expressed in the document. It was produced astonishingly quickly – John Paul had begun work on it the month after his election – and when the head of Vatican Radio launched it he said it represented the views Karol Wojtyla had held throughout his priestly ministry.

The key to the encyclical lies in its first sentence: 'The Redeemer of Man [encyclicals are by tradition known by their opening words in Latin], Jesus Christ, is the centre of the universe and of history.' That, of course, is a statement of the fundamental belief of all Christians, but it was something that John Paul felt was in danger of being forgotten, and he was stating it in a remarkably stark and challenging way. *Redemptor Hominis* refocuses everything – in the Church and the world – on Jesus Christ as God made man, and the manner in which John Paul reflects on the doctrine of the Incarnation includes passages of real beauty. He says that through the Incarnation 'the son of God *in a certain way united himself with each man* [original italics]. He worked with human hands, he thought with a human mind. He acted with a human will, and with a human heart he loved.' So someone who wants to understand him- or herself must first seek to understand Christ:

He must, so to speak, enter into Him with all his own self, he must 'appropriate' and assimilate the whole of the reality of the Incarnation and Redemption in order to find himself. If this profound process takes place within him, he then bears fruit not only of adoration of God but also of deep wonder at himself. How precious must man be in the eyes of the Creator, if 'he gained so great a redeemer'.

Thus Jesus Christ becomes the source of the dignity of the individual and, by extension, of his or her human rights. 'The name,' John Paul argues in an especially striking phrase, 'for that deep amazement at man's worth and dignity is the Gospel, that is to say, the Good News. It is also called Christianity.'

It is inspiring – if slightly mystical – stuff, but it raises some awkward questions: most notably, if the mysteries of the Incarnation and the Redemption are the guarantors of human rights, where does that leave the rights of those who do not believe in them? In due course some sober voices of concern were heard; Michael Walsh, in his biography, pointed out that

> It had been the teaching of the Church's philosophers and theologians for centuries that the dignity of the individual rested upon the natural law, upon a philosophical assessment of human need and capability, upon a conviction that ethics did not require a revelation. But the 'greatness, dignity and value' that belong to humanity, asserts the pope, are to be found in the act of redemption. As the guardian of the gospel message, therefore, the Church can claim a privileged status when the dignity of the person is being debated. It also meant that there was no longer any common ground when talking of moral issues with those who did not share the Christian faith.

Those who later complained that they felt surprised and betrayed by John Paul's authoritarian instincts would have found unambiguous warnings if they had paid close heed to the text of *Redemptor Hominis*. Freedom for John Paul was not an absolute good that can stand on its own; it is only 'true' freedom if it is based on faith in Christ, otherwise it is 'illusory' or 'superficial'.

So only the Church really understands what freedom is: 'Since man's freedom is not found in everything that the various systems see and propagate as freedom, the Church, because of her divine mission, becomes all the more the guardian of this freedom.' And it is quite clear that when John Paul uses the word 'Church' he has in mind the Church as expressed through the papacy and the Vatican; he describes papal infallibility as a 'gift' from Christ himself, and follows that up with a passage which is clearly intended as a warning to adventurous theologians. They were told they must 'seek to serve the Magisterium [the body of official church teaching]'; 'when theologians,' writes John Paul, 'as servants of divine truth, dedicate their studies and labours to ever greater understanding of that truth, they can never lose sight of the meaning of their service in the Church.' The encyclical takes a very high view of John Paul's own mission ('there is a link between the first fundamental truth of the Incarnation . . . and the ministry that, with my acceptance of my election of Bishop of Rome and Successor to the Apostle Peter, has become my specific duty in his See') and if you read it with a soberly secular perspective it has a slightly scary millenarian tone at times ('We are, in a certain way, in a season of a new Advent, a season of expectation' and so on).

The pace of papal activism during these early days of John Paul's pontificate never seemed to slacken – it is especially awe-inspiring when set against the tortoise-like progress of his successor, Pope Benedict XVI, who in his first six months of office only really attracted the attention of the world's news editors because of a controversy about his views on Harry Potter. *Redemptor Hominis* was published on 3 March 1979 – by Easter week the pope had produced another big document, a letter to the world's priests. He lectured them about the value of celibacy, and told them that the priesthood 'cannot be renounced because of the difficulties we meet and the sacrifices asked of us'. A ban on the 'laicisation' of priests who wanted to get married was introduced.

The climax of John Paul's first year as pope had yet to come. From his earliest days in office he had been explicit in his declaration that his Polishness was to be an essential element in his pontificate. 'The Church in Poland,' he said at his inaugural mass, 'has become an object of great interest by reason of the conjuncture of circumstances which is of such importance to the aspirations of contemporary humanity, of so many nations and states. It has become a church of special witness, toward which the eyes of the world are turned.' The idea that Poland should have an especially prominent place on the agenda of a Polish pope is unsurprising, but John Paul was saying more than that; in keeping with the romantic Polish tradition of his homeland as a 'Christ among nations', the new pope was arguing that Poland had something of great importance to teach the world and the wider Church. And he was unashamed about the way he mixed the personal with the broader principles he was outlining. 'I do this not only by virtue of my episcopal and papal calling,' he declared as he gave Poles a special blessing during his homily, 'but from the deepest necessity of my own heart.' The possibility of a papal visit to Poland had been raised even earlier, on the day after his election, when the Polish bishops issued a statement expressing the hope that John Paul would return to celebrate the 900th anniversary of the martyrdom of St Stanislaw.

The Poland he left behind in October 1978 was brewing up nicely for one of those cyclical crises that had given rhythm to its recent history. In keeping with past patterns, the early years of the new Gierek regime had seen real progress. In 1973 Poland had the third highest national economic growth rate in the world, and real wages increased by 40 per cent during Gierek's first five years in power. What is more, there were goods in the shops to spend the money on; in 1971 the Soviets agreed a huge hard-currency deal to fund Polish purchases in the West, and at the same time Warsaw secured a $25 million credit line from Washington to buy grain. Poland began to produce the 'Polski Fiat' under licence, and cars filled those drab streets described by Christine Hotchkiss in the late 1950s.

But a boom built on borrowing and imports could not, of course, last for ever. Many of the loans taken out early in the Gierek administration came due for repayment as the decade ended, and the Polish government found itself in the classic vicious circle of taking on new loans to service existing debt; by

1979 Poland's foreign debt stood, by the government's own admission, at nearly $18 billion. The domestic economy was in no position to meet the challenge. Polish agriculture remained stubbornly inefficient – in spite of an effort to introduce a measure of capitalism into the system – and it became increasingly difficult to satisfy consumer demand for food from domestic sources. Terrified by the memory of the food riots which had brought it to power, the government inadvertently encouraged people to eat even more by pouring money into subsidies to keep prices down; these subsidies were estimated to represent some 70 per cent of retail costs by 1977. By one of those odd twists sometimes thrown up by the Alice-in-Wonderland eccentricities of the Soviet bloc economies, pork emerged as the big issue of the moment. 'There was something irrational, even aggressive, about the carnivorous obsession that now gripped the Poles,' Neal Ascherson writes in his account of the Polish crisis of the late 1970s and 1980. 'Their per capita meat consumption was higher than that of several western countries, and their insistence on pork at the expense of more plentiful meats like beef or lamb led to queues and shortages. In an act of subconscious aggression, the population was literally eating away the foundations of the political structure.'

The possibility of a papal visit to Poland presented Edward Gierek with an awkward dilemma. With his economic miracle rapidly collapsing around him, his base of domestic support was anything but secure, and the reaction to John Paul's election had left no doubt that any attempt to stop the pope coming home would be very unpopular indeed. But he also had to watch his back with the party bosses in Moscow, and Brezhnev and his politburo were far from enthusiastic about the idea of any pope – let alone a Polish one – visiting a Soviet bloc country. On 24 January 1979 there was a cameo moment in the Vatican which would have brought home to John Paul himself just how little had changed in the Kremlin: Andrei Gromyko, the granite-faced Soviet foreign minister who was such a perennial feature of Cold War diplomacy, paid a courtesy call. When John Paul suggested that the state of religious freedom in the Soviet Union was not quite as it might be, Gromyko gave him a period piece of Soviet flannel.

'This kind of accusation was nothing new to us,' he wrote in his *Memoirs*,

> I replied, 'Not all rumours deserve attention. The West spreads all kinds of misinformation about the state of the Church in the Soviet Union, but the truth is that from the very first day of its existence the Soviet state has guaranteed freedom of religious belief . . . We have religious people, but that doesn't create problems for themselves or for Soviet society.

There was another vintage Soviet moment when Edward Gierek telephoned the Soviet leader Leonid Brezhnev to inform him that he had decided to agree to John Paul's visit to Poland. Gierek, who most historians judge to have been a fundamentally good-hearted man, seems to have regarded his relationship with the Soviet leader Leonid Brezhnev as something close to friendship; I interviewed Gierek at his home in Poland and his wife rather touchingly produced from the cellar an enormous oil painting of the Soviet and Polish leaders together at Brezhnev's retreat in the Crimea, on holiday but both very firmly wearing suits. The friendship ended with the telephone call. Brezhnev first suggested that Gierek get round the problem by telling 'the pope – he is a wise man – that he can declare that he can't come due to illness', a remark which must rank with Marie Antoinette's cake comment as a symbol of leadership which has lost touch with reality. When Gierek explained that the political realities of Poland made it impossible to deny John Paul entry to the country, Brezhnev told him that Gomulka (his predecessor) had been a better communist, and hung up.

Agreement on the visit was made public on 3 March 1979, with the Polish state media warning that it would not alter the 'strictly secular' character of the Polish state. Poland was still a country where symbols, especially religious symbols, carried a high political charge, and the proposed date of the visit had caused one of those communist-era arguments which seem so obscure and unlikely from today's perspective: because St Stanislaw's martyrdom was closely tied to the idea of resistance to the state, the authorities refused to allow John Paul's visit to coincide with its anniversary in May, and the visit was announced for the beginning of June.

A week after the announcement, on 9 March, Cardinal Villot, John Paul's secretary of state, died in Rome, and the Church's top political and diplomatic job fell vacant. The man John Paul chose to fill it, Cardinal Agostino Casaroli, was one of his most successful appointments. The two men had come to know one another during Casaroli's time as Paul VI's envoy to Eastern Europe, but they were certainly not ideological soulmates – Casaroli, as the principal practitioner of the policy known as *Ostpolitik*, was instinctively more accommodating to communist regimes. They were also very different in character; Casaroli was a career civil servant (he first worked in the Curia in 1937), and, a diplomat to his fingertips, he believed his work was best done away from the limelight. But the Casaroli–John Paul partnership, which covered the critical decade leading up to the collapse of communism, turned out to be an extremely effective one.

'It was only when we reached Warsaw's daunting grey Victory Square that we woke up to the sheer scale of what was happening,' remembers ITN's Jon Snow, back with the papal press corps for this second great John Paul pilgrimage.

> There, towering above the square, was not the hammer and sickle of Communism but the cross of Christianity. The Communists had restricted the attendance to a staggering three hundred thousand people. Furthermore, Polish television was covering the event live. It is perhaps hard to comprehend what an extraordinary development this was. Here was a centrally controlled Communist society, an integral element of the Soviet Union's sphere of influence, in whose very capital (that had given its name to the very pact designed to resist the threats of NATO) hundreds of thousands of people were being allowed to do something that millions more were being permitted to watch, that the state was neither authoring nor managing. In more than thirty years of Communist government a Catholic mass had never been shown on Polish television.

Other estimates have put the size of the crowd at John Paul's first open-air mass in Poland even higher – at up to a million people. 'Christ cannot be kept out of the history of man in any part of the globe, at any longitude or latitude,' he told the congregation (if that is not an inappropriate word for such a huge gathering), and, as a contemporary newspaper report described it, 'The applause started and went on and on, in waves . . . dying down in one part of the square and starting up elsewhere.' Parts of the crowds broke out into spontaneous hymns, there were chants of 'We want God', and there was much weeping. It was nearly a quarter of an hour before the pope could quieten the crowd to continue with his address.

Alexander Tsepko has especially vivid memories of that day. Officially an academic working in Warsaw, he was also an adviser to the Central Committee of the Communist Party in Moscow, and he was expected to 'write a report' on the pope's visit for his masters in the Kremlin. As John Paul arrived in Warsaw he positioned himself in Uizdowski Allee, just across the road from the Polish Communist Party headquarters, and he watched as

> Suddenly all the windows . . . opened. All the Party workers sat right on the window-sills – all of them from the third and fourth floors. And it was as if they merged with the crowd. The people were singing 'Ave Maria', and it sounded like a great anti-communist hymn. A fellow academic who was standing next to me said 'Sasha, this is it, this is the end of socialism in Poland.' It happened in a matter of seconds, while the Polish Party workers hung out of the windows. During those seconds, and the hours that followed, power passed to the Church. Nothing, not even martial law, could change that.

The visit lasted for nine days, and John Paul visited all the places that made up Poland's Catholic map: he went to Gniezno, where the first Polish kings had been crowned and where one of those favourite Polish saints of his, St Adalbert, was buried, and, perhaps nostalgic for the camp-fire nights when he was an unofficial university chaplain on holiday, he spent the evening on the balcony of the episcopal palace singing and chatting with a crowd of students who had stayed on after his mass for young people. He spent two nights at the Black Madonna's home of Jasna Gora, and returned to Kalwaria, the hillside of shrines which he had visited often as a child and again as a restless archiepiscopal night-owl. He paid due respect to Wadowice, the town of his childhood, and he visited the camp at Auschwitz/Birkenau, celebrating mass with 150 priests who had survived the death camps. It was a spectacularly successful piece of performance art, and the narcotic of a heatwave added to the sense that it was a season set apart. The visit brought tears to the prose of the most hardened hacks. Neal Ascherson, in what is by and large a tough-minded account of the events leading up to the formation of the trade union Solidarity, was moved to elegy by the memory:

> These were days that at once revealed and matured the nation . . . For anyone who travelled round Poland with John Paul II, it took time to become normal again. In dreams, one still walked over strewn flowers, in the glare of the sun. On the screen of closed eyelids, one saw again those long, long Indian files of men, women and children walking through waist-high meadows on their way to meet this man, carrying crosses and their banners. The curtains rustled in the wind; one started awake, hearing the soft, vast rippling which is the sound of a million human beings clapping their hands.

But was the pope's visit really as important as the pork which Ascherson has also written about so eloquently? Clearly, economic and social pressures had created in Poland what a Marxist might have recognised – if with a degree of irony – as pre-revolutionary conditions. But you do not have to be carried away by Catholic romanticism to argue that the John Paul pilgrimage played the part of a catalyst for the unravelling of the Polish communist state – and by extension the Soviet system. Jacek Kuron, the founder of the Workers' Defence Committee KOR (which played a John the Baptist-like role in preparing the way for Solidarity and all that followed), was struck by the atmosphere in the crowds milling around the streets of Warsaw the night before John Paul's arrival: 'There was extraordinary order on the streets, and it was supervised by the church militia, young people in Catholic organisations. It was amazing, because it was a self-organising society. One of those church militiamen would give a sign – this way or that – and people would immediately obey.' By handing the running of the visit over to the Catholic Church, Edward Gierek (who watched John Paul's first open-air mass in secret from a hotel room overlooking Victory Square) delivered a great victory to his institutional rival for control over the people of Poland; something huge was happening, and it was run by an alternative institutional system.

What is more, because it was being done with the consent of the people, it worked. Jacek Wozniakowski, who had been part of Karol Wojtyla's circle of intellectuals in his Krakow days, attended John Paul's big Krakow mass; 'Everything went so smoothly,' he remembered,

> without the help of the police or the authorities, and with such goodwill and peacefulness towards each other, and this gave many people the feeling that so much could be achieved by such simple means. In every totalitarian system, fear is the elementary weapon. This fear was overcome, vanquished, simply by the fact of people being together with a common voice.

'The fact that people organised themselves,' Jacek Kuron told me, 'gave them in turn the feeling of freedom.'

Half a world away in Washington, events in Poland were being watched with especially close attention by Zbigniew Brzezinski, President Carter's hawkish National Security Adviser. Brzezinski, himself of Polish extraction, had met Karol Wojtyla at his 1976 lecture at Harvard. His judgement on the papal visit to Poland was characteristically punchy and economical: 'The dominant mood until then,' he said, 'was the inevitability of the existing system. After he left the dominant mood was the non-inevitability of the existing system. I think that was a fundamental transformation.'

John Paul himself summed up the visit as he left Krakow airport; never one to show reserve in the way he talked about his doings, he described it as 'without doubt an unprecedented event, not only in this century but in the whole millennium, especially since it was a visit by a Polish pope, who has the sacred right and duty to experience a deep emotional bond with his people'.

9

Changing History

As the turn of the decade approached, the pace of the pontificate became more frenzied than ever. The final months of 1979 saw papal pilgrimages to Ireland, the United States and Istanbul. John Paul began a programme of talks on 'the theology of the body' (it eventually ran to 130 speeches at general audiences spread over four years), addressed the United Nations General Assembly (an hour-long *tour de force* covering the arms race, human rights and the injustices of the world economic system) and – as if the problems of the late twentieth century were insufficient for his wolfish intellectual appetite – declared that the Church's seventeenth-century condemnation of Galileo for stating that the earth moved round the sun should be re-examined. He called the Sacred College of Cardinals together in Rome for its first consultative meeting in four centuries, having created fourteen new cardinals to top up its numbers. And the 1980s began without a pause for breath; there were visits to Africa, France, West Germany, Brazil (he learnt Portuguese to prepare for the trip) and Asia, and there was a veritable outpouring of papal pronouncements (apostolic exhortations, letters and so on), plus another full-blown encyclical.

On 13 May 1981 the whirligig was brought to a halt in the most dramatic manner imaginable – by the first attempted papal assassination of modern times. John Paul had lunched that day with Professor Jerome Lejeune and his wife; the distinguished French geneticist was a leading member of the 'pro-life' move-ment, and the two men had apparently been discussing the 'rhythm method' of birth control. At five he emerged in his popemobile from the Arch of Bells (the clock tower on the left extremity of the façade of St Peter's) for a general audience in St Peter's Square – the usual form at these events was a couple of circuits of the piazza in superstar style before the formal address, which John Paul would give from the dais in front of the basilica. A witness (a Polish nun) remembers him looking 'relaxed, pink and smiling' and reflected, 'How young he looks, how handsome he is.' The popemobile, a white open-topped vehicle somewhere between a jeep and a flatbed truck, moved slowly so that he could interact with people as he was driven down the corridors which were kept open through the mass of pilgrims by wooden crash barriers. Looking back at the pictures of these events there is something touchingly innocent about an age which could be quite so careless of security.

The vehicle would sometimes pause to allow John Paul to pick up and hug one of the children held out to him; he had just handed back a blonde four-year-old girl in the course of his second circuit of the square when, at around quarter past five, Mehmet Ali Agca pulled the trigger of his Browning 9 mm pistol. Agca was standing in the second row of pilgrims behind the wooden barricade – the crowd that day was a relatively modest 20,000 or so strong – so the shots were fired at close to point-blank range. He would later claim that he did not really mean to kill the pope (his accounts of his motivation were many and various) but, as John Paul himself remembered it later, 'Agca knew how to shoot, and he certainly shot to kill.' Most of the first-hand accounts of that moment mention the way the pigeons that habitually scavenge the square were startled into flight by the sound of the gun – an oddly inconsequential detail which perhaps reflects the fact that it took people a little while to grasp the enormity of what had happened. Stanislaw Dziwisz was accompanying John Paul in the back of the vehicle – as he always did – and this is his memory of the way events unfolded:

> The bullet passed through the Holy Father's body, wounding him in the stomach, the right elbow and the left index finger. The bullet fell between the Pope and me. I heard two more shots, and two people standing near us were wounded.

I asked the Holy Father, 'Where?' He replied: 'In the stomach.' 'Does it hurt?' 'It does.'

There was no doctor within reach. There was no time to think. We immediately carried the Holy Father into an ambulance and set off at great speed towards the Gemelli Hospital. The Holy Father was praying *sotto voce*. Then, during the journey, he lost consciousness.

A number of factors would determine whether or not he survived, for example the question of time, the time it took us to reach the hospital; a few more minutes, some obstruction in the way, and it would have been too late.

The journey to the Gemelli took eight minutes – an astonishingly quick journey in the Roman traffic, and a fact which undoubtedly added to John Paul's later conviction that his survival was providential. The account I have quoted above is taken from an informal conversation between two Polish philosophers, Stanislaw Dziwisz and the pope at Castel Gandolfo. It was published as an epilogue to *Memory and Identity*, the book of papal reflections which came out not long before John Paul's death, and it is moving because of the way the double act between Dziwisz and John Paul reveals their closeness:

JOHN PAUL
Yes, I remember that journey to the hospital. For a short time I remained conscious. I had a sense that I would survive. I was in pain, and this was a reason to be afraid – but I had a strange trust. I said to Father Stanislaw that I had forgiven my assailant. What happened at the hospital, I do not remember.

STANISLAW DZIWISZ
Almost immediately after we arrived at the hospital, the Holy Father was taken into the operating theatre. The situation was very grave. The Holy Father had lost a great deal of blood. His blood pressure was falling dramatically, his pulse barely registered. The doctors suggested that I administered the Sacrament of the Sick. I did so at once.

JOHN PAUL
I was already practically on the other side.

John Paul had in fact lost more than six pints of blood – there was 'blood everywhere' according to Professor Crucitti, the surgeon in charge – and the operation to save his life lasted five and a half hours. The bullet had done considerable damage; the professor recorded that there were 'multiple lesions of the small intestine and colon' and noted that 'the mesentery, the membrane which is the starting point for the blood vessels which irrigate the small intestine, was cut in several places'. As he cleaned up he found, 'in the last part of the colon . . . a terrible laceration caused by the direct passage of the projectile'. But Ali Agca's shot had – by the tiniest but most critical of margins – missed John Paul's central aorta. Twenty-two inches of intestine were removed, the colon was sewn up in several places, and a colostomy was inserted. It was close to midnight by the time the operation was over and John Paul was moved to intensive care, where he remained for four days.

What followed looks in retrospect a little like a dress rehearsal for that very public struggle between papal will and the laws of nature which marked the final months of John Paul's life. According to Fr Stanislaw, his first question when he came round from the operation was, 'Did we say Compline?' and the secretary stated that John Paul 'never failed to say his office'. From his hospital bed he managed to broadcast a message to the faithful in St Peter's Square on Sunday 17 May, and he rose to the occasion with characteristic flair – thanking the people for their prayers, empathising with the two tourists who were also injured in the attack (neither was seriously wounded), forgiving 'the brother who attacked me', and offering his sufferings 'for the Church and the World'. With slightly Trollopian humour he insisted on referring to his medical team as 'the Sanhedrin', and although initially a good patient was soon agitating to get back to work. On 3 June, after three weeks in hospital, he was allowed to return to the Vatican, eager, the world was later told, 'to preside over the solemnities of 7 June connected with the anniversary of the Council of Ephesus and the first Council of Constantinople'. He was out at his window blessing the crowd within half an hour of his arrival.

But handsome or not, John Paul was not as young as the impression of the Polish nun who saw him emerge from the Arch of Bells on 13 May suggested; his sixty-first birthday fell on 18 May, the day he was moved out of intensive care. And within a week of his discharge from hospital the fever was back – rising to 104 degrees. His condition was soon causing grave alarm to those around him; his face was 'grey and emaciated' and 'in their black rings his eyes, now an unusual green in colour, did not focus on anyone and simply looked vacant'. The cause of the fever proved elusive, and antibiotics did nothing to lower it. John Paul was put back on a drip, and on 20 June he returned to hospital. There was a wheelchair at the door which, despite an initial attempt to walk to his bed, he was constrained to use.

The problem was eventually traced to cytomegalovirus, which had been carried in one of the emergency blood transfusions he had been given on the evening of 13 May. Since there is no antibiotic treatment for viruses the problem simply had to be managed – with painkillers, rest and so on – until the fever was eventually beaten on 24 June. Once the crisis was over John Paul began to press to have his colostomy dealt with while he was still in hospital, resenting the prospect of yet another stint in the Gemelli at some future date. 'He was,' according to Fr Stanislaw, 'in a hurry to resume his normal activities, which he almost reproached himself for having had to slow down.' At least one of his doctors insisted that it would be wiser to wait until he was fully rested and the weather was cooler, proposing an October date for the colostomy operation. But John Paul insisted on attending the meeting at which the date for the procedure was to be fixed, and lectured his medical team for half an hour on the duty of doctors to give patients some sense of control over their own destiny (patients, he argued, must be allowed to feel that they are 'the subject of their illness' and not merely the 'object of treatment'). They gave way and the deed was done in early August. On the 15th of the month John Paul was able to celebrate the Feast of the Assumption in front of 50,000 people in St Peter's Square, finally back at the helm more than three months after the assassination attempt.

John Paul's belief that his survival was connected with the Fatima story had matured during his weeks in hospital. At an audience a couple of months after his recovery he said that Ali Agca fired his gun not just on the feast-day of Our Lady of Fatima but at 'the hour' when the Virgin appeared to the visionary Portuguese children in 1917, and as we have seen earlier he was incapable of spotting a coincidence without seeing the hand of Providence at work (indeed, he declared at Fatima a year later that 'in the designs of Providence there are no mere coincidences'). On his return to the Vatican he called for the material relating to the Fatima visions, including the infamous Third Secret, a document with such a mysterious and powerful reputation that in the early 1980s a man hijacked an airliner to press the demand that the Vatican should reveal its contents. What he read appears to have persuaded him that he was himself the subject of the Virgin's message.

The Third Secret had an odd history. One of the visionary children, Lucia dos Santos, who was ten in 1917, became a nun as an adult, and in her convent in 1944 she wrote down what she said she remembered seeing. She handed the document to the local bishop with instructions that it should be passed on to the pope, but must remain unopened until 1960. John XXIII took a peep at the appointed time and returned the Secret unpublished to the archives. The vision – which has since been published in full – must have made rum reading, and one cannot help wondering whether John kept it locked up for the simple reason that it seemed so peculiar; a 'Bishop dressed in White' – who Lucia identifies as 'the Holy Father' – is described walking up a hill towards 'a big Cross of rough-hewn trunks' and he passes through 'a big city half in ruins'; 'trembling, with halting step, afflicted with pain and sorrow, he prayed for the soul of the corpses he met on his way'. When he reaches his objective he kneels at the foot of the cross and is promptly 'killed by a group of soldiers who fired bullets and arrows at him'. When the document was finally published in 2000 it was issued under the auspices of the Congregation for the Doctrine of the Faith (CDF), and it is quite fun to read the way the CDF's then Prefect, the theologically fastidious Cardinal Ratzinger, handles the material in his gloss; the future Pope Benedict uses what English Literature academics call Practical Criticism to unlock the vision's meaning, and declares:

the image which the children saw is in no way a film preview of a future in which nothing can be changed. Indeed, the whole point of the vision is to bring freedom onto the scene and to steer freedom in a positive direction ... therefore we must totally discount 'fatalistic' explanations of the 'secret', such as, for example, the claim that the would-be assassin of May 13th 1981 was merely an instrument of the divine plan guided by Providence ... Rather, the vision speaks of the dangers and how we might be saved from them.

It is classic Ratzinger; he simultaneously explains away the obvious inconsistencies thrown up by the John Paul theory (the fact that the pope in the vision dies, for example) and somehow rescues his boss's ideas from slipping into heresy.

Ali Agca was caught at the scene of his crime, and was tried and sentenced to life imprisonment before John Paul had even completed his second stint in hospital. When, in September, the judge delivered the formal written verdict which Italian law requires in trials of grave crimes, he concluded that Ali Agca had not acted alone; 'The threatening figure of Ali Agca suddenly appeared among the crowd,' he wrote, 'to execute, with almost bureaucratic coolness, a task entrusted to him by others in a plot obscured by hatred.' But he also accepted that 'the evidence has not permitted us to uncover the identity or the motives of the conspirators'. Investigators were, however, able to establish something of the killer's past; he had a history of involvement in organised crime – particularly smuggling between Turkey and Bulgaria – and in 1979 he had been involved in the murder of the editor of the liberal Turkish newspaper *Milliyet*. He had confessed when he was arrested five months after the killing, but managed to escape from a military prison by disguising himself as a soldier. He promptly wrote a letter to *Milliyet* threatening to kill the pope when he made his 1979 visit to Istanbul: 'Western imperialists,' the letter declared, 'fearful that Turkey and her sister Islamic nations may become a political, military, and economic power in the Middle East, are sending to Turkey at this delicate moment the Commander of the Crusades, John Paul, disguised as a religious leader. If this visit is not called off, I will definitely kill the Commander pope.'

The *Milliyet* letter was advanced in evidence by those who believed that Ali Agca was a Muslim fundamentalist who had set out to kill the pope for religious reasons. But the conspiracy theory that probably had the widest support rested on the so-called 'Bulgarian connection'. Ten months after his trial Ali Agca identified three members of the staff at the Bulgarian embassy and four other Turks as his co-conspirators in the assassination attempt; he provided details of an escape plan involving a truck which was to have smuggled him to Yugoslavia under Bulgarian diplomatic immunity, and told a strange story of being recruited in the Bulgarian capital Sofia by a mysterious businessman who offered him $400,000 for a 'hit' on John Paul. There was circumstantial evidence for quite a lot of this, and since it seemed unlikely that the Bulgarians would have operated without Soviet approval suspicions turned to the Kremlin.

It is certainly true that John Paul had become a serious irritant to the Soviet leadership. Carl Bernstein and Marco Politi report in their biography *His Holiness* that 'the minutes of the Politburo of the USSR, obtained by the authors of this book, demonstrate the increasing Soviet preoccupation with the pope and the Church – and the Soviet leaders' frustration with Polish authorities for not cracking down on the Church'. And there was colourful stuff in the Soviet press, which was of course always a reflection of official thinking; the pope was a 'cunning and dangerous ideological enemy' and a 'malicious, lowly, perfidious and backward toady of the American militarists' according to one journal. But this kind of thing is very far from conclusive proof of a plot, and although the Bulgarians and Turks implicated by Ali Agca were brought to trial the case collapsed through lack of evidence. The assassination attempt against John Paul II will probably go down as one of the great unsolved mysteries of the twentieth century.

At the time John Paul was reported to have remarked that he was not interested in following the various theories because 'the devil did this thing'. Later, in the conversation recorded in *Memory and Identity*, he said that 'Ali Agca . . . was a professional assassin. This means that the attack was not his own initiative, it was someone else's idea, someone else had commissioned him to carry it out.' Without going into any details he added his view that the attempt on his life 'was one of the final convulsions of the arrogant ideologies unleashed during the twentieth century. Both Fascism and Nazism eliminated people. So did Communism.'

Given the way events had unfolded in Poland after John Paul's 1979 visit, it was probably inevitable that suspicions of a communist hand in the attempt to assassinate him should have lingered on. The summer of 1980 had seen another turn of the Polish cycle, although the immediate cause had more to do with pork than the pope. At the beginning of July that year the government finally gave way to economic incvitability and raised the price of meat. The increases were relatively modest and restricted to products at the top end of the market (Edward Gierek had not forgotten the lesson of the events that brought him to power) but they provoked a series of strikes and inflationary pay settlements across the country. Unrest became full-blown crisis in mid-August when the management of the Lenin shipyard in Gdansk fired the somewhat unlikely figure of Anna Walentynowicz, a crane driver who combined a mousy appearance – 'small, middle-aged, a worried expression behind cheap, thick spectacles' – with formidable powers as an orator and a history of making trouble for the authorities. She was a popular figure, and on 14 August there was a workers' meeting at the shipyard demanding her reinstatement and a 'cost of living' rise for all for good measure. Some accounts suggest the meeting was running out of steam when Lech Walesa, who had been fired from his job at the Lenin works for making a provocative speech four years earlier, turned up at the scene. He was hauled over the perimeter fence and climbed onto a bulldozer to address the workers. The meeting voted for a strike, and the Solidarity story had begun.

From the first days of the strike the pope was a kind of living patron saint of the strikers; his image was all over the gates of the Gdansk shipyard, alongside that of the Black Madonna (Lech Walesa habitually wore a buttonhole pin of the icon in his lapel). John Paul was also, after a fashion, the intellectual godfather of the free trade union movement. During the late 1970s, KOR, the Workers' Defence Committee which he had nurtured during his time as Archbishop of Krakow, had done much to create the political conditions which made the Solidarity strike so much more than an industrial dispute, and KOR activists helped to encourage nationwide sympathy action to support the Lenin shipyard workers in the critical early stages of the strike (300,000 workers had come out across the country by the end of the first week).

John Paul's role in 'managing' events during that dramatic August is difficult to pin down; he certainly was not a puppeteer pulling the strikers' strings in the way some of those in the Kremlin may no doubt have imagined. But there is evidence that he became impatient with the way Cardinal Wyszynski handled things on the ground. The Polish primate seemed ambivalent about the drama unfolding in Gdansk, and his public comments fell far short of clear support for the strikers. On 20 August John Paul, by contrast, said a public prayer with some Polish pilgrims which, although carefully worded ('all of us here in Rome are united with our compatriots in Poland, with the Church in Poland, whose problems are so close to our heart'), was widely interpreted as a blessing for the strike. Three days later he sent the Polish primate a letter ('I am writing these few brief words to say how especially close I have felt to you in the course of these last difficult days') which included what Carl Bernstein and Marco Politi describe as 'a precise political order': 'I pray with all my heart that the bishops of Poland,' declared John Paul 'can even now help this nation in its difficult struggle for daily bread, for social justice, and the safeguarding of its inviolable right to its own life and development.' It was tantamount to a papal endorsement for the strikers' political demands.

But if it was an 'order' Wyszynski ignored it. As the crisis deepened he agreed to a meeting with Edward Gierek, at which the Party First Secretary once again asked him to intervene in the national interest, brandishing the well-used but genuine threat of Soviet military intervention. The cardinal duly appeared on state television appealing for 'calm, poise and circumspection', suggested that there was fault on both sides of the dispute and warned that prolonged strikes could threaten Poland. At the Lenin shipyards in Gdansk there was a strong sense of betrayal among the strikers, and in the Vatican John Paul is said to have made some tart comments about Wyszynski's age and loss of touch. The following day the pope made another carefully worded but supportive appeal for 'peace and justice in our country' at his general audience, and, encouraged by the word from Rome, the Polish episcopate met in emergency session in Czestochowa that afternoon and agreed a lengthy statement of support for the strikers' demands; they rather cleverly quoted the Second Vatican Council's view that 'the right to set up free labour unions is one of the fundamental rights of the human being. These unions should truly represent their members . . . and guarantee each of them free participation in their activities without fear of repression.' The strike held, and the Gdansk Accord which the government accepted on 31 August recognised the first free trade union in the Soviet Empire. Lech Walesa signed the agreement with an enormous pen carrying the image of John Paul, a souvenir from the papal visit. Three weeks later the Church enjoyed some of the fruits of his achievement: Poland's national radio network inaugurated its first regular religious service under communist rule.

The Gdansk agreement did not, of course, end the Polish crisis, which rumbled on in the months leading up to the attempt on John Paul's life and beyond. Edward Gierek left the scene in dramatic fashion – suffering a heart attack on the very day that the Sejm, the Polish Parliament, met to debate the crisis – and was replaced as First Secretary of the Communist Party by Stanislaw Kania. Soviet concern about the inability of the government in Warsaw to control the way events were developing became increasingly shrill: 'the counterrevolution in Poland is in full flood,' Leonid Brezhnev told the Soviet Central Committee in Moscow on 29 October, 'Walesa is travelling from one end of the country to the other, to town after town, and they honour him with tributes everywhere. Polish leaders shut up and so does the press. Not even television is standing up to these anti-socialist elements.' Kania was summoned to Moscow to be told that he should begin preparations to put the country under martial law. Four weeks later, with no sign of an end to the unrest in Poland, he was called back to face an Extraordinary Meeting of the Warsaw Pact, and was explicitly threatened with military intervention.

The West was taking the possibility of a Soviet invasion very seriously indeed by that stage. Two days before the Warsaw Pact meeting, East Germany (the German Democratic Republic, as it was formally named, or GDR) had closed areas around the border with Poland to foreign military attachés, and Western spy satellites picked up signs that Soviet forces were moving to forward positions in Czechoslovakia and the western USSR as well as the GDR. The Soviet ambassador in Washington was called into the State Department and warned against the consequences of military action. On the evening of 7 December the American National Security Adviser Zbigniew Brzezinski telephoned John Paul to say that Washington's intelligence suggested an invasion could begin at any time. We now know – from papers which have emerged since the collapse of communism – that the decision to halt the invasion plans had in fact been taken at the meeting between Kania and the other Warsaw Pact leaders which took place on 5 December, but fear of an imminent Soviet attack continued at a very high pitch indeed. Newspapers in the West were dominated by headlines predicting the worst – I was a very junior trainee at Independent Television News at the time, and vividly remember being given the job of ringing up as many Poles as I could find in London and putting them on stand-by to weep for the cameras when the apparently inevitable had occurred.

Stalin's famously dismissive question 'How many divisions has the pope?' has been much quoted in the debate about John Paul's role in the collapse of communism. In the crisis of that winter he showed how effectively he could use what resources he did have – which were essentially those of the bully pulpit. On 16 December he wrote personally to the Soviet leader Leonid Brezhnev, and the letter is remarkable for the lack of the usual diplomatic circumlocutions. 'I address myself to the preoccupation of Europe and the whole world as regards the tension created by internal events taking place in Poland during these last months,' he begins. The letter dwells on the results of the German invasion of Poland in 1939 – with the clear implication that if the Soviets were to invade in 1980 it would be morally equivalent to what the Nazis had done four decades earlier – and John Paul firmly states his confidence that 'you will do everything you can in order to dispel the current tension, in order that political public opinion may be reassured about such a delicate and urgent problem'.

The following month John Paul invited Lech Walesa and a Solidarity delegation to Rome. Walesa was lionised by the Western media when he arrived, and he disappeared behind the doors of the papal library for a twenty-five-minute private conversation with John Paul. When they emerged for the official welcoming ceremony the pope repeated in public the private message he had sent Leonid Brezhnev: Poland must be allowed to sort out her difficulties without outside interference.

> What is at stake here is, and always will be, a strictly internal matter for the people of Poland. The immense efforts which were made during the autumn, and which must continue, were not directed against anyone. They were directed *towards*, not against, the common good. The right, which is in fact a duty, to make similar efforts is something that every country has. It is a right that is recognised and confirmed by the law of nations.

No modern pope had ever used his office in quite this way. It is true that both John XXIII and Paul VI had made significant statements on international affairs in general – and the Cold War in particular – and John had tried to intervene in the Cuban missile crisis of 1962. But the lack of papal divisions meant that their influence was limited to exhortation from the sidelines; neither would have claimed a direct role in international crisis management. The sheer audacity and flair with which John Paul exploited the moral authority of the papacy had placed him at the centre of the international stage and made him a figure Stalin's heirs could not afford to ignore.

When the Polish crisis blew up again that spring he showed that he also understood the need for tactical flexibility. The Solidarity movement opened another front in its war with the government by demanding recognition of a farmers' union, to be known as Rural Solidarity, and towards the end of March the political temperature rose significantly when the secret police beat up a group of Solidarity leaders in the town of Bydgoszcz. On 27 March there was a four-hour national strike, and Solidarity planned an indefinite general strike to begin on the 31st of the month. Kania and General Wojciech Jaruzelski – the 'military strong man' who had by now been promoted to the prime minister's office at the insistence of the Soviets – were coming under renewed pressure from Moscow, and the threat of Soviet military intervention was once again in the air. John Paul judged the moment right for restraint rather than confrontation. On 28 March he sent a message to Cardinal Wyszynski in which he urged the Solidarity leadership to continue its negotiations with the government rather than bringing matters to a head with a general strike, and Wyszynski duly passed that message on to Lech Walesa. On 30 March, with a day to go before the deadline for the strike, Walesa and his government opposite number announced a compromise: those responsible for the beatings at Bydgoszcz would be punished, and although Rural Solidarity would not be officially recognised immediately it would be allowed to operate. Several members of the Solidarity leadership resigned in protest at what they saw as a climbdown, but John Paul apparently remained convinced that discretion had indeed been the better part of valour on this occasion. A month later he received a visit from Ronald Reagan's CIA director William Casey, and according to a memoir by Casey's deputy, Robert Gates, John Paul told his boss that 'Moscow could not tolerate very much more . . . and that . . . a tactical withdrawal by Solidarity was the only way to avoid suppressive measures'.

The new Polish prime minister Wojciech Jaruzelski – with the Mafia-like dark glasses which never left his eyes and his unnaturally stiff military bearing – was to become famous in the West as the stereotypical Soviet stooge, but he was in fact a much more complicated and interesting character than his image suggested. He had been born a Catholic aristocrat, and in 1939 he and his family were caught up in the Soviet advance and deported to a labour camp as class enemies – the glare of the Siberian sun cracked his eyelids and he injured his back cutting wood there, so his curious appearance was in fact a legacy of Stalin's gulags. He returned to his native land as an officer in the Polish contingent of the Soviet army which entered Poland in 1944. He has given a memorable account of being summoned, in the immediate aftermath of the Bydgoszcz crisis, for another of those 'fraternal conversations' which had by now become such a familiar part of the Polish government's dealings with its eastern neighbour. He and Kania were flown to an airfield near the Soviet border and then driven off into the woods for a late-night meeting in a specially equipped railway carriage. They found the KGB head Yuri Andropov and the Soviet defence minister Marshall Ustinov presiding over 'Piles of sandwiches, tea, coffee and beer – sandwiches with caviar, fish and some meat'. There was a large green baize table in the centre of the carriage, and for six hours the two Poles were lectured about the iniquities of Solidarity and the threat the union posed to 'the achievements of socialism'. They were urged to consider the introduction of martial law, and there were more threats of a Soviet invasion.

Jaruzelski's direct experience of the Soviet Union as an exile and then a soldier during the war years had taught him to take those threats seriously, and he has always insisted that when he finally declared martial law – in a 6.00 a.m. broadcast on 13 December 1981 – it was the only way of preventing a Soviet strike. Mikhail Gorbachev, who was a member of the Politburo in 1981, supported his assertion; in an interview many years later he told me – without any apparent irony about his choice of language – 'Poles were lucky that at that moment General Jaruzelski was at the leadership of the country. God must have taken into consideration the Polish people's religious devotion and given them the General as their leader at such a time.' Evidence that has subsequently come to light suggests that the Soviet leadership had in fact decided against intervention that December, and that Jaruzelski was fully aware of the decision. But at the time John Paul was willing to give the Polish leader the benefit of the doubt.

His first intervention was instinctive – telephone links to Poland were cut and in the immediate aftermath of the general's broadcast it proved impossible for the Vatican to establish contact with the Polish bishops – but proved critical in setting the tone of the Church's response to martial law. The 13th of December was a Sunday, and there was, as usual, a large party of Polish pilgrims waiting in St Peter's Square for John Paul to appear at his balcony at noon. Speaking in Polish – in the sure knowledge that his words would also find their way to the millions of Poles at home who would be tuning in to the BBC and the Voice of America that day – he told them: 'Too much Polish blood has already been shed, especially during the last war. Polish blood must no longer be spilled. Everything must be done to build the future of our homeland in peace.' The call to non-violence – which was directed at both Jaruzelski's government and those disposed to resist it – was followed by a more considered plea in a formal letter to Jaruzelski. Twenty or thirty people were killed in clashes with the security forces in the immediate aftermath of the martial law declaration, and John Paul addressed the Polish president thus:

> Recent events in Poland since the declaration of martial law on December 13th have resulted in death and injury to our fellow countrymen, and I am moved to address this urgent and heartfelt appeal to you, a prayer for an end to the shedding of Polish blood . . . Our history cries out against any more bloodshed, and we must not allow this tragedy to continue to weigh so heavily on the conscience of the nation. I therefore appeal to you, General, to return to the methods of peaceful dialogue that have characterised efforts at social renewal since August 1980. Even though this may be a difficult step, it is not an impossible one.
>
> The welfare of the entire nation depends upon it. People throughout the world, all those who rightly see the cause of peace furthered by respect for the rights of Man, are waiting for this return to non-violent means. All humanity's desire for peace argues for an end to the state of martial law in Poland.

While leaving no doubt with which side the pope stood, the letter offered Jaruzelski the possibility of continuing dialogue with the Church and through the Church with the Solidarity opposition. On 19 December Archbishop Luigi Poggi, the Vatican nuncio-at-large to Eastern Europe, was despatched to make the point to General Jaruzelski in person (he had to travel by train since all flights to Warsaw had been suspended, and the journey took him several days). John Paul's determination to keep the lines of communication open in this way was, in the long term, to prove a decisive factor in the way communism unravelled in Poland. At the time martial law looked like a catastrophic setback – a reversal of everything that had happened in Poland since John Paul's visit in the summer of 1979. With hindsight it looks more like a brief interruption in a process of change which had, in fact, become inevitable.

Even at the time of John Paul's election there were commentators arguing that the papacy had become too big a job for one man. It is perhaps not surprising that, between managing a major international crisis and recovering from an assassination attempt, John Paul failed to spot a nasty scandal brewing within the Vatican itself. The Vatican Bank affair broke as a story when the chairman of the Banco Ambrosiano, Roberto Calvi, was found hanging beneath Blackfriars Bridge in London with $15,000 and a couple of bricks stuffed into his pockets. Years later it emerged that Calvi, who was known as 'God's Banker' because of his close association with the Vatican, had written to John Paul personally two weeks earlier appealing to him as 'my last hope, my very last'; Calvi said he was sure John Paul did not know the full extent of the relationship between his Banco Ambrosiano and the Vatican, and he claimed to have helped set up 'banking services to combat the penetration and expansion of Marxist ideologies' in Latin America. Be that as it may, the nature of the relationship between Calvi's Banco Ambrosiano and the Vatican Bank (the IOR, or Institute for Religious Works, as it was more properly known) which emerged during the investigation that followed Calvi's death turned out to be very dodgy indeed, and the IOR was later forced to pay out nearly $250 million in compensation to Ambrosiano creditors.

The Calvi story unravelled in a manner to gladden the heart of every right-thinking conspiracy theorist: the Mafia, the traditionalist Catholic group Opus Dei and the Masonic Lodge P2 all put in appearances. Twenty-three years after the grisly discovery under Blackfriars Bridge four Italians – including the Mafia's former chief cashier, who was already serving a long sentence on unrelated charges – and an Austrian woman went on trial for Calvi's murder in an Italian court. At the heart of the affair was Archbishop Paul Marcinkus, the colourful American bruiser (he was six foot three and had excelled at American football during his days as a seminarian) who ran the IOR. Marcinkus always maintained that he had never knowingly done anything wrong, and used his diplomatic immunity to fight off any attempt to put him in an Italian witness box. He had, at the very least, kept strange company, and if he really did not see anything odd about some of the arrangements he entered into at the behest of his friend Roberto Calvi he must have been very naïve indeed. Marcinkus also served as John Paul's advance man on his foreign tours – he did the job very much in the style of an advance man working on an American presidential campaign – and the pope relied heavily on his advice. Marcinkus was Paul VI's appointment originally, but his relatively close relationship with John Paul is perhaps another reflection of the fact that the pope was not always the best judge of character.

John Paul made the most significant appointment of his pontificate in late November 1981, as political storm clouds were gathering in Poland. The rapport established between Karol Wojtyla and Cardinal Joseph Ratzinger during the conclaves of 1978 had flourished following John Paul's election, and in early 1980 we find the then Archbishop of Munich expressing admiration for the new pope's championship of traditional Catholic teaching. It was not, he explained during a radio interview, within the pope's power to change what had been handed down to him: 'It is the pope's duty,' he said, 'to preserve the faith intact for our time, and to criticise the ills of Western society.' Joseph Ratzinger's four years in charge of the Munich archdiocese marked a brief interlude of pastoral work in what had been otherwise an almost entirely academic career, and John Paul turned to him as a man with the intellectual bottom for the job of Prefect of the Congregation for the Doctrine of the Faith, the body usually described as the Vatican's theological watchdog. While the John Paul–Casaroli partnership decided the way the Church dealt with the wider world during the 1980s, the much more enduring John Paul–Ratzinger partnership defined the internal life of the Church for the rest of the pontificate, and Cardinal Ratzinger was to prove an absolutely critical player in the way John Paul redesigned the model of the papacy. He probably never expected to inherit the legacy of their joint enterprise himself – as he did when he was elected Pope Benedict XVI in 2005 – and seems to have found the mantle that fell on his shoulders somewhat uncomfortable.

The two men had much in common; although Joseph Ratzinger was born seven years later than Karol Wojtyla, he was equally formed by the experience of growing up in a world of deep and unquestioning Catholic faith. The Bavaria of the 1930s shared much of the religious character of Poland during the same period, and Joseph's father was every bit as pious as the elder Karol Wojtyla; he would sometimes go to mass three times on Sunday. The Ratzingers came from a social milieu not unlike that of the Wojtylas, too; Ratzinger senior was a policeman (a fact that inevitably became the source of much pointed humour when the younger Ratzinger showed his teeth in his Vatican job), and Joseph joined a seminary in 1943, the year after Karol Wojtyla presented himself as a candidate for ordination at the Archbishop's Palace in Krakow. Both men attended the Second Vatican Council – Joseph Ratzinger was there as a *peritus* or theological adviser – and both had formidably productive literary habits (by the time he became pope himself, Joseph Ratzinger had produced more than fifty books, and, in the words of his biographer John Allen, 'a seemingly infinite series of journal articles, popular essays, and lectures').

There were, of course, also significant differences – of both background and character – between them. Joseph Ratzinger's defenders point out that the Hitler Youth movement had been made compulsory when he so famously became a member at fourteen in 1941, and he did not join the German army until he was conscripted along with the rest of his class of seminarians in 1943. He was not a Nazi. But it is impossible to resist the temptation to contrast the image of a bookish young Ratzinger reluctantly sitting at his anti-aircraft battery outside a Munich BMW plant with the altogether more arresting figure of the wartime Wojtyla. Ratzinger seems to have shown no interest in any career or vocation other than the priesthood – and certainly never suffered anything like the young Karol's thespian temptation. John Allen has found no record that John Paul's choice as the Prefect of the Congregation for the Doctrine of the Faith 'had any serious romantic relations as a young man', and it seems unlikely that a Halina figure will emerge from the shadows one day to muse on what life might have been like as Frau Ratzinger. Finally, the German had the natural pessimism of the conservative, while the Pole was animated by the rosy optimism more usually associated with the liberal view of history; later in his career Cardinal Ratzinger began to reflect on the possibility that the Church should become 'smaller and purer', a very different vision from that of the great evangelising pilgrim pope John Paul.

The CDF is the oldest of the Vatican congregations; it was founded in the sixteenth century when the tradition of cardinals acting as papal advisers in a kind of cabinet (the system of 'consisteries') fell away, and it was created as a direct response to the Reformation to rule on matters of faith and heresy. It was originally known as the 'Universal Inquisition', and it was not until the penultimate day of Vatican II, 7 December 1965, that the phrase 'Holy Office' was dropped from its modern title; the Index of books which Catholics were forbidden to read was abolished on the same day, and the title 'general inquisitors' for cardinal members of the organisation went too. The man who ran the Holy Office during the Council, Cardinal Alfredo Ottaviani, had become an almost cardboard cut-out villain for liberal reformers because of the enthusiasm with which he defended the status quo (his motto was *semper idem*, for ever the same, and his first intervention on the floor of St Peter's was a vigorous defence of the Latin mass). By a nice irony the young Joseph Ratzinger had, in the course of his service as a theologian at Council, helped to draft a speech for Cardinal Frings of Cologne which denounced the 'methods and behaviour' of Ottaviani's Holy Office as 'a cause of scandal to the world'.

All that history makes the job of Prefect of the Congregation for the Doctrine of the Faith a natural target for those who want to tease Catholics for belonging to an obscurantist and authoritarian Church. The way Cardinal Ratzinger carried out the role offered Catholicism's enemies the opportunity to go well beyond the old jokes and to accuse the Church of genuine repression.

The Prefect had already shown his willingness to exercise his disciplinary powers as Archbishop of Munich when he blocked the appointment of the distinguished theologian Johann Baptist Metz to a job at the city's university. Once installed in the Vatican he set about deploying the full force of his powers – 'cracking the whip immediately on taking office' as one of his critics put it – and, reflecting the priorities of his master John Paul, he soon turned his attention to the Liberation Theologians of Latin America.

I have spoken to many people in the Catholic Church – from cardinals downwards – who liked and admired the late pope but disliked much of what was done in his name, and I have found that Cardinal Ratzinger – before he became Benedict XVI, at least – was often the lightning rod they used to focus their anger away from John Paul. It is a perfectly natural thing to do, and John Paul's public persona was infinitely more attractive than that of the apparently dry-as-dust academic and ex-member of the Hitler Youth movement who served him (I have met Ratzinger once and he is in fact a surprisingly gentle person who inspired deep loyalty and affection among his staff at the CDF). But it does violence to the facts to separate John Paul from the actions of his closest collaborator. It is true that John Paul could sometimes retreat into a gnomic management style which allowed him to escape taking sides in an argument; there is a story, told to me by a senior member of the church hierarchy, that he once listened to a ferocious debate between a group of French bishops and, when they finally turned to him for a decision, simply said, with great panache, '*Tres bien, nous sommes sur la route,*' leaving them as puzzled about his view on their dispute as they had been when they began. But he and Cardinal Ratzinger came to know one another's minds very well indeed; for more than twenty years the two men would meet each Friday in private to discuss the CDF's work, and there were regular Thursday lunches at which the conversation ranged more widely over a variety of topics in a freewheeling manner.

Moreover, the 1984 *Instruction on Certain Aspects of Liberation Theology*, which marked perhaps the rawest moment in the conflict between the Vatican and the Liberation Theologians of Latin

America, was apparently produced on John Paul's explicit instructions. The papal biographer George Weigel says that Cardinal Ratzinger told him in an interview that 'John Paul charged the CDF with tackling the problem' of Liberation Theology. 'The *Instruction* had its origins in a 1982 conversation involving John Paul II and Cardinal Ratzinger,' writes Weigel. 'The intellectual initiative was John Paul's.' And whatever private conversations had taken place, John Paul had anyway given a very public indication of the strength of his feelings during perhaps the most ill-tempered pilgrimage of his entire pontificate – his visit to the Nicaraguan capital of Managua in March 1983.

All sorts of Cold War and Catholic currents converged in Nicaragua. The Sandinista revolution to oust the old-school Latin American dictatorship of Anastasio Somoza in 1979 had widespread popular support; Daniel Ortega and the Sandinista leadership would in the fullness of time disappoint their supporters mightily, but in the early 1980s they still had the status of revolutionary heroes. At the same time Washington – Ronald Reagan had of course come to power in the presidential election of 1980 – regarded Ortega with profound suspicion. He was seen as a communist stooge in the United States' 'backyard', and he became a favourite bogeyman for stirring up Middle American fears of Soviet tanks grinding up the highway into Texas. America's support for the right-wing rebel movement which emerged to challenge the Ortega regime was in due course to land the Reagan administration in the dreadful mess of the Iran-Contra affair. Nicaragua was, as John Paul vividly described it later, 'a shooting gallery for the superpowers'.

To make things even more complicated, the Catholic Church in Nicaragua was divided against itself. The Church had played a significant role in the Sandinista revolution. In the late 1970s the country's primate, Archbishop Miguel Obando y Bravo, was encouraging peaceful political resistance to the Somoza dictatorship in much the same way that Karol Wojtyla had been fighting communist oppression in Poland; in the middle of 1979, as it became apparent that the Sandinista revolt against Somoza had overwhelming popular support, the country's bishops issued a remarkable statement which endorsed the revolution as a way of ending 'evident and prolonged tyranny, which seriously threatens the fundamental rights of the individual and undermines the common good of the country'. Some priests argued that the oppression and injustice represented by the Somoza regime justified the use of violence – although there is little evidence of active clerical participation in military operations in Nicaragua. And the Sandinistas had strong support among the so-called 'base Christian communities' – the grassroots Catholic groups which Liberation Theology taught were the building blocks of the new Church.

But the radical Marxist character of the Sandinista movement became more and more apparent as its leaders settled into power, and a division opened up between the 'official' Church – led by Obando but by no means restricted to the hierarchy – which found itself increasingly in opposition to the country's government, and the 'popular' Church which continued to support the revolution. Nicaragua's population was a modest three million in the early 1980s, and 80 per cent of them were Catholics; the quarrel was soon marked by the kind of bitterness that only a family argument can generate, and outside pressures – from John Paul's Vatican, Lopez Trujillo and his conservative friends at CELAM and Ronald Reagan's White House – helped to bring this poisonous concoction to a merry boil. 'Priests publicly disowned their bishops, and bishops disowned priests,' writes Penny Lernoux in *People of God*, her history of Latin American Liberation Theology: 'Religious orders divided, as did foreign and Nicaraguan priests and nuns.' The low point came in the summer of 1982, when Obando y Bravo tried to move a pro-Sandinista priest out of his parish. It provoked an open rebellion by the parishioners, who occupied their church and attacked a bishop who was sent to retrieve its sacred objects. The Jesuit Fr Cesar Jerez, who was president of Managua's University of Central America during this period, compared the divisions within the Church to the high-water mark of doctrinal dispute and heresy-hunting of the early church: 'It was as if the times of the councils of Nicaea and Ephesus were with us again,' he said.

A focus for the battle was provided by the four Catholic priests who served in official positions in the Sandinista government: Fr

Edgar Parrales was the minister of social welfare and later the ambassador to the Organisation of American States, Fr Miguel D'Escoto (a Maryknoll Father) was foreign minister, Fr Ernesto Cardenal was minister of culture and his Jesuit brother Fr Fernando Cardenal was the co-ordinator of the government's Literacy Crusade. For the Vatican this was a flagrant example of the excesses to which Liberation Theology could lead, and all four were told that they must either resign their jobs or leave the priesthood – making a choice, as it were, between their ministries and their ministry.

The four argued (and Miguel D'Escoto, whom I interviewed during the preparation for this book, continued to make this case long after he abandoned the Sandinista movement in 1995) that they were simply serving their country at a time of great national need; the forty years of Somoza dictatorship had left a dreadful legacy which urgently needed to be addressed, and it would have been difficult to quarrel with the objectives of programmes like Fernando Cardenal's Literacy Crusade. But contemporary commentators saw much bigger forces at play in the battle over the priests' position: 'Both the Sandinistas and the Vatican understood the stakes,' writes Penny Lernoux.

> If Nicaragua could demonstrate to the rest of Latin America that Christian–Marxist co-operation made Rome superfluous, the Vatican might lose its hold on the most populous Catholic region in the world. As noted by the Irish political writer Conor Cruise O'Brien in a shrewd analysis . . . Catholic Sandinismo was potentially a latter-day version of the split caused in European Catholicism by the Protestant Reformation.

With the benefit of hindsight, that reads like the kind of hysterical nonsense which the febrile character of Cold War intellectual debate sometimes fostered, but it may well have felt that way to the key players as the pope's plane approached Managua airport on 4 April 1983.

There had been intense negotiations between the papal nuncio in Managua and the Ortega regime about the protocol of the visit, because the Vatican was determined to avoid anything that might look like an endorsement of the Sandinista priest-ministers. The cabinet – including the culture minister Fr Ernesto Cardenal – was lined up at the airport to see John Paul arrive, but the plan seems to have been that he would not greet them individually. There is some dispute about how he came to find himself shaking hands all the way down the full ministerial receiving line – some accounts suggest it was a spur-of-the-moment decision by John Paul himself, others that it was the result of a mistake by an over-enthusiastic official who guided him in the wrong direction – but the result was one of the most enduring images of the pontificate. Ernesto Cardenal was an international poet of some distinction, and he had turned out in an appropriately literary style of formal dress – a white smock topped off by a black beret. As John Paul reached him he swept off his beret and knelt to kiss the papal ring. The pope took a step back, pulled away his hands and wagged his fingers in admonition at the kneeling figure, telling him, 'Regularise your position with the Church.'

John Paul lost his temper altogether at his open-air mass in Managua later that day. Instead of the usual field of gold and white papal flags waving above the crowd, he was confronted by posters of Marx and the heroes of the Sandinista revolution. Ortega and the other members of the Sandinista National Directorate sat on a platform and from time to time saluted the crowd with clenched fists, shouting, 'Power to the people!' During his sermon John Paul confronted the idea of a 'popular' Church head on, and he was more or less shouted down by sections of the crowd – many accounts of the event suggest that the barracking was orchestrated, which is perfectly credible. He bellowed, '*Silencio*' in the tone of a man not accustomed to being crossed, ploughed on with his sermon and waved his crozier above his head as a message of solidarity to the loyal Catholics he believed were out there somewhere behind the Sandinista activists (the hugely enthusiastic reception he received when he returned to Nicaragua thirteen years later suggests he was right).

The visit helped to create the highly charged and emotional climate in which the publication of the Vatican's *Instruction* on

Liberation Theology was received the following year. The document was designed 'to draw the attention of pastors, theologians, and all the faithful to the deviations, and risks of deviations, damaging to the faith and to Christian living, that are brought about by certain forms of Liberation theology which use, in an insufficiently critical manner, concepts from various currents of Marxist thought'. Taken as a whole, it amounted to a fairly ferocious condemnation of an approach which Rome said 'subordinates theology to the class struggle'. And the *Instruction* was followed within a month by the interrogation and silencing of the Liberation Theologian Leonardo Boff which, like the Nicaragua visit, quickly became part of media mythology.

Boff, a Brazilian Franciscan, had written a book called *Church Charism and Power* which took the new ideas that the Liberation Theologians had used to analyse Latin American societies and turned them on the Church itself: 'My book is an attempt to show that the Church is only deserving of being liberating if the Church itself is a church of liberty,' he said. Cardinal Ratzinger summoned him to Rome to explain his ideas, and, after a lengthy conversation, imposed a period of 'silence' during which Boff was forbidden to write, teach or speak publicly. It was of course precisely the kind of sentence that human-rights activists complained about in the totalitarian regimes of the communist world and Boff – who turned up in Rome looking suitably humble in the Franciscan habit he seldom wore at home – had a great deal of fun with the notoriety the incident afforded him. He was fond of describing it to journalists, and the story tended to get more dramatic as time went on. It was a day of 'medieval scenes', he told me when I interviewed him fifteen years later. He described being bustled into a car and swept at high speed through the Vatican gardens, past

> an enormous iron gate with huge nails pointing outwards. I asked the official with me if this was the torture chambers. 'You politicise everything,' he said. We walked into a lift guarded by two Swiss Guards in official clothing . . . we crossed an enormous room, I guess it must have been eighty metres wide, with glamorous carpets and huge Renaissance paintings. Right

at the end of this room was a tiny room with two chairs and a small table.

One of the chairs, Boff insisted, had been used by Galileo during his interrogation several centuries earlier. This picture of a callow provincial being terrorised by a naked display of Vatican power needs to be taken with some salt; apart from anything else, Boff knew Ratzinger personally, as the cardinal had supervised his doctorate when he was studying in Germany in the 1960s.

In the midst of all this John Paul pulled off one of those *coups de théâtre* which no other public figure could match; even his most ungenerous critics could not help admiring his decision to visit Ali Agca in his prison cell. John Paul took along Monsignor Dziwisz, two bodyguards and – of course – a photographer. It was two days after Christmas in 1983. Pope and would-be assassin talked in low voices in a corner of the cell, and there was much speculation about the subject of their conversation – John Paul told a visiting Polish priest at breakfast the next morning that Ali Agca had heard about the Fatima story and was worried about being struck down by a vengeful Virgin. But the truth is that it mattered not a jot what they talked about because the image they made was so striking: the two men sitting on plastic chairs in the corner of a prison cell, heads bowed in confidential fashion, one young, dressed in jeans and running shoes, the other dignified in his white cassock, formed a modern icon of the Christian ideal of forgiveness. There was nothing forced or awkward about the picture; if a politician had done something similar there would have been a certain amount of sneering comment about a 'photo-op', but there was nothing remotely hammy about John Paul's performance – a further reflection, perhaps, of his long-held conviction that theatre is a serious business.

In 1985, twenty years after the end of the Second Vatican Council, John Paul called an Extraordinary Synod of Bishops in Rome. I was sent to cover the opening as a reporter, and looking back at the event today it seems a useful punctuation mark for taking stock of the way public perceptions of John Paul's pontificate had changed. The sheer excitement he had generated in his early days in office gave him a remarkably long honeymoon period with Catholics and non-Catholics alike. The part he had played in the Polish drama made him a natural hero in Western Europe and North America, where the Cold War remained the big fact defining the terms of political discourse. Equally, the charm and enthusiasm he exerted on his audience during his foreign travels secured him widespread affection almost everywhere he went in the developing world. But by the middle of the 1980s his conservative theological views were attracting more and more adverse attention, especially in Western newsrooms; actions like the silencing of theologians did not sit well with the instincts of liberal-minded journalists and editors. John Paul's gradual transformation from Cold War hero into conservative bogeyman had begun. The Synod which was called to reflect on the legacy of Vatican II cemented the process.

The modern concept of a Synod of Bishops was itself a product of the Council; it was conceived as the institutional mechanism for reflecting 'collegiality', the idea that the pope, though supreme, is one of many bishops (just as St Peter was one among twelve apostles), and it was designed to counter-balance the doctrine of papal infallibility defined at the First Vatican Council. Those bishops who attend Synods are elected by their episcopal conferences, and although it certainly is not in any sense the 'church parliament' which some at the Council argued for, it is the 'closest thing to an international representative institution in the Catholic Church'. Paul VI's ideas about the way it should work suggest that he believed it could provide a mechanism for the pope and his Curia to listen to the Church in the wider world; the Synod should, he said, 'encourage close and valued assistance between the sovereign pontiff and the bishops of the world', and 'ensure that direct and real information is provided on questions and situations touching upon the internal action of the Church and its necessary activity in the world today'.

But many of those arriving in Rome for the Extraordinary Synod at the end of November 1985 had already concluded that John Paul conceived of the Synod system as a mechanism for making sure that the bishops of the world listened to the Vatican rather than the reverse. The pattern had been set at the first Synod of the pontificate – the Synod on the Role of the Christian

Family in the Modern World in 1980 – and John Paul's view of church democracy is well illustrated by the experience of the English and Welsh bishops on that occasion. The English and Welsh Church had been quietly developing a democratic system of its own – involving consultation between bishops, priests and laity – and in advance of the Family Synod a National Pastoral Congress was held in Liverpool to identify the issues its bishops should carry to Rome. The result, a document called *The Easter People*, reflected a general feeling at the Congress that the Church should consider 'developing' (that was considered a less frightening word than 'changing') its teaching in two highly sensitive areas, the ban on artificial contraception laid down in *Humanae Vitae* and the exclusion of divorced and remarried Catholics from receiving communion. Cardinal Hume, the Archbishop of Westminster, took the document with him on a visit to John Paul at Castel Gandolfo in the summer before the Synod on Family Life, and his reception was less than encouraging; the cardinal later described how he handed the pope a copy of *The Easter People* which he had deliberately opened at the page relating to contraception, only for John Paul to wave it impatiently to one side.

Nevertheless the Family Life Synod opened in a mood of optimism; John Paul attended almost every session, taking copious notes of the 'interventions' but never himself speaking, and entertained as many participants as he could to lunch or dinner in the papal apartments. Cardinal Hume and the other liberal leader of the English Church, Archbishop Derek Worlock of Liverpool, duly reflected the conclusions of the National Pastoral Congress on the floor of the Synod. Worlock was detailed to deal with divorce and told the assembled bishops that 'the Church cannot turn a blind eye to the many family tragedies which are increasingly in society, and no less in the Church itself'. Hume took the contraception brief, and spoke of the 'good, conscientious and faithful sons and daughters of the Church' who 'just cannot accept that the use of artificial means of contraception in some circumstances is *intrinsice inhonestum* [intrinsically evil]'.

But midway through the Synod things took a classic Roman turn. The task of drafting 'Propositions' which the Synod would place before the pope was put in the hands of a team of experts working under the guidance of Cardinal Ratzinger (he was not yet Prefect of the CDF at this stage, but was acting as the Synod co-ordinator). The bishops felt they were being manipulated by the Curia, and promptly rejected everything the Ratzinger team put forward. They insisted on drawing up their own Propositions. The ideas they came up with were, by all accounts, far from radical (they were supposed to be kept secret, but leaked out in bits and pieces, as things in the Vatican usually do) but they went far enough to provoke a stern rebuke from John Paul in his sermon on the final day of the Synod. Nothing more came of the meeting until a year later, when John Paul issued an 'Apostolic Exhortation' which was supposed to reflect the mind of the Synod but in fact did nothing of the kind. *Familiaris Consortio*, as it was called, restated traditional church teaching in a way that makes it difficult to see whether the Synod meeting had really had any point at all. In the final days of the Synod, as it became apparent which way things were headed, Cardinal Hume made a much quoted speech which amounted to a very gentle English tease about the sort of Church the Polish pope was creating. Hume told the bishops he had nodded off during their debate:

> I heard a voice speaking and it spoke of the Church; and in my dream I had a vision. It was a vision of the Church. I saw a fortress, strong and upstanding. Every stranger approaching seemed to those defending to be an enemy to be repelled; from that fortress the voice of those outside could not be heard. The soldiers within showed unquestioning obedience – and that was much admired; 'Theirs not to reason why, theirs but to do or die.' It seemed thus in my dream, and then I remembered, upon awakening – it was only just to do so – that dreams distort reality. They exaggerate.

Hume said later that in his subsequent dealings with John Paul the pope often told him, in good-humoured tones, to 'keep on dreaming', but the English cardinal left the Synod on the Family already convinced of the conservative direction the new pontificate would take. At the time of writing, a quarter of a century after the Synod on the Family, any change in Catholic teaching on contraception or divorce looks considerably less likely than it did then.

By the time of the 1985 Synod the Church's centre of gravity had shifted significantly. It was no longer a question of how fast progressive bishops could push along the revolutionary path that began with Vatican II: they were instead fighting a rearguard action to prevent a counter-revolution. The tone for the meeting was set by the publication of a book entitled *The Ratzinger Report*, a long interview which John Paul's man at the CDF had given to the Italian journalist Vittorio Messori. The cardinal tactfully spoke of 'restoration' rather than counter-revolution, but there seemed little doubt about what he had in mind. 'If by "restoration" we understand the search for a new balance after all the exaggerations of an indiscriminate opening to the world, after the overly positive interpretations of an agnostic and atheistic world,' he told Vittorio Messori, 'then a restoration understood in this sense (a newly found balance of orientation and values within the Catholic totality) is altogether desirable and, for that matter, is already in operation in the Church.' Cardinal Godfried Danneels, the Archbishop of Malines-Brussels, who had the task of co-ordinating the responses to the questionnaires sent out to episcopal conferences in advance of the Synod, faced so many questions about *The Ratzinger Report* at his press conferences that he eventually snapped: 'This is not a Synod about a book, it is a Synod about Council.'

But it was certainly a Synod about the ideas in that book: "The issues at the Synod were, in large part, those discussed by Cardinals Wojtyla and Ratzinger prior to the conclaves of 1978,' wrote George Weigel. Many of the items on the agenda – the theological status of episcopal conferences, for example, or the enculturation of the liturgy – were somewhat 'churchy', and did not excite huge interest among the men and women in the Clapham pew, but there was in fact a very great deal at stake. The Synod, according to Weigel, 'did mark the end of a period of Catholic history. The Council [Vatican II] that had taken the gamble of not providing authoritative keys to its interpretation had been given an authoritative interpretation by the Synod.'

The Synod's Final Report recognised that Vatican II was 'a legitimate and valid expression and interpretation of the deposit of faith as it is found in the Sacred Scripture and in the living tradition of the Church' – not perhaps the warmest words of endorsement one could have come up with – but said that there had been 'partial and selective' readings of some of its documents and a 'superficial interpretation' of some of its conclusions. It is no accident that the Synod's most significant decision was that the Church needed a new Catechism, 'a compendium of all Catholic doctrine regarding faith and morals' to clear up post-Conciliar confusion about what the faithful were supposed to believe and what they could and could not do. 'Restoration', every bit as much John Paul's project as it was Cardinal Ratzinger's, was underway.

Two days before the Synod began, the Anglican Archbishop of Canterbury, Dr Robert Runcie, wrote a letter to John Paul which must have weighed heavily on the pope's mind – especially in view of the Synod's reaffirmation of the need to pursue Christian unity. It was part of a correspondence between Rome and Lambeth Palace on the vexed question of women priests, and when the letters were published in full the following summer – simultaneously in London and Rome – it became apparent that they marked a very serious break in progress towards closer relations between Anglicanism and Roman Catholicism. John Paul had begun the exchange himself; when it became apparent that the Church of England was serious about following other Anglican communions on the road to the ordination of women, he sent Runcie what the archbishop described in his reply as a 'frank' letter warning that this would be a serious obstacle – 'an element of grave difficulty' – to reconciliation between the two churches.

Robert Runcie was a class act, adept at managing the intellectual contortions which his office demanded – archbishops of Canterbury are the nominal leaders of a communion which is almost as far-flung and disparate as the Roman Catholic Church, but they enjoy nothing like the same authority as the pope. His response took eight months to formulate, because, he said, he needed to consult with the churches around the world for which he was responsible. It was elegantly argued, and recognised the seriousness of the step the Church of England was taking. But it stated clearly 'the most substantial doctrinal argument, which is seen not only to justify the ordination of women . . . but actually to require it': Christ redeemed all humanity, and since the priesthood had a 'representative nature' it made no sense to exclude from it 50 per cent of those whom Jesus had spilt his blood to save. Runcie wrote in similar terms to Cardinal Johannes Willebrands, the President of the Secretariat for Promoting Christian Unity, and received a letter in return which was every bit as courteous, theologically thoughtful and, in the end, blunt. The Vatican was not going to buy into any of the arguments which had been aired on the floor of the General Synod of the Church of England, and the decision to publish the exchange of letters on 30 June 1986 reflected a joint recognition of the severity of the disagreement. Any hope of unity between Roman Catholicism and its closest Protestant cousin had disappeared for at least a generation, and perhaps for ever.

It was a painful moment. The Anglican and Roman Catholic Churches had been in conversation since the late 1960s through a forum known as ARCIC – the Anglican–Roman Catholic International Consultative Commission. In 1982 the Commission produced a document which it claimed represented 'substantial and explicit agreement' on a number of the issues which had traditionally divided the two churches. And John Paul's extraordinarily successful visit to Britain in the summer of 1982 had created a climate of high optimism among both British Catholics and Anglicans; one of the high points of the trip was John Paul's visit to Canterbury Cathedral, an event which produced some breathtakingly beautiful television images, as the two church leaders walked the cathedral's ancient and once Roman Catholic cloisters, and prayed together before the altar where Thomas à Becket was slain. As Cardinal Basil Hume's biographer Tony Howard has said, 'while 1982 may justifiably be seen as a year of hope, it can also be regarded as one that witnessed a mirage. For a moment the sight of it was thrilling, but the promise it held out proved to be neither lasting nor permanent.' John Paul's flair for image-minting could make people dream, but it was not on its own enough to deliver.

The publication of the exchange of letters on women priests did not prevent Robert Runcie being given a prominent role in another of those 'snapshot' moments which took place three months later and still stands out in many memories of John Paul's pontificate – the inter-religious World Day of Prayer for Peace at Assisi in the autumn of 1986. It was, as the papal biographer Michael Walsh notes in a somewhat wry account of the proceedings, 'an odd gathering':

> Pride of place – next to the pope who was, after all, the host – was given to other Christian denominations, above all to Robert Runcie, the Archbishop of Canterbury, but when they all came together they met in a circle. There were Buddhists and Moslems, Shintoists and Sikhs. There were African and Amerindian animists; the latter passed round a pipe of peace. There was a walk, supposedly a pilgrimage, around the streets of Assisi with John Paul at its head and Robert Runcie trying, not too successfully, to make conversation. There was also prayer, each in his or her own way, though the various strands of Christianity got together in the Our Father which the pope led, a reading of the Beatitudes (by Runcie) and a prayer for peace from the Vice-President of the Lutheran World Federation who was, seemingly, the only woman entitled to call herself a religious leader in the sense of the meeting at Assisi. There was a waving of olive branches and a release of doves. Catholics, admitted the pope with a sideways glance at the crusades which Francis of Assisi had tried, and failed, to halt, had not always been peacemakers. 'Either we learn to walk in peace and harmony, or we drift apart and ruin ourselves and others,' he said.

It was all too easy to dismiss the Assisi event as gesture politics, which in a sense it was. The conservatives in the Curia thought it smacked of syncretism, the heretical habit of trying to mix Christianity with the doctrines and practices of other faiths (a tendency which would in due course much engage Cardinal Ratzinger's attention), and it did not stop John Paul causing grave offence to several other Christian denominations and non-

Christian faiths in subsequent years of his pontificate. But it was unprecedented, and in John Paul's obituaries in 2005 the Assisi meeting was cited widely in the non-Catholic press as an illustration of his originality and generosity of spirit. He himself called it 'the religious event of the year' when he addressed a group of Roman clergy in December 1986.

The following month John Paul welcomed General Wojciech Jaruzelski to the Vatican for an official visit; it was a little more than six years since the declaration of martial law, and the mere fact of the visit was a tribute to how much had been achieved by the pope's determination to keep the lines of communication open to Poland's communist leadership. The balance he had struck in the immediate aftermath of the martial law declaration – pursuing negotiation with the government while giving unambiguous support to the aspirations expressed in Solidarity – became a settled policy. When he had visited Poland in 1983, for example, John Paul had taken care to meet both Lech Walesa and General Jaruzelski; he had promised the general that he would work for the lifting of Western economic sanctions against Poland, and the meeting helped provide Jaruzelski with the political cover he needed to lift martial law a month later. John Paul's message of non-violence also proved extraordinarily effective; in 1984 Fr Jerzy Popieluszko, an outspoken critic of the government, was murdered by the secret police and dumped in a reservoir near Warsaw. It was one of those critical moments when the country could have erupted into civil war. The funeral was attended by several hundred thousand people – some estimates put the figure as high as a million – but it passed off without incident.

There was a third papal pilgrimage to Poland in the summer of 1987, and this time John Paul felt sufficiently confident of the way things were going to turn up the pressure on the Jaruzelski regime. He insisted on visiting Gdansk – which the government had succeeded in excluding from his 1983 itinerary – and repeatedly used the word 'solidarity' in his sermons (he managed seven solidarities within three minutes during his open-air mass at the port of Gdynia). Jaruzelski was provoked into responding with a good old-fashioned communist rant at a farewell meeting with the pope ('May the word "solidarity" flow from our Polish soil to those people who still suffer racism and neo-colonialism, exploitation and unemployment, persecutions and intolerance,' he declared), but it was becoming apparent to everyone by this stage that the days of the old-style communist hegemony the general represented were numbered. Post-war Poland's first non-communist prime minister, Tadeusz Mazowiecki, was elected almost exactly two years later.

The new factor in the Cold War equation was, of course, Mikhail Gorbachev, who had succeeded Konstantin Chernenko as Soviet leader in 1985 and had been engaged in an increasingly dramatic diplomatic dance with the American president Ronald Reagan ever since. In the summer of 1988 John Paul despatched his secretary of state, Cardinal Casaroli, to the Kremlin with a warm letter for the Soviet leader: 'I have personally followed the events of international life,' the pope said, 'and first and foremost the initiatives in favour of peace that you have undertaken. In recent times my special attention has been drawn to the promising developments created by the encounters and agreements in these last months between the Soviet Union and the United States of America, especially as regards disarmament, which have given such relief to the whole world.'

On 1 December 1989 the Soviet leader visited John Paul in the Vatican. In many ways the occasion was a postscript to the Cold War; the Berlin Wall had come down the previous month, the communists no longer held power in Poland, and the Soviet Union itself would soon begin to unravel. Moreover, Gorbachev's account of the meeting in his autobiography records exchanges between the two men of really quite stunning banality ('Under-lining the honourable mission of His Holiness in the modern world,' he recalled, 'I noted certain coincidences in both his and my statements. That means a simple thing – there should be coincidences in our basic thoughts'). But the meeting probably does deserve that much over-used journalistic sobriquet 'historic'. Europe suffered three great traumas during the twentieth century, but if you look at them from the perspective of a Pole born in 1920, the Great World War, the Second World War and the Cold War can appear to be one long conflict interrupted by anxious and uncertain periods of peace. That conflict defined John Paul's life, and both he and the man sitting opposite him in his library that day had played decisive roles in bringing it to an end. Gorbachev was a convinced atheist, but John Paul would frequently refer to him as a 'providential man'.

Towards the end of his life, in a conversation recorded in *Gift and Mystery*, John Paul reflected on his role in the collapse of communism:

> I am constantly aware that in everything I say and do in fulfilment of my vocation, my mission, my ministry, what happens is not just my own initiative. I know that it is not I alone who act in what I do as the Successor of Peter.
>
> Let us take the example of the communist system. As I said earlier, a contributory factor in its demise was certainly its deficient economic doctrine, but to account for what happened solely in terms of economic factors would be a rather naïve simplification. On the other hand, it would obviously be ridiculous to claim that the Pope brought down Communism single-handedly.

John Paul turns to Luke's Gospel for two occasions on which Jesus speaks to the disciples about the mission they are carrying out in his name and tells them to think of themselves as 'unworthy servants'. The pope then picks up the theme and applies it to his own mission: 'Unworthy servants . . . The sense of being an "unworthy servant" is growing in me in the midst of all that happens around me – and I think I feel at ease with this.' The analysis of the balance of causes behind the collapse of communism is clear-eyed and probably fair. The way John Paul places himself in the gospel context is both humble – which is no doubt how he would have felt it – and gigantically hubristic; there is a complete absence of irony in the manner in which he compares himself with the disciples and assumes for himself such a prominent role in the divine plan.

10

Taking on the World

In the summer of 1989, as the Cold War divisions in Europe melted away with breathtaking speed, the American diplomat and academic Francis Fukuyama published an essay which established him as the prophet of the new world order – to use a phrase which would soon be capitalised and popularised by Dr Fukuyama's president, George Bush senior. The piece carried a bold title, 'The End of History', and when Dr Fukuyama later expanded it into book form he précised his case in his Introduction thus:

> I argued that a remarkable consensus concerning the legitimacy of liberal democracy as a system of government had emerged throughout the world over the past few years, as it conquered rival ideologies like hereditary monarchy, fascism, and most recently communism. More than that, however, I argued that liberal democracy may constitute the 'end point of mankind's ideological evolution', and 'the final form of human government', and as such constituted 'the end of history'.

In the economic sphere, Fukuyama argued, history had delivered the victor's crown to free market capitalism ('the world's only viable economic system'), and 'the logic of modern natural science' was the driving force behind human affairs in his brave new post-ideological world:

> Technology makes possible the limitless accumulation of wealth, and thus the satisfaction of an ever-expanding set of human

desires. This process guarantees an increasing homogenisation of all human societies, regardless of their historical origins or cultural inheritances. All countries undergoing economic modernisation must increasingly resemble one another; they must unify nationally on the basis of a centralised state, urbanise, replace traditional forms of social organisation like tribe, sect and family with economically rational ones based on function and efficiency, and provide for the universal education of their citizens. Such societies have become increasingly linked with one another through global markets and the spread of a universal consumer culture. Moreover, the logic of modern natural science would seem to dictate a universal evolution in the direction of capitalism.

For a short while, 'Fukuyama-ism' was an extremely successful faith. Obviously history was not over in the sense that 'events' had stopped happening, but the sense that History with a capital H had in some way resolved the wrenching ideological clashes which had tossed humanity around so horribly during the twentieth century chimed with the mood of optimism with which the 1990s began. With the poison of ideological struggle drawn from the international political system, problems seemed almost bewilderingly easy to solve; country after country embraced democracy without anyone dying (Romania seemed in those heady days to be the exception that proved the rule rather than a harbinger of a frightening new Balkan trend), and the biggest and most obvious piece of unfinished business in Europe – the re-unification of Germany – was tidied up within a matter of months with the minimum of fuss. When Saddam Hussein invaded Kuwait in August 1990 the international community responded just as the Gospel of the New World Order said it should; former enemies united to condemn an obvious wrong by an old-fashioned tyrant who had not noticed the way the world had changed, the United Nations – which had laboured under the burden of ideological discord almost from the moment of its founding – suddenly began to function as the guarantor of international law it was supposed to be, and American military might was deployed in its service.

John Paul was the only big international figure who consistently

challenged the American strategy which led to war in Iraq
(François Mitterrand and Mikhail Gorbachev both had their
reservations, but in the end they followed the logic of American
power). Between August 1990 and January 1991 President George
Bush senior and his secretary of state, James Baker, painstakingly
put together a political and military coalition against Saddam
Hussein through a series of UN resolutions, and steadily turned
the diplomatic screw on the Iraqi leader with the threat that force
would be used if he did not comply with the Security Council's
demands – according to the logic of the American position, a
credible threat of force represented the only real hope of achieving
a peaceful solution, because it was the only pressure Saddam
would take seriously. Throughout those months John Paul was
equally assiduous in trying to ensure that war never happened –
he preached, wrote letters and bent ears in a campaign that
continued right up until the last moment and beyond; on 12
January – three days after the American secretary of state James
Baker and his Iraqi opposite number Tariq Aziz had met at a
hotel in Geneva for what was clearly the last possible opportunity
to find a peaceful solution – John Paul argued that peace was still
a real option in his New Year address to the diplomatic corps of
the Holy See. On 15 January, the day before hostilities began, he
wrote to both George Bush and Saddam Hussein appealing to
each for a change of heart. When the bombs began to fall on 16
January itself he telephoned the American president to say that
he hoped the coalition would win, but his public comments were
still giving a priority to the push for peace before all else – there
was a delegation of Iraqi Christian leaders in Rome that day and
he used the occasion to call for the withdrawal of all foreign
armies from the region, and to describe the UN trade embargo
against Iraq as 'a ghastly crime against humanity'.

John Paul was, of course, simply wrong in his obstinate belief
that the breach of international law represented by the invasion
of Kuwait could be reversed without the use of force – or, at the
very least, without that threat. There is no evidence whatever that
Saddam Hussein would have been persuaded to pull out of Kuwait
by months of patient diplomacy; his only real strategy during the
conflict was to keep back enough men and weapons to be able to

deal with the insurgency which followed the war, and he continued to cause trouble for the rest of the 1990s through a combination of tricksy diplomacy and (we now know) a systematic subversion of the UN system through the corrupt debauching of the oil-for-food programme. And yet if you look back at what John Paul said during the lead-up to the first Gulf War, it does have an unsettlingly prophetic quality. He warned that violence would not settle the region's problems and that the conflict would have 'unforeseeable, but certainly disastrous consequences'; writing after another Gulf War and the appalling internecine blood-letting that followed the downfall of Saddam Hussein it is difficult not to concede his prescience. He also tried to place the Gulf crisis in the wider context of the other conflicts in the Middle East, and spoke forcefully of the need to address the Palestinian question. At the time that looked a little like a naïve willingness to accept the Iraqi regime's agenda – Saddam Hussein sought repeatedly to deflect attention from what he had done in Kuwait by raising the issue of the Palestinians – but again, today that kind of thinking is mainstream.

When the Gulf crisis erupted, George Bush senior had replaced Ronald Reagan as President of the United States, and the split between the White House and the Vatican which it revealed is sometimes put down to a generally less harmonious relationship following the change of administration in Washington. During the 1980s John Paul and Ronald Reagan had found themselves – broadly speaking – on the same side in both Eastern Europe and Latin America, and when Carl Bernstein and Marco Politi brought out their biography *His Holiness: John Paul II and the Hidden History of Our Time* in 1996 they caused a stir by arguing that there had been a kind of grand anti-communist alliance between the two – the picture they painted was enticingly filled out with details of the way William Casey, Ronald Reagan's Roman Catholic CIA director, would slip into the papal apartments to provide John Paul with classified American intelligence. The thesis provided plenty of ammunition for those disposed to caricature John Paul's role as a political figure – whether they were right-wing American ideologues who wanted to claim him as one of their own or left-wing critics who liked to see him as a Reaganite lackey – but he was in fact every bit as independent-minded in his approach to the United States as he had been on every other big issue that had confronted him, from his attitude to Jews as a young boy and his response to the Nazi occupation onwards.

John Paul's critique of the model which America offered the world had always been bracingly tough, and even during the period of his alleged ideological and political intimacy with Ronald Reagan he was saying and writing things the Washington administration did not want to hear or read; on his 1987 American tour, for example, he laid into the inequalities in American society, drawing attention to the obvious but politically unpalatable fact that 'the black community suffers a disproportionate share of economic deprivation' and telling Reagan's America that 'far too many of your young people receive a less than equal opportunity'. At an open-air mass in San Antonio, in Texas, he also told the congregation of 350,000 – which included many Mexicans who had slipped over the border illegally to work in the United States – that he supported the Sanctuary Movement, a church-sponsored organisation which Ronald Reagan's administration accused of illegal activities because of the way it looked after migrants and political refugees from Latin America. And at the end of that year he wrote one of his social encyclicals – *Sollicitudo Rei Socialis,* or *On the Social Concerns of the Church* – which so upset conservative circles in the United States that a deputation of leading right-wing Catholic intellectuals was despatched to Rome to lobby the Vatican. The document seemed to suggest that 'liberal capitalism' and 'Marxist collectivism' were in some way morally equivalent, both 'imperfect' systems 'in need of radical correction'. It declared that 'each of the two *blocs* (capitalist West and communist East) harbours in its own way a tendency towards imperialism . . . or towards neo-colonialism; an easy temptation to which they frequently succumb'. It blamed the increasing economic gap between the developed and developing worlds on the way the richer nations had used their power and wealth over the previous decades. And that word 'solidarity' was back, used now in a way that almost seemed a tease to the Reaganites who had been so full of enthusiasm for it when it had a capital S and was seen as a mechanism for giving the Soviets a bloody nose; in *Sollicitudo Rei*

Socialis solidarity is a Christian virtue which obliges the rich to help the poor.

His next foray into the field of superpower politics and economic theory was made in the immediate aftermath of the Gulf War, in May 1991. Communism had of course more or less disappeared by then – at least as a serious force in European politics – so talk of a moral equivalence between two blocs no longer made much sense, and in *Centisimus Annus* John Paul is much more generous in his treatment of capitalism, which he describes as 'the victorious social system'. But the encyclical still contains plenty of warnings about the signs of decadence the pope identified in the advanced societies of Europe and North America – drug abuse, pornography and the like – and the principles of Christian humanism which had formed the bedrock of John Paul's objections to communism now tempered his enthusiasm for capitalism. 'The Church acknowledges the legitimate role of profit as an indication that a business is functioning well,' he wrote, but

> profitability is not the only indicator of a firm's condition. It is possible for the financial accounts to be in order and yet for the people – who make up the firm's most valuable asset – to be humiliated and their dignity offended . . . In fact, the purpose of a business is not simply to make a profit, but is to be found in its very existence as a community of persons who in various ways are endeavouring to satisfy their basic needs, and who form a particular group at the service of the whole society.

The month after the publication of *Centisimus Annus* John Paul gave vent to a series of jeremiads against the Cold War's ideological victors. The occasion was yet another trip to Poland, and he spoke with the high emotion that his journeys home almost invariably inspired. Poland was now led by the hero of Solidarity, Lech Walesa, but it showed no signs at all of becoming the kind of ideal Catholic society John Paul had once dreamed of – quite the reverse, in fact. The collapse of communism had deprived the Church of its unique appeal as the only source of resistance to an oppressive state. Many Poles now seemed more interested in pursuing Western goods and Western values than they were in their faith, and they resented the way priests and bishops tried to use their influence in their newly open society. There was a national debate in progress about a church-backed parliamentary bill to restrict abortion, and, to the pope's great distress, several prominent Catholics stood in open opposition to the Church's position. What was more, discussion of Poland's future relationship with the European Union was being conducted in a manner which he saw as materialistic and shallow.

For nine days in June John Paul stomped up and down the country hectoring and lecturing. He called the consumerism he saw around him 'a freedom that enslaves', and characterised Western Europe as 'a whole civilisation of desire and pleasure which is now lording it over us, profiting from various means of seduction'. 'Is this civilisation or anti-civilisation?' he demanded. There was more than a hint of wounded national pride in some of his comments: 'We do not have to *enter* Europe,' he declared, 'we created it. We created it, incurring greater hardships than those who are credited with, or credit themselves with, being the keepers of the European spirit.' Sometimes his feelings about the European Union and abortion became entangled with one another: 'And what should be the criteria for Europeanism?' he demanded. 'Freedom? What kind of Freedom? Freedom to take the life of an unborn child?' Many of these comments were made off the cuff, and even John Paul seemed to realise that he overstepped the mark from time to time. 'Pardon my burning words,' he said, 'but I had to say them.' John Paul's angry tone was badly out of harmony with the public mood in Poland, and the visit left a bitter after-taste; Jonathan Kwitny quotes a former Solidarity activist and papal fan who told him, 'It was as if he had lost touch with the country. We had so many problems. Instead of talking about them, he talked about these things we were sick and tired of – abortion. Instead of trying to understand us and teach us he was wagging his finger: "Everything that comes from the West is corrupt – liberalism, capitalism, pornography."'

Part of this was personal disappointment. Poland had fulfilled the first part of her destiny by spearheading the final assault on communism in the East, but she was failing woefully in the other role John Paul had assigned to his homeland – that of providing a shining Catholic example which would reinvigorate the Christian character of the West. But the early years of the 1990s also marked the moment when, in a more general way, John Paul fell out of love with modernity – or at least with modernity as it was manifest in the gospel according to Francis Fukuyama. In one sense the Fukuyama view of the world was very similar to that of John Paul: it was premised on the idea of history as progress towards the realisation of an ideal human condition. However, neither Christ nor sin get so much as a mention in the index of Fukuyama's seminal work, and at another level Fukuyama-ism – in which the End of History is defined in largely materialist terms and peoples give up their 'historical inheritances and cultural inheritances', becoming more homogenised as technology and economic efficiency determine their destiny – was something close to hell for John Paul; for him History would end with Salvation. With his direct experience of Nazism and communism, this mystic Pole believed that culture was the only way a nation could preserve its soul.

There were physical trials to match his spiritual distemper. In the summer of 1992 John Paul experienced stomach pains which led to the discovery of a large – though benign – tumour in his lower intestine. The operation to remove it took four hours, and several gallstones were extracted at the same time. John Paul came through it as well as could be expected, but he was a seventy-two-year-old man by then, and it took him a couple of months – at Castel Gandolfo and in a cottage in the Dolomites – to recuperate. Speculation about his death and successor began in earnest and would continue for the rest of the decade, and there were two more blows to his health to come. In November the following year he slipped on a piece of newly installed carpet after an audience in the Vatican and fell down several of the steps near his throne. An X-ray revealed that he had broken his right shoulder – although he still managed to greet people with his left hand in the immediate aftermath of the accident. The plaster cast meant giving up his practice of writing in longhand in his chapel, and an amanuensis was called in with a lap-top computer. Four months later there was an even more serious incident – John Paul fell over in his bath and had to make yet another trip to the Gemelli Hospital, this time for a hip replacement. Vatican Radio somewhat melodramatically declared, 'Once again the pope is a pilgrim in the world of suffering – of his own personal suffering – he who already bears on his shoulders the weight of sorrows of humanity.' Thereafter John Paul walked with the help of a cane.

In the midst of these painful reminders that he had long passed the age at which most modern leaders leave public life, John Paul produced his most significant document. If the sermons of his Polish trip seemed at times like a scatter-gun assault on the modern world, the encyclical *Veritatis Splendor* – 'The Splendour of Truth' – was a magisterial rolling barrage. It is intellectually muscular, meaty enough to be published as a small book, and informed by an unrelenting seriousness of purpose which makes it a compelling read. It also contains passages of real beauty. The encyclical brings together most of the big themes of John Paul's life, and the confrontational clarity with which he makes his case suggests he intended it to be controversial. The reaction it provoked in some quarters was extreme indeed; the distinguished moral theologian Bernard Haring told the readers of the London-based Catholic magazine *The Tablet* that 'After reading the new papal encyclical carefully, I felt greatly discouraged. Several hours later I suffered long-lasting seizures of the brain, and looked forward to leaving the Church on earth for the Church in heaven.'

John Paul declares that his purpose in writing the encyclical is to address a crisis in the Church:

> Today . . . *it seems necessary to reflect on the whole of the Church's moral teaching* [the italics are his] with the precise goal of recalling certain fundamental truths of Catholic doctrine which, in present circumstances, risk being distorted or denied . . . It is no longer a matter of limited and occasional dissent, but of an overall and systematic calling into question of traditional moral doctrine.

But the tone of the encyclical is anything but 'churchy' – its sweep embraces the broadest possible critique of the post-communist world, and its argument draws deeply on John Paul's lived

experience of the great currents of twentieth-century history.
Thus

> Today, when many countries have seen the fall of ideologies
> which bound politics to a totalitarian conception of the world –
> Marxism being the foremost of these – there is no less grave a
> danger that the fundamental rights of the human person will
> be denied and that the religious yearnings which arise in the
> heart of every human being will be absorbed once again into
> politics. This is the *risk of an alliance between democracy and
> ethical relativism*, which would remove any sure moral reference
> point from political and social life, and on a deeper level make
> the acknowledgement of truth impossible. Indeed, 'if there is
> no ultimate truth to guide or direct political activity, then ideas
> and convictions can easily be manipulated for reasons of power.
> As history demonstrates, a democracy without values easily
> turns into open or thinly disguised totalitarianism.'

John Paul is quoting himself at the end of that passage, and these
are the mature reflections of someone with the clear-eyed and
deep understanding of totalitarianism I have tried to describe in
earlier chapters; the memory of the randomness of evil which he
had experienced in wartime Krakow had not left him.

John Paul's answer to the crisis of modernity is to reassert the
general principle that there is such a thing as absolute truth, and
specifically that there are some actions which are 'intrinsically
evil' in an absolutely true sense: 'there exist acts which *per se* and
in themselves, independently of circumstances, are always seriously
wrong by reason of their object.' He swats away the relativist
argument that the moral character of these actions can be
determined only by reference to the motivation of the person
taking them:

> If acts are intrinsically evil, a good intention or particular
> circumstances can diminish their evil, but they cannot remove
> it. They remain 'irremediably' evil acts; *per se* and in themselves
> they are not capable of being ordered to God and to the good
> of the person . . . circumstances or intentions can never trans-

251

form an act intrinsically evil by virtue of its object into an act 'subjectively' good or defensible as a choice.

And John Paul quotes St Paul's first letter to the Corinthians to suggest that those guilty of intrinsically evil acts will not 'inherit the Kingdom of God'. To put the case crudely, 'sins are an objective reality, and don't think you will get away with it on Judgement Day by trying to claim you had good reasons for committing one'. It is bracing stuff.

The source of the difficulty many people had with the encyclical becomes apparent when you look at the list of acts which are judged to merit the 'intrinsically evil' sticker; there are some trendy modern ones which John Paul draws from a Vatican II document – genocide, 'physical and mental torture and attempts to coerce the human spirit', prostitution and people-trafficking, 'degrading conditions of work which treat labourers as mere instruments of profit' among them – and some good old-fashioned ones courtesy of Saints Paul and Augustine – fornication, adultery, theft, blasphemy and so on. And slipped into the middle of these, with a paragraph all to itself, is our old friend 'contraceptive practices whereby the conjugal act is intentionally rendered infertile'. The way the passage is written allows for a tiny area of ambiguous wriggle room, but, as John Wilkins, then the editor of *The Tablet*, put it, 'clearly contraception is envisaged as one of those acts which are always and everywhere forbidden irrespective of intention and consequence'. That effectively closed off any future debate about whether contraception might be legitimate if it was used to prevent a greater evil (such as HIV infection), and it was a startling statement to make in the context of the many millions of Catholics who – as the pope perfectly well knew – had long ago reached the settled conviction that contraception is at worst morally neutral and in many circumstances a positive blessing. When John Paul wrote *Love and Responsibility* in the 1950s he was concerned about the pastoral problem of selling a difficult doctrine to men and women whose lives he knew and cared about; when he writes about the same issue in the 1990s it is thrown down like a kind of gauntlet, a challenge to the world's Catholics to prove their fidelity.

'The pope is confident that he has a binding duty to proclaim his teaching with no calculation whatsoever about the foreseeable practical consequences for the people concerned and for the whole church,' wrote Bernhard Haring in his commentary on the encyclical. 'He would consider such considerations unlawful and dangerous, because they take into account a weighing of values. Whatever the risk, whatever the danger, he believes that his insights brook no dissent, but can be met only with obedience.' His distress about the encyclical reflected the fact that – like John Paul's first encyclical, *Redemptor Hominis* – *Veritatis Splendor* has some tough words for Catholic theologians who, the pope writes, have a duty to 'set forth the Church's teaching and to give loyal assent, both internal and external, to the Magisterium's teaching in the areas of both dogma and morality'. 'John Paul's starting point is a high sense of duty, combined with an absolute trust in his own competence, with the assistance of the Holy Spirit,' retorts Haring through his fit of the vapours in *The Tablet*, 'and this absolute trust in his own powers is coupled with a profound distrust towards all theologians (particularly moral theologians) who might not be in total sympathy with him.' Others seemed to admire the way John Paul had apparently boxed in liberals like Haring. 'Liberals who dissent from the doctrine reaffirmed in the encyclical now have only three choices,' wrote Germain Grisez, the professor of Christian ethics at Mount St Mary's College in Maryland, in the same magazine, 'to admit they have been mistaken, to admit they do not believe God's word, or to claim that the Pope is grossly misinterpreting the Bible.'

Veritatis Splendor was published on 5 October 1993. During a few crowded months the following spring the pace of the pontificate picked up again in a way that recalled the papal activism of the early 1980s. But John Paul's tone was very different now; admonition had replaced optimism, and with his great spiritual *oeuvre* now out there as a challenge, he really did seem determined to take on the modern world and all its works. Reproduction and the role of women were to be the principal battlegrounds.

The Church of England's General Synod finally gave a proposal for women priests the necessary two-thirds majority in November

1992, and in March 1994 thirty-two women were ordained in Bristol Cathedral. John Paul had, as we have seen, made it as plain as he could to the Anglican Church that this would not be a welcome development, but two months after the service in Bristol Cathedral, while still confined to his hospital bed recovering from his hip operation, he took matters much further with the publication of a new ruling on the question. The apostolic letter *Ordinatio Sacerdotalis* – 'On Priestly Ordination' – is a relatively brief document, but its impact will be felt for many decades to come.

The significance of the document lay not in its ideas but in the degree of authority it claimed. The traditional position of the Church on the question of women priests has rested on the fact that Jesus called only men as his apostles – that makes it, goes the argument, a matter of divine will rather than human choice. John Paul now took it upon himself to declare that the divine origins of the ban on women priests meant that 'the Church has no authority whatsoever to confer priestly ordination on women and that this judgement was to be definitely held by all the Church faithful' – in other words, it was not so much that he or any other pope would not change the rules: rather, they *could* not. John Paul made the statement, he wrote, 'in order that all doubt may be removed regarding a matter of great importance, a matter which pertains to the Church's divine constitution'. And to close any remote possibility that the individual conscience of some Catholics might find a little wriggle room here, Cardinal Ratzinger issued a commentary on the document stating that it was 'a doctrine taught by the ordinary Papal Magisterium in a definitive way; that is, proposed not as a prudential teaching, nor as a probable opinion, nor a mere matter of discipline, but as certainly true', and that the document required the 'full and unconditional assent of the faithful'.

Since the *Ordinatio Sacerdotalis* contained no new arguments – it was simply an order to think in a particular way – it is difficult to imagine that it changed many minds. Nor did it quite succeed in closing down debate as it was clearly intended to do – or at least not immediately. Cardinal Martini of Milan, a distinguished Jesuit scholar and at the time regarded as the great liberal hope for the papal succession, said that although the document 'does not admit of either rebuttal or reformability' its truth was not a 'truth of faith'; he rather cleverly suggested that it meant the issue of women priests could not be discussed 'in this millennium', which of course had less than six years to run its course (many people believed that Martini would be pope by the time it ended, but when the next conclave finally took place in 2005 he was too sick himself to be considered a serious candidate). In Germany and the United Kingdom there were challenges to the document from lay groups and organisations representing women's religious orders and, unsurprisingly, there was an eruption of anger in the United States. In the midst of the ensuing ruckus a bishop raised what is known as a *dubitum*, a request for a ruling on the exact status of the teaching in *Ordinatio Sacerdotalis*. The answer which eventually came from Cardinal Ratzinger's Sacred Congregation for the Doctrine of the Faith is worth quoting as an example of the kind of language which earned the man sometimes called the 'Panzer Cardinal' his fearsome reputation – it even included a reference to that most controversial of concepts, infallibility:

> This teaching requires definitive assent, since, founded on the written Word of God from the beginning constantly preserved and applied in the Tradition of the Church, it has been set forth infallibly by the ordinary and universal Magisterium . . . Thus, in the present circumstances, the Roman Pontiff, exercising his proper office of confirming the brethren (cf Luke 22:32), has handed on this same teaching by a formal declaration, explicitly stating what is to be held always, everywhere, and by all as belonging to the deposit of the faith.

You really cannot get much more definite than that, and – again unsurprisingly – it provoked further rhetorical detonations. The English Catholic theologian Nicholas Lash – professor of divinity at Cambridge – accused John Paul and the Vatican of a 'quite scandalous abuse of power', Cardinal Ratzinger's old sparring partner Hans Kung said they were trying to 'scare, to repress, to forbid discussion', and in Germany a petition for the ordination of women was got up, attracting the signature of one and a half million German Catholics. *Ordinatio Sacerdotalis* was in a way John Paul's *Humanae Vitae*; like the birth control encyclical, it was premised on the idea that what had always been taught in the past must always be taught in the future. The crisis in authority it provoked was not as grave as Paul's – simply because contraception in the 1960s was, for obvious reasons, more important to more people than women priests were in the 1990s – but it was real and deep nonetheless. Unlike Paul VI, John Paul was unabashed by the furore; he later published an apostolic letter – accompanied by another Ratzinger commentary – which spelt out the consequences of dissenting from his view. *Ad Tuendam Fidem* updated Canon Law to deal with those theologians who violated their oath to uphold the Church's teachings in this and other matters – an oath which had itself been introduced by John Paul. Theologians who questioned what John Paul had said on women priests would no longer be considered as in communion with the Church – or, to put it in a blunter and more old-fashioned way, they would be excommunicated.

Ordinatio Sacerdotalis is one of John Paul's most significant legacies. His immediate successor, Pope Benedict, of course had no intention of changing tack on the question of women priests because he was, as Cardinal Ratzinger, intimately involved in developing and implementing John Paul's position. But if some future conclave does elect a pope who is sympathetic to the idea he will find it very difficult indeed to create an elegant way of getting round the fact that any reform would mean declaring John Paul (who will almost certainly be 'St John Paul' by then) spectacularly, definitively and absolutely wrong. The position that the ban on the ordination of women is of divine and not human origin is extremely difficult to retreat from, and it is made even more so when such enormous theological resources have been invested in fortifying it as a stronghold that should never be surrendered.

It has been argued that *Ordinatio Sacerdotalis* was timed to pre-empt any discussion of women's ordination at a conference on religious life planned for the autumn of 1994. The affair certainly crystallised the sense among many Catholic women in Europe and North America – particularly those serving the Church in religious orders – that John Paul was fundamentally at odds with modern ideas about who women are and what they can do; that he was, if one is to be blunt about it, a male chauvinist. The record – of both his views and his feelings – is in fact mixed. He had produced what he liked to style a 'new feminism' in an 'exhortation' called *Mulieris Dignitatem* ('On the Dignity of Women'). The document includes a strikingly original reading of the story of the woman taken in adultery in the Gospel of St John; John Paul argues that with the penetrating challenge, 'Let him who is without sin among you be the first to throw a stone at her', Jesus draws attention to the perennial phenomenon of women taking the fall for male wickedness: 'A woman is left alone, exposed to public opinion with "her sin", while behind "her" sin there lurks a man – a sinner, guilty "of the other's sin", indeed equally responsible for it,' he writes. Male domination of women is, he argues, a distortion of the proper relationship between the sexes, and arises from Original Sin. 'The overcoming of this evil inheritance is,' he declares, 'generation after generation, the task of every human being. For whenever a man is responsible for offending a woman's personal dignity and vocation, he acts contrary to his own personal dignity and his own vocation.' It is a nice reversal of the old Christian misogyny based on the idea that women are responsible for passing on Original Sin from one generation to the next, and *Mulieris Dignitatem* is in many ways a surprisingly radical document – particularly in view of the age and background of the author.

But there is plenty there for feminists to take issue with, too. John Paul insists on the essential difference between men and women and states

> even the rightful opposition of women to what is expressed in the biblical words 'He shall rule over you' (Genesis 3:16) must not under any condition lead to the 'masculinisation' of women. In the name of liberation from male domination women must not appropriate to themselves male characteristics contrary to their own feminine originality. There is a well-founded fear that if they take this path they will ... deform and lose what constitutes this essential richness.

That richness seems above all to consist in a woman's role as a mother, and, in characteristically ambitious intellectual style, John Paul builds a perilously tall metaphysical pyramid on the idea of 'motherhood'; it is said to involve 'a special communion with the mystery of life', and John Paul claims that 'each and every time that *motherhood* is repeated in human history it is always *related to the Covenant* which God established with the human race [John Paul's italics]'. Even virgins – particularly those in religious orders – can, it seems, enjoy what John Paul calls 'spiritual motherhood'.

In the aftermath of the publication of *Ordinatio Sacerdotalis* there was a celebrated encounter between John Paul and Dr George Carey, who succeeded Robert Runcie as Archbishop of Canterbury. Dr Carey records in his autobiography that when he asked John Paul to state his objection to the ordination of women the pope 'gave a simple and direct reply: "Anthropology." That is to say, women *qua* women cannot be ordained.' Many people interpreted that as the moment when John Paul let his misogynist cat out of its bag, but he was almost certainly referring to the complex and careful – even if contentious – analysis of the differences between men and women which he had developed in *Mulieris Dignitatem*. It should also be said that no one has ever suggested that he showed any signs of clerical misogyny or even awkwardness in his direct personal and professional dealings with women; he collaborated with a number of women academics during his time as a philosophy don, and there is no evidence that he approached them with anything other than the assumption of intellectual equality.

Overwhelmingly the most important factor in deciding his attitude to women was of course his devotion to the Virgin Mary. Mary, he wrote, 'sheds light on *womanhood as such* by the very fact that God, in the sublime event of the Incarnation, entrusted himself to the ministry, the free and active ministry, of a woman' and he says that women can find in her 'the secret of living their femininity with dignity and achieving their own true advancement'. A good deal of the argument in *Mulieris Dignitatem* is dedicated to dispelling the old idea that Mary offers a model of feminine submission, but it is worth noting that one of the *causes célèbres* of John Paul's pontificate in the 1990s involved a theologian who tried to present the Virgin as a kind of revolutionary heroine. In *Mary and Human Liberation*, Fr Tissa Balasuriya turned the traditional image of Mary – humble, other-worldly and accepting of her destiny – inside out and made her a feminist icon and political activist. I have interviewed Fr Balasuriya and he struck me as above all a tremendous tease, but John Paul's Vatican did not think his book was at all funny; it earned him a brief period of formal excommunication.

Anyone who imagined that age and illness had diminished John Paul's appetite for engaging in controversy in the wider world was disabused by the way he went about tackling his other principal preoccupation in the spring of 1994 – the preparations for the United Nations Conference on Population scheduled for the spring of that year. The previous UN conference on the subject, which took place in Mexico ten years earlier, had ended with an agreement that abortion should not be promoted as a method of family planning; it was a modest Vatican victory, and had been achieved largely through pressure from the Reagan administration. As the planning for the 1994 meeting got underway it rapidly became apparent that the Clinton administration took a very different view. A senior Vatican diplomat, Archbishop Jean-Louis Tauran, was despatched to sound out the State Department; George Weigel records that the official charged with implementing American policy, the former Democratic Senator Tim Wirth, kept a 'condom tree' as a desk ornament and that 'the tree was removed for Archbishop Tauran's visit . . . but little else was achieved'. The draft summit statement of a Programme of Action which began circulating in the spring was 'a disturbing surprise' for the pope, because it proposed what he saw as 'general international recognition of a completely unrestricted right to abortion', threatened the institution of the family and failed to take account of 'the sacredness of life'.

John Paul's Cairo campaign kicked off with a confrontation which, like the finger-wagging incident at Managua airport a decade earlier, entered popular papal mythology and helped define the way he was perceived. In March he was visited at the Vatican by Mrs Nafis Sadik, the UN's under-secretary responsible for the conference. Mrs Sadik, who was a Pakistani gynaecologist, later gave an account of the meeting in which she said she had been hectored and glowered at and treated with something close to discourtesy – she suggested that John Paul barely waited for her to sit down before he launched into his tirade. The argument went back and forth for forty minutes, with Mrs Sadik insisting on a woman's right to abortion when she becomes pregnant against her will. This is how her version of the heart of the encounter is reported in the Bernstein–Politi biography *His Holiness*:

'Don't you think,' John Paul II interjected, 'that the irresponsible behaviour of men is caused by women?'

Sadik froze. 'My jaw dropped,' she reported afterward. John Paul saw the shock etched on the face of his interlocutor and tried to change the subject.

But the woman in the sari stopped him. 'Excuse me, I must respond to your statement about the behaviour of women. In most of the developing countries men look on marital relations as their right, and the women have to comply. Men come home drunk, have sexual relations with their wives, and the wives get pregnant . . .'

The pope's look was stern; his eyes, usually so affectionate, had taken on a cold glitter. To Sadik, he seemed as taut as a spring. Nothing had prepared her for such a reception.

'Why is he so hard-hearted,' she was wondering, 'so dogmatic, so lacking in kindness? He could at least say, "I really feel the suffering of these people; but the best way is the moral way."' She told friends after the discussion, 'He's not at all the benevolent person his image makes him out to be.'

George Weigel has questioned Mrs Sadik's account of the meeting in his biography of John Paul. It is certainly true that the claim that he blamed women for the behaviour of men sits oddly with the imaginative reading of the story of the woman taken in adultery in *Mulieris Dignitatem*. However, she held to her account of John Paul's words when interviewed about the meeting by the BBC's *Panorama* programme in 2003, and her picture of an angry pope is convincing. 'He gets angry because people won't do what he wants them to,' one cardinal told me in the last year of John

Paul's life, and the way the pope set about fighting for changes in the Cairo document bears testimony to his passionately strong feelings about what was at stake. His secretary of state, Cardinal Sodano, summoned all the ambassadors to the Holy See into the Vatican for a meeting at which he spelled out the Church's position, and the entire corps of 140 papal nuncios were recalled from their postings around the world for a council of war. They were instructed to drum up support from old allies – Catholic countries in Latin America and Africa – and to seek new friends in the Islamic world (Archbishop Tauran made trips to Iran and Libya, not countries which would normally feature near the top of the list of Vatican-friendly nations).

In an even more intensive personal campaign than the one he had fought over the Gulf War three years earlier, John Paul wrote letters (to the UN secretary-general Boutros Boutros-Ghali and to the world's heads of government), preached (no fewer than twelve Angelus addresses were devoted to the topic during the summer months) and lobbied (ringing Bill Clinton directly in the White House and then putting his case to the American president all over again during an audience in the Vatican). The fall in his bath and his subsequent hip-replacement surgery took place in the middle of all this; it did not slow down the pace of his attack on the UN plans, but it did prompt a new twist in his providential thinking. In his first address in St Peter's Square after his release from hospital he thanked God for the 'necessary gift' of suffering and, in millennial mood, added,

> I meditated on all this and thought it over again during my hospital stay . . . I understood that I have to lead Christ's Church into this third millennium by prayer, by various programmes, but I saw that this was not enough: she must be led by suffering, by the attack thirteen years ago and by this sacrifice. Why now, why this, in this Year of the Family? Precisely because the family is under attack. The Pope has to be attacked, the Pope has to suffer, so that every family and the world may see that there is . . . a higher Gospel: the Gospel of suffering, by which the future is prepared, the third millennium of families, of every family and all families.

Even by the standards of some of his past statements about his own place in God's plans this was strong stuff; a quite deliberate and frankly acknowledged policy of self-dramatisation to make a point for the whole human race.

John Paul's efforts were to some degree rewarded; when the UN Population summit finally met in September the Vatican delegation managed to filibuster the debate until the meeting produced a final document which again stated clearly that abortion should not be promoted as a method of family planning. But his international campaign had significantly changed the way the diplomatic landscape looked when viewed from St Peter's; at Cairo the Church found most of its allies in the developing world and was isolated from the United States and the nations of Western Europe. It was a natural development of the diplomatic trend that became apparent during the Gulf crisis, and to some extent an accurate reflection of both the way John Paul now saw the West and the way the West saw him.

There was disappointment in some quarters about the way he responded that year to the great challenge of the Church's future in Africa. John Paul had first put forward the idea of a special Synod for the African Church in 1988. He loved his visits there; he had made nine trips to the continent by 1994, and responded naturally to the enthusiasm and theatricality of the way he was welcomed whenever he went. During his first African pilgrimage in 1980 he told a crowd in Kenya – having memorably put on an ostrich-feather head-dress and brandished the matching accessories of leopard-skin shield and assegai – 'Christ was not only God, but also man. As a human being he is also an African.' The African Church grew like Topsy throughout John Paul's pontificate, and many of its leaders shared his conservative moral instincts. But the public image of a new planting in the Christian vineyard growing vigorously in harmony with the Mother Church in Rome belied the reality of an institution with some very serious problems.

Many of them could be traced back to the way the priesthood was viewed in Africa. Some young men were – and, indeed, are at the time of writing – coming forward for ordination not so much out of a sense of vocation but because the priesthood can offer a path to social and educational advancement. Inevitably, not all of them have been prepared to make the sacrifices required by their calling, and the problem of priests who lived more or less openly with 'wives' became a serious source of scandal. In *The Pope in Winter* John Cornwell reports an even graver corruption of the priesthood by the systematic abuse of nuns, who, he suggests, became an especially attractive option for sexually active priests with the spread of AIDS. He quotes a report on the matter prepared for the Vatican in 1994 by one Sister Maura O'Donohue, a doctor and member of the Medical Missionaries of Mary. 'Sadly,' she wrote,

> the sisters report that priests have sexually exploited them because they too had come to fear contamination with HIV by sexual contact with prostitutes and other 'at risk' women . . . For example, a superior of a community of sisters in one country was approached by priests requesting the sisters would be made available to them for sexual favours. When the superior refused, the priests explained that they would otherwise be obliged to go to the village to find women, and might thus get AIDS.

There was also the extremely delicate question of how far the African Church should be allowed to go down the road of what is known as 'inculturation', the process, greatly encouraged by the Second Vatican Council, of giving the Catholic message a distinctive local expression. John Paul seems to have been genuinely torn about this. On the one hand his statement that Christ 'is also an African' reflected an authentic attachment to the ideal of the universality of the Christian message. On the other he had a natural cultural bias of his own towards many of the Western expressions of the Church's life – like the use of Latin – and his close adviser Cardinal Ratzinger was ever vigilant against the possibility that inculturated expressions of the Christian message – adaptations of the form of mass to reflect local traditions, for example – would subtly change the message itself. The balance was particularly difficult to strike in a Church which was growing very fast but was not always deeply rooted; many African Catholics, for example, have continued to consult witchdoctors. Some cultural attitudes common in Africa – disapproval of gay sex, for example – sat easily with Catholic teaching; other traditions, like polygamy, did not.

The original plan had been to hold an African Synod on African soil, but the continent's hideously complex politics made it almost impossible to find a host country that would not provoke controversy. The Synod finally opened in Rome in the spring of 1994; the delay and the decision to abandon the idea of an African venue inevitably created a suspicion that John Paul and the Vatican wanted to ensure control over the outcome. Furthermore, the fact that the meeting took place against the dreadful backdrop of the massacres in Rwanda certainly did not help the atmosphere – confirmation that eight Tutsi priests had been killed at a Catholic centre in Kigali coincided with the Synod's opening ceremony, and the news from one of the few countries in Africa where Catholics were in the majority went on getting grimmer as the Synod progressed.

Some of the ideas which emerged from the Synod bore fruit. More than a hundred of the bishops who attended signed an open letter to their European and American *confrères* asking them to work for the cancellation of Africa's foreign debt; debt relief would in due course become one of John Paul's great campaigns of the new millennium. But the internal difficulties which the African Church faced were, for the most part, left to fester. The bishops talked about some of the issues they had to deal with – priestly celibacy and polygamous marriage among them – with real frankness, but when John Paul eventually gave his response to their propositions he offered little in the way of solutions to the challenges. 'The worship services in Rome sizzled with movement and colour, and the discussions were conducted with zest,' observed *The Tablet* in its obituary of John Paul. 'But in his conclusions, made known the following year, the Pope gave only limited approval to the adaptation of the Gospel to local African cultures, and said very little about the pastoral problems of marriage in Africa and the need to overhaul priestly formation, though bishop after bishop had raised these subjects during the Rome assembly.'

The year 1994 combined intense intellectual and political

activity with a serious deterioration in John Paul's health after the hip operation – Mrs Sadik mentioned a 'shaking' in one of his hands in her account of her meeting with him, and the signs of Parkinson's became more and more evident as the decade wore on – and it is possible to see that year as the second 'tipping point' in his pontificate. His willingness to barge into the world of 'secular' politics so robustly – whether he was fighting communism in Eastern Europe, the 'culture of death' at Cairo or African enslavement to foreign debt – had by then permanently changed the role of the papacy. The Vatican's diplomatic profile was vastly increased under John Paul – the number of countries with which it enjoyed diplomatic relations at ambassadorial level rose by seventy during his first two decades in office – and one of the main considerations of the cardinals who gathered to choose his successor a decade later was the need to pick a pope with the stature to perform on the world stage. But his ready engagement with secular politics meant that most secular commentators judged him in secular political terms, and in the European and North American press the polemics of 1994 confirmed the caricature of John Paul as a right-wing old buffer and finger-wagging apostle of an earlier and less tolerant age. He had the stoop and he had the stick, and in the view of many people he had now shown that he had the views to match.

Secular coverage of his pontificate thereafter consistently underestimated his immense importance as a spiritual leader to millions of people – a failure of journalism which to some extent explains the widespread surprise in the secular press about the popular reaction to his death in 2005. I have referred above to some of the criticism aimed at his views on women. Here is a very different picture of John Paul during this period drawn by the writer Leonie Caldecott, in an essay praising his 'new feminism' (in Oddie's *John Paul the Great*). She is describing an address he gave to an international conference on the role of women in Rome:

I listened with a mixture of awe and sympathy as he delivered, in a weakened voice, his address to us in French. But the real surprise was still to come. At the end of the address he told

Cardinal Stafford, who was hosting the conference, that he wished to greet each one of us individually.

There followed an extraordinary scene as hundreds of women, from all corners of the world, filed past Pope John Paul II. A number of women had brought with them albums or writings, like children in a show-and-tell session. Through it all, the ailing pontiff remained on his feet, his head bowed in part by his illness, in part by the intimacy of each encounter, patiently smiling and blessing each and every one as she passed. As I got closer and closer to the Holy Father, I realised that some women were thanking him, as well as telling him things. I also noticed that instead of looking more and more tired, he was actually looking stronger and steadier. It was as if he was drawing strength from us, just as we were drawing encouragement from him. I was suddenly overwhelmed with the desire to be a part of that exchange.

Whether or not one feels sympathy with that kind of emotion is beside the point; any balanced account of John Paul's life has to reflect the fact that he inspired very large numbers of people in that way. Towards the end of 1994 *Crossing the Threshold of Hope*, the collection of personal reflections from which I have sometimes quoted, was published. It grew out of a never-realised project for a television interview to mark the fifteenth anniversary of his election; because of the press of other engagements the anniversary came and went without the interview, but the Italian journalist Vittorio Messori was allowed to submit his questions in writing. That, of course, meant there was no chance for the sort of follow-up challenges that an authentic face-to-face interview might have produced, but many of John Paul's responses were genuinely conversational, and the tone was quite unlike that of his formal writing in encyclicals, apostolic exhortations and so forth. *Crossing the Threshold of Hope* was a publishing phenomenon. The initial sales figures for the hard-cover edition – as recorded four years after publication – were 1.2 million for the United States, 957,000 for Italy and 300,000 for Catholic Spain, and even in secular northern Europe the book did startlingly well, with 200,000 copies going in Germany and 145,000 in Protestant Britain. And when

John Paul visited the Philippines at the beginning of 1995 he attracted what is thought to have been the biggest crowd in history; estimates for the number of people who turned out for his mass in Manila were between five and seven million.

Secular coverage of John Paul's last decade was further flawed by a failure to find an adequate language to describe some of the positions he took. Calling him 'right-wing' or 'conservative' simply did not reflect the complexity of much of what he was saying, as he dramatically demonstrated with his next lament on the spirit of the age, the encyclical *Evangelium Vitae* ('The Gospel of Life'), which came out in the spring of 1995. Much of the language is apocalyptic in the extreme (the encyclical's conclusion quotes from the book of Revelation and evokes the 'portent which appears in heaven', '"a great red dragon" which represents Satan') and John Paul paints the modern world in a *chiaroscuro* of moral light and dark, with the Church, 'the people of life', holding out against the 'culture of death'; his target, John Paul declares, is 'the extraordinary increase and gravity of threats to the life of individuals and peoples . . . new threats are emerging on an alarmingly vast scale'. All the usual suspects – secularism, the 'contraceptive mentality' and the 'eclipse of the sense of God' – come in for the usual sweeping condemnation, but along with the familiar attacks on abortion and euthanasia there is a very significant rewriting of Catholic teaching on the death penalty. The purpose of a judicial system is defined thus:

> Public authority must redress the violation of personal and social rights (which occur when a crime takes place) by imposing on the offender an adequate punishment for the crime, as a condition for the offender to regain the exercise of his or her freedom. In this way authority also fulfils the purpose of defending public order and ensuring people's safety, while at the same time offering the offender an incentive and help to change his or her behaviour and be rehabilitated.

Judicial punishment should therefore, John Paul argues, mean the death penalty only 'in cases of absolute necessity; in other words, when it would not be possible otherwise to defend society'.

And he concludes that 'Today . . . as a result of steady improvements in the organisation of the penal system, such cases are very rare, if not practically non-existent.'

That form of words was much tighter than traditional Catholic teaching, and John Paul's new *Catechism of the Catholic Church* (which had been begun after the Extraordinary Synod of 1985 and was first published seven years later) was revised to reflect it. It put a little more distance between John Paul and the United States, it was certainly not a 'right-wing' position, and it is likely to prove one of his enduring legacies.

In early October 1996 John Paul was admitted to the Gemelli Hospital for the sixth time; he had been suffering discomfort in his abdomen and his doctors decided to remove his appendix. The following month he celebrated fifty years as a priest, and marked the occasion with the publication of another book of personal reflections, *Gift and Mystery*. Speculation that a papal era was drawing to a close became common currency in well-informed Catholic circles as well as in the press, and there was evidence that John Paul himself had been reflecting on what would happen after his death; never modest in his ambitions, he had published, in the spring of that year, a new set of rules for choosing future popes. It was partly a question of tidying up some of the more baroque bits and pieces of the papal election system which had been inherited from the past; he formally abolished the provision for electing popes 'by acclamation', for example, a mechanism that is portrayed to great effect in the film *The Shoes of the Fisherman* but has never actually been used to elect a pope. John Paul ruled that future conclaves would be decided by 'scrutiny', or voting, which was already well established by custom and practice.

But he made one significant change. The old rules stated that the election of a pope required a two-thirds majority; John Paul decided that if a succession of ballots produced no result the conclave could decide to move to a decision by a simple majority. Quite what was in his mind when he came up with this refinement to the conclave tradition is not clear; perhaps he wanted to ensure that there would never be a return to the bad old days of the Middle Ages, when conclaves could sometimes last for months. It meant that if a group of cardinals supporting a particular candidate found themselves just short of the traditional winning post of two-thirds of the votes, they had a strong incentive to hold out until the conclave decided to opt for a decision by a straight majority. Ironically, the system might have militated against John Paul's own election if it had been in place in 1978, because it would have made sense for the Siri supporters to dig in their heels. John Paul also ordered the construction of a new hostel, the Domus Santae Martae, or St Martha's House, where the cardinals could stay during a conclave in considerably greater comfort than the circumstances endured by members of the Sacred College in 1978.

As the decade advanced it became increasingly difficult for outsiders to get a real sense of what was happening to John Paul's health – not least because the Vatican was less than frank about his condition. Even those who met him face to face sometimes came away perplexed. Dr George Carey, the Archbishop of Canterbury, recalls being shocked by the way he carried himself at a private meeting in 1997:

> I was dismayed by how tired the Holy Father looked. He spoke in a low, expressionless voice, and seemed almost uncomprehending at times. Cardinal Cassidy [the head of the Pontifical Council for Christian Unity] had to prompt him occasionally, and he looked like a man at the end of his ministry. When I mentioned *Ut Unum Sint*, Edward Cassidy had to remind him that it was the encyclical he had written on unity.

Yet later that same day – at lunch – Dr Carey found the pope transformed: 'he was alert, focused and engaged. There was none of the "absence" I had felt earlier. We had a wide-ranging discussion about the mission of the Church and relations with Islam . . . On every topic his view was informed and intelligent. The contrast with his earlier exhaustion was staggering.' As Dr Carey observes in his autobiography, 'Later it became clear that the Pope's alertness and ability to function in public were significantly affected by the quality of the drugs he was taking to combat his Parkinson's, and the time at which they were taken.'

Yet John Paul could still surprise, and still showed himself open to the opportunities offered by technology; at the beginning of April 1997 the Holy See launched a website, and was able to report 2.9 million 'hits' in the first three days of its operation. The foreign trips continued apace despite everything; there were six in 1997, and although the number was down to three in 1998 those included the first ever papal visit to Cuba. Fidel Castro, who was himself into his seventies by this stage, put on a suit instead of his usual combat fatigues to greet John Paul at Havana airport, and the sight of these two grand old men together was a cherishable moment for Cold War connoisseurs everywhere.

The milestones came and went. On 25 May 1998 John Paul became the longest-serving pope of the twentieth century, and on 16 October that year he notched up twenty years in the job. The occasion was marked by a mass in St Peter's Square two days later, which also celebrated the fortieth anniversary of his consecration as a bishop. John Paul concelebrated with forty cardinals, 100 bishops and 800 priests, most of them from his diocese of Rome. The congregation was 10,000 strong. In his sermon he said:

> After twenty years of service in the Chair of St Peter I cannot fail to ask myself a few questions today. Have you observed all this? Are you a diligent and watchful teacher of the faith in the Church? Have you sought to bring the great work of the Second Vatican Council closer to the people of today? Have you tried to satisfy the expectations of believers within the Church and that hunger for truth which is felt in the world outside the Church?

Few present would have questioned the sincerity of his efforts to fulfil those obligations – it was an emotional occasion, and the pope cried as children from a Roman parish brought him presents – but there were plenty of people out there in the wider Catholic family with doubts about the way he had gone about it.

By the time of his twentieth anniversary celebrations John Paul had created 159 new cardinals, and 101 of the 115 members of the Sacred College who were entitled to vote in a conclave (the right is restricted to those under eighty) were his 'creations'. Fully 2,650 of the Church's bishops – well over half the total, and roughly the number who had gathered for the Second Vatican Council – had been named by him. It was, not surprisingly, a church leadership very much in his own image; in Latin America, for example, victory over Liberation Theology had been consolidated by a steady stream of appointments of men who reflected John Paul's theological perspective. And it had produced an odd inversion of the usual pattern of generational politics: the younger bishops and cardinals formed the conservative vanguard of Cardinal Ratzinger's project of 'restoration', while the liberals among the Church's leaders tended to be the old men, those who had come to prominence on the back of the revolutionary waves that flowed from Vatican II. And some big figures like Cardinal Konig, who was, by common consent, one of the giants of the Council, were less than happy about what was happening to the great project which they had begun. When I interviewed König in 1997 he was deeply disillusioned by some of the things his candidate in the 1978 conclave had done, and felt personally slighted by the way John Paul's Vatican had treated him since his retirement. He was, however, extremely reluctant to make his views public.

Cardinal Hume of Westminster found himself in a similar dilemma. Hume was extremely old-fashioned in his ideas about the loyalty and restraint which his position demanded, but the reservations he had expressed in his 'Dream Speech' at the Synod on the Family in 1980 had grown with the passing of the years. He had become convinced of the need for a re-examination of the discipline of priestly celibacy, and believed that it was unwise to rule out the possibility of ordaining women to the priesthood at some time in the future (indeed, he told one friend, a lay woman, that he was himself a closet supporter of women priests, but felt that it would be wrong to say so publicly). He had also crossed swords with the Vatican at an institutional level, and very much disliked being treated like the office junior by the curial bureaucrats in Rome. His biographer turned up the draft of a broadside he directed at Cardinal Ratzinger in the archives of the archdiocese of Westminster; the letter was apparently provoked by one of the CDF's periodic denunciations of the wickedness of homosexuality, and its tone provides a spicy flavour of the kind

271

of arguments that were going on behind the scenes in the Catholic Church during the 1990s.

> Your Eminence,
> I am sending you a copy of my reflections on the Church's teachings on homosexual persons. The reason why I have had to prepare this document is because of the considerable distress, anger and misunderstanding which the document emanating recently from your Congregation has caused. I note that the document to which I am referring, entitled 'Some Considerations Concerning the Response to Legislative Proposals on the Non-Discrimination of Homosexual Persons', was not signed nor is it clear initially with what authority it had been issued.
> I should emphasise that great distress has been caused by this latest document, and not only to homosexuals. Moreover, there are many homosexuals who would never think of acting in a militant manner who feel that the Church has abandoned them . . .

In the late 1990s Hume told a priest whom he had come to know well that he was preparing to go public with some of his views because his age (he was into his late seventies, and had passed the official retirement age for bishops) meant he no longer had anything to lose. In the event illness intervened, and Hume's attack on John Paul's Vatican was made – in the words of one British headline writer – 'from beyond the grave'.

The cardinal was diagnosed with terminal cancer in the spring of the last year of the millennium. He announced the news in a letter sent to each priest of his archdiocese, which was an expression of a particular, very English Christian approach to death, understated in its claims but clearly designed to offer an inspiration:

> Dear Father,
> You may have heard that I have recently been in hospital for tests. The result: I have cancer and it is not in its early stages.
> I have received two wonderful graces. First, I have been given

time to prepare for a new future. Secondly, I find myself – uncharacteristically – calm and at peace.

I intend to carry on working as much and as long as I can. I have no intention of being an invalid until I have to submit to the illness. But nevertheless, I shall be a bit limited in what I can do. Above all, no fuss. The future is in God's hands. I am determined to see the Holy Year in.

This is an opportunity for me to thank you all for your friendship, your patience and, not least, your good humour.

I know that the diocese has a great future. The Gospel must live again in our society. May that grace be given to us all in the Holy Year. You, dear Fathers, have a key role to play in that.

Please pray for
Yours devotedly
Basil Hume

That phrase 'Above all, no fuss' came back to me almost exactly six years later as I stood in St Peter's Square watching the high drama unfolding around the death of John Paul. Anthony Howard reports in his biography of Hume that after watching a news broadcast which gave the release of the letter the lead slot, the cardinal remarked – before settling down to his Saturday afternoon habit of watching *Grandstand* on the BBC – that the last thing he wanted was to become a 'celebrity invalid'.

Hume's diagnosis was in mid April. Within a month it was apparent that the disease was moving very fast indeed, and it was becoming increasingly difficult for him to fulfil his public engagements; in particular it was evident that a journey to the United States, where he was due to address the Conference of the American Bishops in the summer, was out of the question. Two years earlier Hume had been extremely helpful to a BBC team – of which I was part – making a series of television programmes about the Catholic Church, and his advisers decided to call in a favour. The cardinal had got on especially well with the series' producer, Farah Durrani, a Muslim; could the cardinal borrow Farah and a BBC crew, came the request from Archbishop's House, to make a video for the American bishops? By the time the result was shown to the American bishops Cardinal Hume was dead, but the issues raised in the video were still very much alive:

> If I now proceed to sound a note of criticism, it is out of fraternal charity and love of the Church. For instance, some of us have been surprised by the form and tone of some letters from curial offices. There are concerns about the manner of some Episcopal appointments and the length of time taken to make them. Not all appointments have been satisfactory. There is often unease about the way in which theologians and their writings have been investigated. There can be a sense of frustration at not having been consulted on issues which are important to us as local bishops.

There was more of the same kind of thing in another speech which was read out on Hume's behalf at a conference in Washington DC a week later:

> It is important always to be strict concerning principles and endlessly compassionate and understanding concerning persons. It does happen that a person or group may take up a position on some issue against the teaching of the Church. How should one act? A first instinct may be to exclude from the community those who dissent. We must rather keep them within the community and work – sometimes very hard – to lead them to take up positions consistent with the Church's teaching.

The idea that John Paul's church management somehow replicated the ideologically driven repression of free speech of Stalinist regimes is, of course, absurd, but there is something very sobering about the fact that a figure of Hume's loyalty and seniority should end up smuggling his anxieties into the public domain in a kind of posthumous samizdat.

11

A New Millennium

Not long after his election, in March 1979, John Paul wrote a brief Last Will and Testament. It was his practice to reread it during his 'spiritual exercises' each spring, and sometimes he would add to it. It is a dignified document, and distinctively John Paulish (he switches between the first and third persons in a slightly queasy-making way, and there is a good sprinkling of Latin tags). This is from his entry in March 2000:

> When, on October 16th 1978, the conclave of cardinals chose John Paul II, the primate of Poland, Cardinal Stefan Wyszynski, told me 'The duty of the new pope will be to introduce the Church into the Third Millennium' . . . In this way I was prepared in some manner for the duty that presented itself to me on October 16th, 1978. As I write these words, the Jubilee Year 2000 is already a reality. The night of December 24th, 1999, the symbolic Door of the Great Jubilee in the Basilica of St Peter's was opened, then that of St John Lateran, then St Mary Major – on New Year's – and on Jan 19th the Door of the Basilica of St Paul's-Without-the-Walls . . . As the Jubilee Year progresses, day by day the 20th century closes behind us and the 21st century opens. According to the plans of Divine Providence, I was allowed to live in the difficult century that is retreating into the past, and now, in the year in which my life reaches 80 years (*octogensima adveniens*), it is time to ask myself if it is not time to repeat with the biblical Simeon '*Nunc dimittis*'.

When the Testament was published after John Paul's death there was much speculation that the reference to Simeon's famous words ('Now thou dost dismiss thy servant, O Lord, according to thy word, in peace' Douay-Rheims Bible) indicated that he had considered resigning. It is much more likely that he had his own mortality in mind. During the late 1990s it sometimes seemed that a sheer determination to 'see the millennium in' was all that kept him alive. The ceremonies at which he opened the Jubilee doors in the four basilicas of Rome marked what he saw as the climax of his pontificate.

The brilliant scholar and Jesuit Cardinal Martini remarked that since Jesus was probably born in 6 BC the millennium should really have been celebrated in the mid 1990s. That sort of sophisticated joke was a very long way from the high seriousness with which John Paul viewed this milestone in Christian history. Preparations for the millennium had formally begun as far back as the summer of 1994, when, in the midst of his frenzied pre-Cairo summit campaigning, he called the Sacred College of Cardinals together in Rome for an Extraordinary (in the technical rather than the descriptive sense) Consistory to consider how the moment should be marked. Part of the programme he laid before them called for a general examination of the Church's conscience and an acknowledgement of 'errors committed by its members, and, in a certain sense, in the name of the Church'. Luigi Accattoli, an Italian journalist who made the search for papal *mea culpas* his speciality, calculated that by this stage John Paul had already apologised for at least forty instances of sins and errors: 'for the treatment of Galileo, the Jews and the Muslims, Hus and Luther; the Indians; the injustices of the Inquisition, the Mafia, racism; religious integralism, schism and the papacy, wars and injustice, and the treatment of Blacks'. He was now proposing that this mania for saying sorry should become official church policy.

Not all the cardinals liked the idea. The criticisms voiced in the course of their two-day meeting were not published at the time, but one of the nay-sayers, Cardinal Giacomo Biffi of Bologna, took the very unusual step of going public with some of his views in a book which came out the following year. 'Is the Church,' he asked rhetorically, 'precisely, guilty of any sins? No; considered in the very truth of its being, the Church has no sins, because it is the "total Christ". He is the head of the Church and the Son of God, to whom nothing morally objectionable can be imputed.' The cardinal did allow that the Church 'can and ought to make its own the sentiments of sorrow and regret for the personal transgressions of its members', but he warned that John Paul's millennial project 'could become a source of ambiguity and even spiritual uneasiness, especially among the young and the simple faithful'. John Paul thus found himself in a curious position; at the very moment when he was being attacked as an obstructive reactionary for some of his opinions – this was, of course, taking place amid the fallout from his edict on the question of women priests – he was coming under criticism from within the church leadership for being too radical.

The pope was apparently no more swayed by Cardinal Biffi's arguments than he had been by those of Mrs Nafis Sadik. When he published his manifesto for the millennium celebrations (the sonorously entitled *Tertio Millennio Adveniente*), he declared,

> It is fitting that the Church should make this passage with a clear awareness of what has happened to her during the last ten centuries. She cannot cross the threshold of the new millennium without encouraging her children to purify themselves, through repentance, of past errors and instances of infidelity, inconsistency, and slowness to act. Acknowledging the weakness of the past is an act of honesty and courage which helps us to strengthen our faith, which alerts us to face today's temptations and challenges, and prepares us to meet them.

The first Sunday of the first Lent of the new millennium, 12 March 2000, was duly declared a Day of Pardon, and at a remarkable service in St Peter's seven cardinals, all dressed in penitential purple, queued up at a microphone next to the High Altar to make their confessions of sins on behalf of the whole Church; they said sorry for intolerance and violence against dissidents, for the Crusades and the wars of religions, for torture during the Inquisition, for executions and persecutions and abuses of human rights. Some of those who had crossed swords with

Cardinal Ratzinger may have been amused by the role he was assigned; he read the introduction to the 'Confession of Sins Committed in the Service of the Truth', which went like this: 'Let us pray that each one of us, looking to the Lord Jesus, meek and humble of heart, will recognise that even men of the Church, in the name of faith and morals, have sometimes used methods not in keeping with the Gospel in the solemn duty of defending the truth.'

There was an apology too to the Jewish people, and a prayer, read by Cardinal Edward Cassidy of the Pontifical Council for Christian Unity, that 'in recalling the sufferings endured by the people of Israel throughout history, Christians will acknowledge the sins committed by not a few of their number against the people of the Covenant'. The following day the *Jerusalem Post* welcomed the gesture as 'one of the most significant acts of [John Paul's] papacy', and declared that 'contrition for past anti-Semitism is now an integral part of Catholic liturgy'. The ceremony, in the *Post*'s view, went 'a long way toward creating the proper atmosphere' for a papal visit to Israel. John Paul had wanted to make a pilgrimage to the Holy Land ever since his election – he had been persuaded to abandon a plan for a trip for sound political reasons right back in 1979 – and the moment had at last arrived.

There had been a good deal of groundwork done in the intervening two decades; the effort to establish better relations between Jews and Catholics and between the Vatican and the State of Israel was one of the perennial themes of John Paul's pontificate, and he had shown himself willing to pay a significant emotional cost in pursuit of his objectives. In the mid 1980s a group of Carmelite nuns moved into an abandoned building on the edge of the Auschwitz concentration camp; their stated intention was to offer their lives of prayer in reparation for what had been done in the camp, but the action was inevitably seen by many Jews as an unwelcome Catholic intrusion at this most powerful and iconic reminder of the Holocaust. Difficult negotiations between international Jewish and Catholic leaders in Geneva in 1987 produced an agreement to build a new interfaith centre just outside the Auschwitz complex where the nuns could set up shop, but they refused to move, and things began to turn ugly. It was an extremely sensitive issue for John Paul, not least because of his own past relationship with the Carmelite Order; his fascination with the Carmelite spirituality of St Theresa of Avila and St John of the Cross had played an important part in his decision to become a priest, and he had at one stage seriously considered entering a Carmelite community himself. But he intervened decisively in the Auschwitz row in the spring of 1993, writing personally to the nuns instructing them to move. The ugly ghosts from Poland's past which the controversy had stirred up were laid to rest again, and later that year the Vatican and the State of Israel signed a Fundamental Agreement leading to the establishment of full diplomatic relations.

John Paul's determined focus on Jewish–Catholic relations paid dividends when the time for this climactic pilgrimage was finally judged to be ripe. The Israeli prime minister, Ehud Barak, gave the visit advance billing as 'a monumental turning point in the relationship between the Christian world and the Jewish world', and in a Gallup poll in the run-up to the pope's arrival 60 per cent of those interviewed said they viewed it positively. The pilgrimage, which began on 21 March 2000, was pregnant with possibilities for high symbolic drama, and, like the great showman he was, John Paul showed that age and illness had not deprived him of that sure touch which had so delighted the crowds in the earlier, more energetic days. Yad Vashem, the Holocaust Memorial outside Jerusalem, is a challenging stage for any public figure; the enormity of the event it commemorates is so powerful that almost any response other than silence risks appearing disrespectful. John Paul showed that flair for public humility he could call upon when he greeted a group of Holocaust survivors. 'The weight of history became almost unbearable when the Pope walked slowly across the Hall of Remembrance to greet seven Holocaust survivors,' said one observer, '. . . the Pope was not receiving the survivors, he was honouring their experience and their memories by walking, with difficulty, to meet them.' Among them was the woman who said she remembered the young Karol Wojtyla helping her when she emerged from a Nazi concentration camp in 1945, ravaged by tuberculosis; she recalled a 'handsome young stranger', who had given her 'a piece of bread and a cup of tea', and then carried her on his back for two miles from the train station where he had found her.

John Paul used his infirmity to theatrical effect again during another high point of the trip, his visit to the Western Wall in Jerusalem. The cliff-face of vast stones is all that the Romans left of Herod the Great's rebuilding of Solomon's Temple when they sacked the city in AD 70, and it is Judaism's holiest place. John Paul walked painfully to the Wall – 'slowly and haltingly', in the words of the *Jerusalem Post* – bowed his head and, in the manner of a Jewish supplicant, placed a prayer in one of the joints between the stones. It was another plea for forgiveness for the sins of Christian anti-Semitism; the liberal Israeli daily *Ha'aretz* observed, 'The image of the pope of a billion Catholics deep in prayer at the Western Wall needs no words, other than the ones the pontiff placed there. It was the crowning point of his papacy's two decades of working for Catholic–Jewish reconciliation, and it was not just the Jews he asked for forgiveness, but their God – and his.' This is one of those points at which those of us who had dismissed John Paul's importance as a world figure by this stage have to offer our own apologies. The *Jerusalem Post* endowed the trip with an importance to match the millennium moment: 'The remarkable pilgrimage of Pope John Paul II resonated through the land with meanings not yet fully grasped,' it declared. 'Hard-edged assumptions by Catholics and Jews about one another, shaped over two millennia, had been touched, softened, perhaps transformed during the six-day visit. The age-old relationship between "Christ-killers" and "pogromists" had, it seemed, yielded to something benign.' 'We fell in love with the man,' the Israeli public security minister Shlomo Ben-Ami told a reporter at the farewell ceremony. 'He is an extraordinary person, full of goodwill, a man of heart, and a man of justice.'

There were other great spectaculars of the Jubilee year. In May there was an ecumenical service to celebrate Christians of all denominations who had borne witness to the faith during the twentieth century. The ceremony took place in the history-soaked and visually compelling setting of the Colosseum; nearly 13,000 men and women were included in the list of those who were honoured, and the headings under which they were grouped helped to cement the sense that John Paul's story and the story of modern Christianity were almost one and the same. 'Christians who bore witness to their faith under Soviet totalitarianism' were top of the list, closely followed by 'Confessors of the faith who were victims of Nazism and Fascism'. The small change of Christian politics was forgotten for a moment as John Paul declared that 'the ecumenism of the martyrs and the witnesses to the faith is the most convincing of all; to the Christians of the twenty-first century it shows the path to unity. It is the heritage of the Cross lived in the light of Easter: a heritage which enriches and sustains Christians as they go forward to the new millennium.'

What, then, are we to make of the fact that later that same year this same pope presided over the publication of a document which insulted other Christian denominations more comprehensibly than almost any Vatican statement of the previous century? Perhaps if John Paul's mood could change as quickly in a single day as Dr Carey's evidence of three years earlier suggests, we should not be too surprised that the signals he sent out to the wider world should reverse themselves so completely over a period of months – or perhaps it is simply unreasonable to expect consistency from any public figure who is over eighty, suffering from Parkinson's, and working at full tilt.

Dominus Jesus – 'Our Lord Jesus' – was issued by Cardinal Ratzinger at the Congregation for the Doctrine of the Faith in the autumn of the millennium year, and it continued the campaign against the modern error of relativism which John Paul had prosecuted with *Veritatis Splendor* ten years earlier. In a style and manner characteristic of some of his later utterances, the CDF's prefect had found a new 'ism' as a focus for his invective, 'Subjectivism', which 'by regarding reason as the only source of knowledge, becomes incapable of raising "its gaze to the heights, not daring to rise to the truth of being"'. It also declared that the Roman Catholic Church was the 'one true Church of Jesus Christ', and that Christian churches which, in the Vatican's view, 'had not preserved the valid episcopacy and the genuine and integral substance of the Eucharistic ministry' were not in fact churches 'in the proper sense'.

This was particularly hard medicine for Anglicans to take. In 1896 Leo XIII had issued a papal bull declaring that Anglican orders were 'absolutely null and utterly void'. A fine example of the Vatican taste for otiose qualifiers – 'null and void' would have done fine – the declaration was inspired by the unrealistic expectations of the then Archbishop of Westminster, Cardinal Vaughan; himself a convert from the Anglican Church, he mistakenly believed that it would prompt a rush of conversions among anxious Anglican vicars. The bull had been allowed to recede quietly into the background but technically it remained the Roman Catholic Church's formal position, and with the publication of *Dominus Jesus* the Vatican seemed to be confirming that it did indeed regard Anglican priests, the Archbishop of Canterbury included, as little more than misguided persons with a taste for fancy dress on Sundays.

Dr Carey got an advance copy of the document and was horrified by what he read. He issued a press release stating that the Anglican Church 'believes itself to be part of the One, Holy, Catholic and Apostolic Church of Jesus Christ' and criticising the tone of what the Vatican had said. He then put in a telephone call to Cardinal Edward Cassidy who, as President of the Pontifical Council on Christian Unity, was his principal point of contact in the Catholic hierarchy (the two men had presided over productive talks on inter-church relations at a big conference in Canada just a few months earlier), and was given a striking illustration of the kind of thing that was going wrong in the higher reaches of the Vatican by this stage in the pontificate. It turned out that Cardinal Ratzinger and the CDF had published *Dominus Jesus* without consulting Cardinal Cassidy's Council about its contents and their likely impact; in Whitehall terms it was a little as if Downing Street had threatened war against a friendly nation without bothering to let the Foreign Office know in advance.

The biggest event of the millennium calendar – and the one which John Paul later said he had enjoyed most – was the World Youth Day meeting that August. The tradition of these biennial international gatherings was John Paul's own creation – he had held six already, in Buenos Aires, Santiago de Compostela, Czestochowa, Denver, Manila and Paris – and for the millennium event two million people turned out in the baking Roman summer heat. Hundreds of priests were stationed in the Circus Maximus to hear confessions (it was estimated that 300,000 young people came forward for absolution), and the celebrations reached a climax with a huge rally at the Tor Vergata field, part of a university campus on the outskirts of the city.

For John Paul fans (and the word seems appropriate in this context) the pop-festival-like crowd demonstrated his remarkable instincts for making the Catholic message relevant to the young. Some Catholics took a more jaundiced view. The writer John Cornwell attended the event, and there is a strong undercurrent of distaste in the way he describes it. In the high-octane atmosphere he detects 'resonances for an older generation of rallies of a different nature'. 'As the evening wore on,' he records, 'the meeting grew steadily more emotional, with the young taking it in turns to be "witnesses to faith" in the style of evangelicals, followed by a group "profession of baptismal faith", "renouncing Satan and all his works and pomps".' The pope's sermon was repeatedly interrupted by chants of 'John Paul Two, we love you', and the old theatrical magic returned in the way he managed the crowd. Whether his message really got across is another matter: 'When the Tor Vergata arena was cleaned up,' writes Cornwell, 'the workers, it is reported, found drifts of condoms outside one of the larger tents.'

After the success of his visit to Israel in March 2000, John Paul experimented with the use of papal apology as diplomatic technique again the following January. The occasion was a visit to Greece, part of a journey 'In the Footsteps of St Paul' which he hoped to use to further his long-cherished ambition for better relations with the Eastern churches. The visit had provoked ferocious opposition within the Greek Orthodox Church, some of it of a distinctly un-Christian character; monks joined street protests against the visit, and on Mount Athos – the 'Holy Mountain' where beats the heart of the Greek Orthodox monastic tradition – whole communities held all-night prayer vigils in the hope of preventing it happening. There was no representative of the Greek Orthodox hierarchy to meet John Paul at the airport, the streets were empty as he drove into Athens, and a few churches marked the moment 'with a mournful ringing of funerary bells'. There were sightings of Orthodox clerics with placards denouncing the pope, in the words of the book of Revelation, as a 'two-headed grotesque monster'. When the Greek Orthodox primate, Archbishop Christodoulos, welcomed John Paul he delivered himself of a litany of Orthodox grievances against the Catholic Church.

The pope's response was to say sorry to Orthodox Christians for the behaviour of members of the Fourth Crusade in 1204. If this sounds like a somewhat *recherché* apology, it was not; the passing of eight centuries had not altered the fact that the Crusader sack of Constantinople remained a real source of resentment throughout Orthodox Christianity. Having been told by their bishops that the 'Greeks were traitors and murderers, and also disloyal . . . and were worse than Jews', the Crusader armies attacked the capital of the Eastern Christian Empire and either stole or destroyed everything of value they could lay their hands on. 'It is tragic that the assailants,' John Paul said, 'who had set out to secure free access for Christians to the Holy Land, turned against their own brothers in faith. The fact that they were Latin Christians fills Catholics with deep regret.'

'Securing free access for Christians to the Holy Land' is perhaps a slightly generous characterisation of what the Crusaders were up to, but John Paul reached for a striking phrase to condemn their actions against their fellow Christians; 'How,' he asked, 'can we fail to see here the *mysterium iniquitatis* at work in the human heart?' The 'mystery of wickedness' is a phrase taken from a particularly apocalyptic passage referring to the devil in St Paul's second letter to the Thessalonians: 'For the mystery of iniquity already worketh; only that he who now holdeth do hold, until he be taken away. And then that wicked one shall be revealed, whom the Lord Jesus shall kill with the spirit of his mouth and shall destroy with the brightness of his coming' (2 Thess 2:7–8, Douay-Rheims Bible). Most biblical scholars agree that 2 Thessalonians was almost certainly not written by St Paul himself, but John Paul was pretty cavalier about such scriptural niceties, and this kind of apocalyptic tone was becoming more and more common in his pronouncements.

The gesture was well received by Archbishop Christodoulos, but John Paul never secured the 'Leap Forward' in Catholic–Orthodox relations he hoped for, and it was one of the great disappointments of his last years. The collapse of communism had seemed to offer a unique opportunity to bridge the divide between Eastern and Western Christianity, and it was an aspiration which greatly appealed to John Paul's sense of his providential role in history. But there were raw nerves in Catholic–Orthodox relations right across the Orthodox world. In Russia the Orthodox hierarchy were extremely sensitive to the accusation that they had been compromised by the way they had reached an accommodation with the old Soviet authorities, and they did not at all relish the challenge of a Catholic renaissance in the post-communist era. The religious picture in Ukraine was hideously complicated: 'Uniate' Catholics – Christians who had maintained their Orthodox liturgy but accepted the primacy of Rome – competed with an Orthodox Church which split into three factions, and the country's religious divisions carried a strong colouring of its broader nationalist and cultural fault lines. In the end the big, old facts of Balkan and East European rivalries proved less susceptible to John Paul's particular brand of charm and politico-religious imagination than either communism or the deep-rooted and bloody division between Christians and Jews.

But the failure of John Paul's Orthodox initiatives cannot be entirely blamed on the legacy of the Crusaders or the church leaders who excommunicated one another with such vigour in the Great Schism of 1054 – some of his closest advisers served their master's cause very ill indeed. Cardinal Angelo Sodano, who had taken over the job of secretary of state when Agostino Casaroli retired, had little background in Eastern Europe – his principal diplomatic experience was in Latin America, where he had ten years' service as the nuncio in Pinochet's Chile under his belt – and he was, by many accounts, woefully lacking in the diplomatic sensitivity which had distinguished his predecessor. He was responsible for a spectacular diplomatic gaffe in the very early days of the post-communist era which soured the new relationship with the Orthodox Church before it even had a chance to flourish.

In 1991 the Vatican decided to establish a hierarchy of Catholic bishops in Russia and Byelorussia to take advantage of the new atmosphere of religious freedom in the former Soviet Union. However, Orthodox sensitivities about the threat of Catholic 'poaching' on Orthodoxy's home turf had to be accommodated; it was decided that those bishops operating within Russia itself should be given 'apostolic administrations' rather than fully fledged dioceses, and John Paul insisted that the Orthodox leaders in Moscow should be fully informed about the proposal in advance of any announcement. The task of managing this delicate matter fell to the diplomats of the Secretariat of State, but Cardinal Sodano not only failed to warn the Orthodox hierarchy about what was happening: there is evidence that he actively conspired to keep everything under wraps until the news of the new bishops was made public. Just a few days before the official announcement was made, Metropolitan Kyril of Smolensk, the Orthodox leader charged with responsibility for relations between the churches, had visited Rome and had met Sodano himself, yet the secretary of state had given him no hint whatever of what was in the pipeline.

The Orthodox hierarchy was, unsurprisingly, enraged when the appointment of the new bishops was announced. Metropolitan Kyril's private feelings of betrayal were given full voice at a meeting he had later that year with Fr Oliver McTernan, a London parish priest who had been travelling in the Soviet Union since the 1970s on behalf of the Catholic organisation Pax Christi and had come to know the Orthodox leaders well. McTernan made a minute of the meeting and passed it up the line to his archbishop, Cardinal Hume. 'Metropolitan Kyril,' he reported,

> was quite open in expressing the personal hurt he felt over a visit to Rome earlier this year. He had been received by the Holy Father in a gracious and brotherly way, but he had been 'greatly insulted' by the reception he received at the Secretariat of State . . . even though his visit to the Vatican came only a few days prior to the announcement of new bishops for the Soviet Union, no one in the Secretariat of Sate seemed to consider it appropriate to communicate this information to him.

The Metropolitan also 'explicitly expressed the fear that the new appointees were either unaware of or insensitive to the delicacies of political and Church life in the former Soviet Union. He found their initial attitudes most unhelpful.'

McTernan stated in an accompanying note to Cardinal Hume that he had tried to write the report in a way that would make it possible to pass it on to the Vatican; 'they – in Rome – NEED to have a direct and frank feedback', he said, but he added a 'Confidential Post-script' which was clearly not designed for curial eyes. 'Kyril considered the personal approach and attitudes of Cardinal Sodano particularly unhelpful,' it said. 'In their recent meeting in the Vatican Sodano began by asking Kyril why he should want to meet with him when "his level" of dialogue was that of Cardinal Cassidy.' In other words, Sodano had kicked the meeting off by suggesting that the Metropolitan was not really grand enough for an audience with the Vatican's secretary of state. It was scarcely the way to treat the representative of what John Paul was fond of describing as a 'Sister Church'. 'He [Kyril] feared that there was a certain "arrogance" which made constructive relationships difficult and that many of the present problems would not have arisen had Cardinal Casaroli still been in office,' McTernan reported.

In the mid 1990s Basil Hume decided to approach the Orthodox hierarchy independently of the Vatican in an initiative one can only describe as diplomatic freelancing; the way the Church of England was moving towards women priests had led him to conclude that the cause of a Catholic union with Anglicanism was, for the moment at least, hopeless, and he had established good relations with the Orthodox leaders who had occasionally passed through London. He also had a powerful ally in the person of Cardinal Godfried Danneels, the Archbishop of Malines-Brussels, who was similarly convinced that the opportunity for closer relations with the Orthodox churches had not been fully exploited. Both men were patrons of a Catholic charity with extensive interests in the old Soviet Union, and that gave them bureaucratic 'cover' to pursue their contacts with Orthodox leaders. The climax of the two cardinals' ecumenical efforts was a meeting with the Russian Orthodox Patriarch, Alexy II, in 1996.

The correspondence surrounding their visit to Moscow has not been published before, and it provides an illuminating insight into what was going wrong in relations between the two churches.

The advance work for the visit was done by Oliver McTernan, who met Patriarch Alexy in December 1995 and prepared a briefing paper for the two cardinals. The Orthodox anxiety about aggressive Catholic proselytising he had encountered in his meeting with Metropolitan Kyril four years earlier had become even more acute, and the poisonous subtext of the nationalist tensions which lay behind the region's religious rivalries came through to the surface in his conversation with the Patriarch. 'One of his many concerns at present was the inter-church situation in Byelorussia,' McTernan reported.

> There, he claims, no less than one hundred and five Catholic priests are of Polish origin and the Orthodox Church are having to contend not only with proselytism but also Polish nationalism. It was a very unhealthy situation. He also claimed that despite the fact that most of the original German Catholic communities had moved away from the Volga region, the Catholic Church are reopening chapels and re-establishing parishes and preaching in Russian to attract former Orthodox people.

The Patriarch raised the issue of Byelorussia again when he sat down with the two cardinals at the end of January 1996. The three-hour meeting was summarised in a memo which detailed the Patriarch's lengthy complaints; he had other examples of 'poaching' by the Catholic Church. 'In the Yaroslav Region,' he said, 'the Catholic Organisation Dom Marii and the "Pro Fratribus" Movement have bought property and are actively proselytising among young people. The local Orthodox Bishop claimed "Orthodox souls are being bought"', and 'In the Seminary in St Petersburg, many of the students were baptised in the Orthodox Church. Their Russian Christian names are frequently changed for more Western sounding names.'

The official Vatican guidelines for the way new Catholic bishops and priests should operate in the territories of the former Soviet Union had been laid out in a document in June 1992 which stated clearly – and much to the satisfaction of the Orthodox leadership – that

> They are in no way intended to bring the Catholic Church into competition with the Russian Orthodox Church or with other Christian Churches in the same territory. So-called proselytism, meaning the exercise of any sort of pressure on people's consciences, whatever form it may take and by whoever it may be practised . . . is certainly not the method being used by the Pastors of the Catholic Church.

But all that, the Patriarch declared, was being ignored in practice, and his pleas to the Vatican on this score had apparently gone unheeded. 'The Patriarch claimed,' the memo continued,

> that all of these concerns have been expressed in official meetings with representatives of the Pontifical Council for the Promotion of Christian Unity. These meetings, however, had so far failed to go further than reaching what he described as 'paper discussions'. He said that these agreements are clearly not being adhered to by Catholics, and this calls into question the seriousness of our ecumenical co-operation.

Hume and Danneels were persuaded that there was a case for the Catholic Church to answer here; their memo concludes that there was a 'factual basis to at least some of the Patriarch's anxieties'. The two cardinals composed a personal letter to John Paul and despatched the memo to the Vatican. 'It is clear,' they told the pope, 'that the Russian Orthodox Church is still uncertain of the intentions and pastoral priorities of the Latin Rite Catholic Church in Russia. There is an urgent need to build trust and confidence, and to give a clearer witness to our belief in the Orthodox Church as a "sister" Church by avoiding any impression of rivalry.' Given the seniority of the two cardinals – Hume had been a member of the conclave which elected John Paul and Danneels had been a cardinal for thirteen years – the document should have carried real weight in Rome. Furthermore, Hume and Danneels, two old hands when it came to dealing with the

Curia, took care to send copies of their memo to the relevant officials in Rome; one went to Cardinal Sodano, one to his deputy in charge of external relations, Archbishop Tauran, and one to Cardinal Cassidy at the Council for Christian Unity.

John Paul never answered the letter at all – Hume later questioned whether it had even been allowed to reach him. Cardinal Cassidy sent a polite but noncommittal response after a delay of several months – as the *Dominus Jesus* incident had demonstrated, his power was limited when the big beasts of the Curia were on the prowl. There was magisterial silence from the secretary of state, Cardinal Sodano, and from Jean-Louis Tauran a quite spectacularly rude bureaucratic brush-off. His response – dated 3 May 1996 – was just three brief paragraphs, only one of which was of any substance:

> In expressing to your Eminences my heartfelt gratitude for your kind attention in this matter, I wish to assure you that in the bilateral meeting between a Delegation of the Patriarchate of Moscow and representatives of the Holy See, which took place in the offices of the Pontifical Council for the Promotion of Christian Unity on 12 and 13 January, every effort was made to find satisfactory solutions to most of the concerns expounded to your Eminences by the Patriarchate.

In other words, 'get your tanks off our lawn' and leave this to the professionals. Hume was incandescent; despite a striking personal humility he had a strong sense of the dignity of his office, and he was not used to being addressed like that by a mere archbishop. He had, moreover, invested a good deal of time, energy and thought in the enterprise which was so lightly but so decisively dismissed by Rome. However, there was little he could do about it, and the Hume–Danneels initiative was quietly forgotten.

The professionals, of course, never delivered; Pope John Paul died without achieving his dream of a visit to Moscow, and his ambition to heal the Great Schism of 1054 remained unfulfilled. The way the Vatican conducted itself in its dealings with the Orthodox Church led some Orthodox leaders to question John Paul's sincerity. A much more convincing interpretation of what went wrong is that his capacity to dream great dreams was not always matched by his capacity to pick the right people and manage them towards his own objectives. Oliver McTernan, still somewhat bruised by his encounter with the Curia, believes that John Paul's plans faced an even more formidable opponent in the person of Cardinal Ratzinger. He says the Prefect of the CDF actively worked against his master's agenda because he feared the implications of unity between the Eastern and Western churches. The Orthodox tradition allows both married priests and remarriage for divorcees, and the far-sighted and ever-clever Ratzinger – so the argument goes – could see the challenge that would present to Roman Catholic teachings if unity were ever to become a realistic prospect.

When John Paul heard about the attack on the Twin Towers in New York on 11 September 2001, his response was swift and clear, but there was little to make it stand out in the torrent of condemnation pouring in from leaders all over the world. From his summer retreat at Castel Gandolfo the pope sent a telegram to President Bush ('I hurry to express to you and your fellow citizens my profound sorrow and my closeness in prayer for the nation at this dark and tragic moment') and issued a statement expressing his horror at the 'inhuman terrorist attacks'. But two days later – entirely by coincidence – he was presiding over a ceremony to welcome the new American ambassador to the Holy See, and although his address on that occasion attracted little attention at the time it was strikingly different in tone from most of the public comment we were hearing as the wounded American eagle stirred itself to strike back. There was no mention at all of the United States' right to defend itself; instead, John Paul declared,

> I pray that this inhuman act will awaken in the hearts of all the world's peoples a firm resolve to reject the ways of violence, to combat everything that sows hatred and division within the human family, and to work for the dawn of a new era of international co-operation inspired by the highest ideals of solidarity, justice and peace.

291

Just two days after the attacks – long before this kind of comment became permissible in polite political society elsewhere in Europe – he was already flagging up concerns about the way Washington might respond: 'In facing the challenges of the future, America is called to cherish and live out the deepest values of her national heritage; solidarity and co-operation between peoples; respect for human rights; the justice that is the indispensable condition for authentic freedom and everlasting peace.'

The American-led attack on the Taliban in Afghanistan began so quickly that there was no real space for John Paul to develop the kind of independent diplomatic drive for peace he had undertaken during the first Gulf crisis. Indeed, for a while there seemed to be confusion among those close to him about whether the Catholic Church considered that the Afghan campaign met the classic criteria for a Just War – this kind of muddle was becoming more and more commonplace, reflecting John Paul's increasingly uncertain grip on the Church's tiller. But by the time the United States and Britain had completed their diplomatic and military preparations for the much more serious enterprise of another assault on Iraq, John Paul was enjoying another Indian summer of energy.

The mix of public admonition and private pressure was reminiscent of his anti-war campaign of twelve years earlier. One senior Vatican envoy, Cardinal Pio Laghi, was despatched to Washington to plead with President Bush against the invasion, and another, Cardinal Roger Etchegary, was sent to Baghdad to meet Saddam Hussein. Etchegary reported afterwards that the Iraqi leader had listened 'long and deeply' to the papal plea for peace, and Tariq Aziz, the deputy prime minister who had become so well known as the public face of the Iraqi regime, was granted an audience in the Vatican in return. John Paul also talked face to face to the UN secretary-general Kofi Annan, and to the British prime minister Tony Blair and the Spanish prime minister Jose Maria Aznar, both of whom were, of course, important supporters of the American policy, and also gave an audience to the anti-war German foreign minister Joska Fischer. True to form, he went on pleading his case long after any realistic hope of success had been exhausted. 'There is still room for peace. It is never too late,' he declared on the day hostilities commenced. Once the invasion got underway it was reported that John Paul was especially distressed by the fact that Saddam Hussein invoked the name of Allah, while George Bush ended his speeches with the words 'God bless America'.

John Paul may have failed twice to persuade the world's only superpower to restrain itself from the use of military force, but the morality of war is one of the areas where he brought about a significant shift in Catholic thinking which is likely to endure. He was not an out-and-out pacifist; during the Balkan crisis in the early 1990s he was among those calling for 'humanitarian military intervention'. And he did not claim the full authority of his office for his judgements about the two Gulf campaigns in the way he had, for example, done in the matter of women priests; the Vatican is a world where nice distinctions about degrees of truth and authority matter greatly, and Cardinal Ratzinger stated on John Paul's behalf that 'The Pope has not proposed the [anti-war] position as the doctrine of the Church, but as the appeal of a conscience illuminated by the faith.' But his instincts were towards pacifism, and he did put his full – and considerable – personal moral authority behind them. During the run-up to the second Gulf campaign he said that after what he had lived through during the Second World War he wanted to deliver a warning to younger generations, and there is no doubt that his passion for peace owed much to his youthful encounter with history. In *Centisimus Annus*, a decade earlier, John Paul had written, 'No, never again, war, which destroys the lives of innocent people, teaches how to kill, throws into upheaval even the lives of those who do the killing and leaves behind a trail of resentment and hatred, thus making it all the more difficult to find a just solution of the very problem which provoked the war,' and the invasion of Iraq was the last great cause which really stirred him to action. Benedict XVI's publicly expressed views on the campaign were very similar to those of John Paul, and it is difficult to imagine a future pope endorsing anything remotely similar to the American campaign – particularly in view of the ample evidence that John Paul's fears were justified.

John Paul left the other great question raised by the attacks of

11 September – Catholicism's relationship with Islam – to be addressed by his successors. He had notched up his usual clutch of 'firsts' in the field. When he spoke to a crowd of 80,000 young Muslims at a stadium in Casablanca in 1985, he became the first pope to give a formal address to a Muslim audience at the invitation of a Muslim leader. 'The trip I made to Morocco at the invitation of King Hassan II can certainly be defined as a historic event,' he declared later. 'The openness of the young people to the Pope's words was striking.' And in 1991, during his journey 'In the Footsteps of St Paul', he was the first pope to step inside a mosque (the Umayyed mosque in Damascus, which is said to contain the head of John the Baptist). He had also included Muslims in his inter-faith 'Day of Prayer for Peace' at Assisi in 1986, and he invited them back for more prayers for peace in St Francis' home town in the aftermath of 11 September in January 2002.

But his reflections on Islam in his 1994 book *Crossing the Threshold of Hope* revealed deep-seated reservations. Comparing the Koran to the Christian Bible, he writes that 'In Islam all the richness of God's self-revelation, which constitutes the heritage of the Old and New Testaments, has definitely been set aside.' He judges the God of the Koran to be 'a God who is *only Majesty, never Emmanuel*, God-with-us, *Islam is not a religion of redemption*'. And although he does allow that '*the religiosity of Muslims deserves respect* – it is impossible not to admire, for example, *their fidelity to prayer*' – there is a patronising edge to this faint praise. Given his own view that freedom must be rooted in religious (i.e. Catholic) truth, one cannot help smiling at the irony bubbling to the surface in the statement that 'In countries where *fundamentalist movements* come to power, human rights and the principle of religious freedom are unfortunately interpreted in a very one-sided way – religious freedom comes to mean freedom to impose on all citizens the "true religion".' (All the italics are his.)

None of this was particularly surprising; there was an ever-present tension between John Paul's instinctive openness to other faiths and his strong sense of Catholicism's unique access to truth. During his time as pope there had been incidents of real persecution of Christians by Muslims in some parts of the world, and in *Crossing the Threshold of Hope* he complained of the 'terribly disturbing' situation of Christians in some countries. 'Fundamentalist attitudes,' he declared, 'make reciprocal contacts very difficult.' The task of responding to 11 September was further complicated by the way the attacks of that day took the issue of formulating a response to Islam to a qualitatively different level. For most of John Paul's pontificate, friction between Islam and Christianity was localised along inter-religious fault lines in Africa and Asia, and it remained a matter that could often be dealt with at a local level. But 11 September gave that friction a global dimension. Moreover, the war on terrorism which followed focused attention on the difficulties of accommodating Islam *within* Christian-based Western societies. These were huge challenges, and it would have been unreasonable to expect a man of John Paul's age and condition to meet them creatively. Church leaders who felt a sense of drift at the top during his final years put Islam near the top of their list of neglected topics.

The most serious church crisis of John Paul's pontificate began with a report in *The Boston Globe* on 6 January 2002: 'Since the mid-1990s, more than 130 people have come forward with horrific childhood tales about how former priest John J. Geoghan allegedly fondled or raped them during a three-decade spree through a half-dozen Greater Boston parishes,' it began. 'Almost always, his victims were grammar school boys. One was just four years old.' The individual stories of abuse, many of which are included in an instant book brought out by the *Globe* team that spring, make for extremely painful reading. Many of the victims were from vulnerable backgrounds – poor families and broken homes – and most were pre-pubescent or adolescent boys. In almost all cases there was a strong relationship of trust between the abused and the abuser. The way their stories are told is not prurient, but the detail of the way abusing priests mixed sex and religion is sickening. Most victims had kept quiet for years because they were too frightened to speak, or did not think they would be believed, or felt that they were in some way themselves to blame for what had happened. But as the *Globe* story gathered momentum more and more came forward; in the first few months of 2002, the paper's investigative team reported, more than two hundred victims of Boston-area victims con-tacted *The Globe*, most in confidence, to relate their stories. Hesitant at first, and often in tears, many said they now regretted having kept the abuse secret. They would never have dreamed of telling – or dared to tell – their devout parents. Some admitted that they have suffered in such profound silence that they have been unable to confide in even close friends, siblings or spouses.

It was investigative journalism of a high order and, in the best traditions of the country that gave us Watergate, it was the cover-up as much as the offences themselves which proved explosive. On 31 January the *Globe* shifted the focus of its reporting from the priests who had committed the abuse to the church leaders who had concealed it.

> Under an extraordinary cloak of secrecy, the Archdiocese of Boston in the last 10 years has quietly settled child molestation claims against at least 70 priests. In the public arena alone, the *Globe* found court records and other documents that identify 19 present and former priests as accused paedophiles. Four have been convicted of criminal charges of sex abuse, including former priest John J. Geoghan. Two others face criminal charges. But those public cases represent just a fraction of the priests whose cases have been disposed of in private negotiations that never brought the parties near a courthouse, according to interviews with many of the attorneys involved.

Most damagingly, the report included evidence that Cardinal Bernard Law, the Archbishop of Boston and one of American Catholicism's most influential figures, had known about the allegations against Fr Geoghan within six months of taking up his post in 1984. And the Geoghan case, it soon became apparent, was symptomatic of something much wider. 'The stories' were, in the words of the *Globe*'s book (called, appropriately, *Betrayal*), 'almost too horrible to be true.' Law and other members of the hierarchy 'were not only aware of the abuse but had gone to considerable lengths to hide the scandal from public view'. They 'had moved abusive priests around' from parish to parish 'like pawns on a chess board', usually without warning anyone local about the men's backgrounds. In the process, of course, they had exposed dozens, probably hundreds, of young boys to the risk of abuse.

Cardinal Law's early attempts to contain the scandal were ham-fisted. In early February he declared publicly and definitively that 'there is no priest known to us to have been guilty of the sexual abuse of a minor holding any position in this archdiocese'. Within little more than a week of that statement, two more priests had disappeared from suburban Boston parishes after the archdiocese found evidence that they had been accused of past abuse, and within a fortnight another six had gone after a further trawl through the archdiocese's personnel files. Confidence in the once popular archbishop went into free fall, and the way he resisted the growing clamour for his resignation (he held out until 2003) soon made him, in the American media phrase, the 'poster-child' of the scandal. But the firestorm touched off by the *Globe*'s story soon spread well beyond Law's own bailiwick. Church authorities across the United States began to review their files, and so too did law-enforcement agencies. Throughout February and into March more and more cases of abuse and cover-up emerged: in Philadelphia, in Cleveland (where an accused priest shot himself in the head rather than face an interview with his superiors), in New York, in Cincinnati, in Detroit and in the nation's largest archdiocese, Los Angeles.

Throughout all this John Paul kept his peace. Then in Holy Week – in his Maundy Thursday letter to priests – he delivered himself of the following sentiments.

> We are personally and profoundly afflicted by the sins of some of our brothers who have betrayed the grace of ordination in succumbing to the most grievous forms of the *'iniquitatis mysterium'* at work in the world . . . A dark shadow of suspicion is cast over all the fine priests who perform their ministry with honesty and integrity . . . the Church shows her concern for the victims and strives to respond in truth and justice to each of these painful situations.

The most striking aspect of these comments is, of course, that John Paul so clearly places the reputation of the priesthood ahead of the pain of the victims – who apparently only merit 'concern'. But perhaps even odder is the choice of that curious phrase '*iniquitatis mysterium*', which he had used about the thirteenth-century sack of Constantinople the previous year, to describe the distressingly contemporary and searing sin of priestly paedophilia; to many 'it seemed', in the judgement of the *Globe*, 'more evidence of an aloof, arrogant, out-of-touch hierarchy whose inability to see beyond its own needs had the effect of rubbing salt into raw, open wounds'. And this first public statement on the crisis from the pope included no mention at all of the culpability of the church leaders like Cardinal Law who had been covering up what was going on.

Past rebellions which John Paul had faced – whether over Liberation Theology or women priests – could credibly be laid at the door of the list of liberal 'usual suspects' who had, in the judgement of the pope and his ideological soul-mate Cardinal Ratzinger, misunderstood the true meaning of Vatican II. But the howls of anguish which were now reaching the Vatican from across the Atlantic came from within the pope's own constituency. There were no militant nuns or way-out theologians among the Boston victims; by a poignant process of self-selection, the most loyal Catholics were the most likely to have been caught up in the abuse – simply because they were the families which provided the altar boys and filled the Sunday schools and the choirs. They were also often the most traditional members of the Church: people with old-fashioned ideas – of which John Paul would heartily have approved – about a priest's role as the father of his flock. Above all, they were people who had bought into the two fundamental ideas which underpinned the celibate priesthood: that there is a special bond of trust between a priest and his parishioners, and that celibacy allows priests to devote themselves completely to their flocks without the rival claims of love and duty which a family would represent. More than two million of Boston's 3.8 million inhabitants were Catholic, and it was the only archdiocese in the United States where Catholics accounted for more than half the population. It was a world where the influence of the Church extended from the most intimate areas of private life to the broadest fields of public discourse – the closest the United States had to offer to the religious culture which Karol Wojtyla had known in Poland.

Secular critics of the Church and liberal Catholics soon piled into the debate, and it became a scandal of national dimensions. By April John Paul had been forced to recognise the gravity of the crisis by calling an emergency summit of American cardinals in Rome, and the leaders of the American Church were, unsurprisingly, facing a tsunami of questions about the lessons that could be learnt from the scandals which continued to erupt all over the United States. The issue of celibacy as a factor that might have contributed towards priestly abuse was raised again and again, and some leaders of the American Church seemed sympathetic to the idea that it might be reconsidered. Cardinal Roger Mahoney of Los Angeles was asked about it at a news conference and responded that 'All these questions are open', and the Vice-President of the American Bishops' Conference, Bishop William Skylstad of Spokane, said in similar vein that celibacy 'is not a doctrinal matter. It's a discipline. I feel it has great merit, but it is not a closed issue.' Cardinal Francis Stafford was one of the few Americans to have reached the higher echelons of the Vatican Curia (he was President of the Pontifical Council for the Laity at the time) so when he told the *New York Times* that he expected celibacy to be on the agenda of the emergency meeting of American cardinals it generated considerable interest. But it was not to be. 'The value of celibacy as a complete gift of the self to the Lord and his Church,' Pope John Paul told a group of Nigerian bishops, 'must be carefully safeguarded.' It was clear that celibacy was not going to be up for discussion at the emergency meeting, and looking back at the long history of John Paul's repeated expressions of attachment to the concept of the celibate priesthood, it was fanciful to expect anything else.

Since both celibacy and the possibility of the resignation of Cardinal Law had been excluded from the agenda before the emergency meeting in Rome even began, it was difficult to see where it could go. There is a painfully telling official photograph of John Paul reading his address to the American cardinals in his library; he is slumped at a slightly odd angle in his throne, and even though he has been given a microphone to amplify his voice – in what was anyway not an especially big room – most of their eminences are following his words from written copies of the text. On the one hand he did seem to recognise – at last – the gravity of the crimes which had been revealed; the sexual abuse of children was, he said, 'by every standard wrong, and rightly considered a crime by society. It is also an appalling sin in the eyes of God.' At the same time he seemed determined to generalise the blame. 'The abuse of the young is a grave symptom of a crisis affecting not just the Church but society as a whole,' he said. 'It is a deep-seated crisis of sexual morality, even of human relationships, and its prime victims are the family and the young. In addressing the problem of abuse with clarity and determination, the Church will help society to understand the crisis in its midst.' The idea that priestly paedophilia was a 'societal problem, not . . . a reflection of structural problems within the Church' was similarly reflected in the comments of Cardinal Castrillon Hoyos, the head of the Vatican's Congregation for the Clergy, in the press conference which concluded the two days of the American cardinals' emergency talks. He talked of the crisis as a problem of 'pan-sexuality and sexual licentiousness' and demanded, 'I would like to know the statistics from other groups, and the penalties others have received, and the money others have paid to victims.'

The papal biographer George Weigel remarked that 'anyone who has watched this man for 23 years cannot but understand that his heart is breaking', and it is impossible not to feel sorry for John Paul at this time. He was very old, and very ill, and his mind – as was natural at this season of life – was turning increasingly to reflection on the things that had really mattered to him. Chief among these was the priesthood. We have already seen that at the time of his ordination he had a very elevated view of the path he was taking, and his understanding of priesthood had become, if anything, higher with the passing of the years. In *Rise, Let Us Be On Our Way*, another of his best-selling cocktails of musings and autobiography, he recalls a youth mass in Madrid which took place while the Boston scandal was still boiling away.

During my last pilgrimage to Spain, I confided in the young people: 'I was ordained a priest at the age of twenty-six. Fifty-six years have passed since then. Looking back, and remembering those years of my life, I can assure you that it is worth dedicating yourselves to the cause of Christ, and for the love of Him, dedicating yourselves to the service of others. It is worth giving your lives for the Gospel and for your brothers and sisters!' The young people understood the message and echoed my words by chanting over and over again: '*It's worth it! It's worth it!*'

It is hard to begrudge him memories like that – which reaffirmed his life's work – and to confront the really tough questions which the paedophile priests scandal raised would have been a searing experience.

It is difficult for most of us to imagine the kind of sacrifices demanded by the celibate life, but it seems reasonable to suppose that it requires the suppression of many natural emotions, including those felt by a biological parent; that must make it difficult for all the faithful celibates at the top of the Catholic Church, popes included, to understand how painful priestly abuse has been for Catholic parents. In John Paul's case, moreover, he had, for nearly four decades before his election to the papacy, worked within the embattled fortress of the Polish Church, and the habit of mind which put the institutional interests of the Church before almost anything else would have been very difficult to shake. Saying sorry for past sins was one thing, but confronting the possibility of a fundamental design fault in the Church he had known all his life was quite another. In the midst of the Boston revelations a Polish archbishop, Juliusz Paetz, whom John Paul knew personally, was forced to resign after the rector of his own seminary complained that he had been making 'continual advances on the young men there who were training for the priesthood'. Robert Kaiser, an American writer who had been covering Vatican affairs since the 1960s, reported that one of his sources told him, 'We cannot tell the Holy Father about Paetz today, the shock would kill him.'

But the record shows that John Paul had had ample opportunity to come to grips with the issue of paedophile priests long before the Boston scandal erupted. There had been a steady stream of incidents around the world in the previous two decades, and one especially notorious case involved a controversial archbishop whom John Paul had himself appointed in the face of considerable local opposition. The choice of the conservative Hans Hermann Groër to replace Cardinal König as the Archbishop of Vienna greatly distressed the grand old man of Vatican II liberalism; I have heard an eye-witness account of König hiding behind his hat when the two men passed one another in the Vatican. Cardinal Groer – as he duly became – was later accused of abusing a pupil when he was a headmaster and 'soliciting in the confessional during the time he had been abbot of a monastery'. He resigned – on grounds of age – in 1995, but not before the affair had led to thousands of defections from the Austrian Church and the creation of a powerful lay-led reform movement known as 'We are Church'.

And yet when the Boston story broke, those at the heart of John Paul's circle still instinctively looked for their villains where they had always done – in that secular culture they saw flourishing beyond the walls of the Vatican, and especially in the secular press. At a meeting in Spain in November 2002 Cardinal Ratzinger was asked a sympathetic question about 'the space dedicated by the media to scandals attributed to priests'. John Paul had given the Congregation for the Doctrine of the Faith juridical responsibility for dealing with accusations against priests in May 2001. The crisis in the United States had marched on at an unrelenting pace throughout 2002, and the damage being done to the Church's reputation was painfully apparent. But the future Pope Benedict XVI appeared to put the whole thing down to press malice. 'In the Church, priests are also sinners,' he acknowledged,

> But I am personally convinced that the constant presence in the press of the sins of Catholic priests, especially in the United States, is a planned campaign, as the percentage of these offences among priests is not higher than in other categories, and perhaps it is even lower. In the United States, there is constant news of this topic, but less than one percent of priests are guilty of acts of this type. The constant presence of these

news items does not correspond to the objectivity of the information or the statistical objectivity of the facts. Therefore, one comes to the conclusion that it is intentional, manipulated, that there is a desire to discredit the Church.

It is worth spending a moment or two unravelling the layers of falsehood in that statement, because it is revealing both about the man who made it and about the intellectual atmosphere which John Paul had allowed to flourish around him. It was, first, based on inaccurate information. The claim that 'less than one percent of priests' had been accused of abuse which the cardinal quoted with such certainty was based on a study of priests in the Chicago area that pre-dated the eruption of the Boston crisis. A study which the American bishops commissioned from the John Jay College of Criminal Justice in New York later came up with more accurate and alarming figures: 4.3 per cent of diocesan priests and 2.5 per cent of priests in religious orders had faced at least one accusation of sexual abuse between 1950 and 2002. More importantly, perhaps, the statement completely missed the point about why priestly abuse is different in kind from other types of paedophile crime. The Church makes exceptionally high claims for its status and the status of the priests who represent it, so the betrayal of trust involved in paedophilia by those priests is especially shocking – and because in the 'restored' Church of John Paul and Cardinal Ratzinger priests were being asked to sell a very hard line on sexual morality, the discovery that they were themselves behaving in a manner that was both criminal in law and abhorrent to morality was even more likely to cause disillusionment with the Catholic Church as a whole. Cardinal Ratzinger's comments, like John Paul's Maundy Thursday letter, made no reference at all to the persistent and deliberate cover-up which had been revealed by *The Boston Globe*, nor to the fact that large numbers of young Catholics had been put through the ordeal of abuse because of the way the hierarchy had protected abusers and kept them within the parochial system and the Church's institutions. Finally, the statement was an example of Joseph Ratzinger's tendency to conjure up conspiracies without naming conspirators; who, one has to ask, was responsible for the 'manipulation' he saw around him? Later, at the mass he celebrated to open the conclave that would elect him pope, the cardinal would talk about a 'dictatorship of relativism' without naming any would-be dictators.

Joseph Ratzinger did penance for the abusive priests of Boston. He was as conscientious as ever in the way he fulfilled the special responsibility for the problem which John Paul had placed on his shoulders; by the time he became Pope Benedict XVI he was, in the words of his biographer John Allen, 'one of the few churchmen anywhere in the world . . . to have read the files of virtually every Catholic priest credibly accused of sexual abuse in recent decades'. It is not an experience that any Catholic would wish on a co-religionist. But Benedict's election to the papacy was to a very great extent dictated by the posthumous influence of John Paul in the conclave of 2005, and the model of the Church which the two of them had created placed severe limits on the new pope's ability to respond in an imaginative way to the deep-seated problems which the Boston scandal had revealed. Since celibacy had been ruled out as a matter of debate and the press had been vindicated, the only remaining villains the Vatican could find were gays. John Paul's personal spokesman, Joacquin Navarro-Valls, declared his hand in March 2002, when, under intense pressure to reveal his master's mind on the burgeoning crisis, he snapped, 'People with these inclinations just cannot be ordained. That does not imply a final judgement on people with homosexuality. But you just cannot be in this field.' In November 2005 Pope Benedict's administration took the prejudices those comments revealed to their natural ecclesiological conclusion with the publication of its *Instruction* on the admission of gays to the priesthood. The document declared that those with 'deep-seated homosexual tendencies' and those who 'support the so-called gay culture' should be banned from entering seminaries. It was woolly thinking – uncharacteristic of Joseph Ratzinger – it offended huge numbers of serving gay priests, and it left the deep questions raised by John Paul's most troubling crisis unresolved.

Amid the unrelenting grimness of the paedophile priests scandal, the ceremony to mark the canonisation of Padre Pio, the

Capuchin friar who had so impressed the young Karol Wojtyla when he was a student in Rome, must have come as a welcome pleasure. John Paul loved making saints – it was a commonplace of his obituaries that he canonised and beatified more people than all his predecessors combined, and Padre Pio brought the number he had raised to the altar to 457. This prodigious figure was in part the result of a change in the rules for the process of canonisation which came into force in the early years of his pontificate, when the post of the so-called 'Devil's Advocate' was abolished. There was a sound practical reason for this colourful tradition: the Promoter of the Faith, as he was more properly called, introduced an adversarial element into the saint-making process so that a candidate's claim was more rigorously tested. Once it had gone, everyone involved in a 'cause' – as the process of recognising a saint is known – had an interest in a positive outcome, which might explain cases like that of St Juan Diego, the Mexican peasant who may not have existed.

St Juan Diego was a good example of John Paul's particular penchant for saints from the developing world; he felt that they could give people in the Church's far-flung provinces more of a sense of what we might call 'ownership' of their faith. Padre Pio's canonisation is an illustration of his finely tuned ear for popular piety. I have noted some of the doubts the church hierarchy felt about Padre Pio's authenticity in an earlier chapter, but he retained a huge following among ordinary Catholics, and his canonisation in June 2002 attracted one of the biggest crowds Rome had ever seen. Like two of his leadership peers in the early days of his pontificate – Ronald Reagan and Margaret Thatcher – John Paul was remarkably good at communicating with his core constituency over the heads of the elite.

There was another, even more controversial canonisation in October that year: that of Jose Maria Escriva de Balaguer, the founder of the Opus Dei movement. Kenneth Woodward, a *Newsweek* journalist who has written an authoritative book called *Making Saints*, has said that Escriva 'enters the list of saints with a huge asterisk after his name' because 'his process was faulty on a number of counts'. It is certainly true that Escriva shot through the system in record quick time; he died in 1975, was beatified in

1992 and canonised ten years later. By way of a yardstick for the way these things usually work, it is worth noting that many of the sixteenth-century Catholic martyrs of the English Reformation did not complete their journeys to sainthood until the 1970s. Moreover, Opus Dei has deep pockets, and the group's leaders were only too happy to reach into them to secure the honour of canonisation for its founder; the writer John Allen quotes, in his book *Opus Dei*, a figure of $1 million for the whole process, including $150,000 for the preparation of testimony and documents for the beatification proceedings alone. There were also accusations that critical voices were excluded from the tribunal which examined the cause, and two members of the beatification panel actually voted against it. The church historian Eamon Duffy has said that 'The canonisation of the founder of Opus Dei is the most striking example in modern times of the successful promotion of a cause by a pressure group, in order to extend and legitimise the objectives of that group; here the saint becomes a mascot and a means to an end for the group who venerate him.'

However much of the heat surrounding the beatification and canonisation of Escriva was related not to the process but to the broader message it sent out about John Paul's relationship with Opus Dei, 'The Work', as it is sometimes called, enjoyed a long period as an object of distaste and suspicion among liberal Catholics and gave those who liked to see the Church as the Whore of Babylon plenty of scope for scandalised titillation. Its sinister and cultish reputation has now largely been dispelled by a policy of greater openness, but there is enough truth in the stories of strange practices to preserve something of the frisson attached to its reputation – the more committed members of the group, known as Numeraries, are given to strapping a spiked chain around their thighs for a couple of hours each day and occasionally whip themselves while praying – and there is no doubt that it promotes a very traditional brand of Catholicism.

John Paul's links with the group went back to the 1970s; his friend Andrzej Deskur, the Vatican insider who did so much to help the future pope network with the right people on his visits to Rome, was an enthusiastic Opus Dei supporter and introduced

Karol Wojtyla to some of the movement's leaders. At a relatively early stage in his pontificate – in 1983 – John Paul granted the movement the status of a 'personal prelature', a special mark of papal favour. One of the most visible members of John Paul's entourage, his personal spokesman Joacquin Navarro-Valls, was an Opus Dei member, and for those with a taste for conspiracy theories there were plenty of examples of members turning up at critical moments of ideological conflict during his pontificate; for example, when Cardinal Ratzinger held a press conference to launch *Dominus Jesus*, the document which caused such offence to George Carey and the Anglican Church, the Vicar General of Opus Dei, Monsignor Fernando Ocariz, was by his side – it turned out he had been one of the principal authors of the report. John Paul's enthusiasm for the group was part of a more general strategy of encouraging grassroots Catholic moments which he believed could revitalise the Church. A long list of such groups – including Focolare, the Neocatechumenate, the Legionaries of Christ and the Daughters of Charity – received his support, and the phenomenon of these mass movements was another reflection of his capacity to speak directly to rank-and-file Catholics of a particular kind.

The twenty-fifth anniversary of John Paul's pontificate – 16 October 2003 – was marked by what his obituary in *The Tablet* described as 'an emotional celebration with a valedictory air'; at the Anniversary Mass John Paul was able to read only the beginning and end of his sermon, and a Vatican official did the honours for the rest. The anniversary also proved to be the occasion of a revealing dispute between the Vatican and the BBC, which suggested that those close to John Paul had learnt little from the paedophile priests affair when it came to dealing with the secular media.

The Corporation's *Panorama* programme marked the milestone by putting together an edition with the provocative title 'Sex and the Holy City'. The programme's reporter, Steve Bradshaw, laid out the theme in his introduction:

Imagine a land in which love is a reality and ideal sex [is too] – simultaneous climax between a loving couple. And in this land all couples are married. No barriers to perfect self-giving; no barriers to childbirth; no condoms, IUDs or pills. Abortion is illegal too. This land does not exist, but these ideals do in the work and thought of Karol Wojtyla, now Pope John Paul II. This is a film about what happens when those ideals clash with reality.

The programme team turned up some powerful stories. They talked to very young rape victims in Catholic Nicaragua where legal abortion is almost impossible to obtain; one child had been eight when she was raped, and the programme interviewed two teenage sisters who had borne children as a result of being abused by their own father. They found a nine-year-old mother in the Philippines who was too afraid to use contraception because of what she had been taught by the Church, and they talked to nuns in Kenya who worked with the victims of HIV/AIDS but refused to countenance the use of condoms.

The evidence that really caused trouble was the consistent message they heard from church leaders and workers – in Latin America, Asia and Africa – that condoms were not safe because they could be penetrated by the HIV virus. The programme's producer told me that he and Steve Bradshaw assumed that whatever the Vatican's view on the moral dimension of condom use, it would not want to be associated with dodgy science, and it was in this spirit that they put the matter to Cardinal Alfonso Lopez Trujillo, the President of the Pontifical Council on the Family. But the cardinal – whom we last met trying to stitch up Liberation Theologians in Latin America – eagerly took on the role of expert scientific witness; the condom, he said, 'is not a safe device', because

the AIDS virus is roughly 450 times smaller than the spermatozoon. The spermatozoon can easily pass through, as we know, the 'net' that is formed by the condom. And so scientists know that there is a margin of uncertainty, it may be 15 per cent, it may be 18 per cent, it may be 20 per cent. These margins of uncertainty – from a scientific standpoint or from the point of view of hygiene . . . should represent an obligation on the part of health ministries . . . to act in the same way as they do with regard to cigarettes, which they state to be a danger.

He insisted his position had a sound scientific grounding, and the programme included the following exchange:

TRUJILLO: . . . this is something which the scientific community accepts, and doctors know what we are saying. You cannot talk about safe sex. One should speak of the human value, about the family, and about fidelity.

BRADSHAW: But I have spoken to the World Health Organisation and they say it is simply not true that the HIV virus can pass through latex from which condoms are made.

TRUJILLO: Well they are wrong about that, no dialogue is possible at that level, scientifically speaking, because this is an easily recognisable fact.

The broadcast of the programme provoked eruptions on several fronts. Relations between the BBC and the Catholic Church in Britain were going through a difficult patch for other reasons at the time, and the bishops of England and Wales declared that the film (together with another BBC programme) was 'biased against and hostile to the Catholic Church' and had 'given offence to many Catholics'. The bishops declared that 'For many decades the BBC has deserved and enjoyed a world-wide reputation for fairness and objectivity, especially in its News and Current Affairs. This reputation is increasingly tarnished.' Organisations involved in fighting the spread of AIDS in the developing world had a rather different take on the affair – many of them were enraged by Cardinal Trujillo's suggestions that condoms were unsafe. The Brazilian government hired a plane to fly over Ipanema Beach trailing a banner which read, 'Nothing gets through a condom. Use it and Trust it.' The European Union's then Development Commissioner, Poul Nielsen, spoke of 'the harshness, the aggressivity and the insensitivity and the lack of love for human beings and the unwillingness to take things seriously' which he saw in the Vatican position. And Dr Catherine Hankins, the chief scientific adviser to the United Nations agency UNAids, stated flatly that 'Latex condoms are impermeable. They do prevent HIV transmission.'

Cardinal Trujillo himself was unabashed. At the beginning of December he issued his 'reflections' on the matter in the form of a document entitled *Family Values Versus Safe Sex*. In meticulously footnoted detail, the cardinal reviewed the scientific evidence and built his case for saying that sex using condoms is tantamount to 'Russian roulette', all the more dangerous because users believe they are safe; 'leading people to think they are fully protected . . . is to lead many to their death,' he wrote. The President of the Pontifical Council on the Family argued that, far from preventing the spread of AIDS, condoms actually made the situation worse by encouraging promiscuity. The footnotes proved his undoing; in a second programme ('Can Condoms Kill?') *Panorama* tracked down some of the scientists quoted in *Family Values Versus Safe Sex*. 'I think it's misleading,' said one expert of the way Trujillo had quoted from his research. 'He didn't pay attention to the paper, he took a number out of it, and basically misused it.' The programme did find some support for the cardinal's belief that changing behaviour and attitudes to sex should be part of the battle against AIDS – 'Catholic' virtues such as abstinence and fidelity are, for example, a prominent element in Uganda's much praised anti-AIDS campaign. But the overwhelming impression created by the affair was of a Vatican cheerfully cooking the scientific data to suit its doctrinal position.

Reading Cardinal Trujillo's thoughts on the tensile strength of latex, the respective merits of petroleum-based and water-based lubricants and the impact of body heat on condoms kept in wallets, one cannot help wondering whether from time to time he asked himself whether this was really what God had called him to do. Some of the writing brings to mind the more technical passages in Karol Wojtyla's 1960 work *Love and Responsibility*, but that book was prompted by the young cleric's genuine concern about the problems brought to him as a parish priest. The Polish lakes and forests where he would discuss his ideas about sex around the camp fire with his kayaking friends were a very long way indeed from the AIDS-afflicted villages of twenty-first-century sub-Saharan Africa. The issue of contraception had eaten up a quite astonishing quantity of papal energy in the intervening years, but somehow John Paul and those around him had missed the way the moral dynamic of the debate had been transformed by the AIDS crisis. The point was made with clarity by one of the leading – and few remaining – progressives in the College of Cardinals in the aftermath of the row over 'Sex and the Holy City'. Cardinal Godfried Danneels, the Archbishop of Malines-Brussels who had accompanied Cardinal Hume on his Moscow adventure, put the moral position thus:

> When someone is HIV-infected and his partner says 'I want to have sexual relations with you', I would say, do not do it . . . But if he does so all the same, he should use a condom. Otherwise he adds a sin against the fifth commandment, Thou shalt not kill . . . It is a matter of prevention to protect oneself against a disease or against death. You cannot judge that morally to be on the same level as using a condom as a method of birth control.

That autumn saw the most serious health scare there had been to date: cardinals were packing their bags and choirs were being placed on stand-by in the way I have described at the beginning of this book. But that formidable constitution, toughened perhaps by the privations of wartime Poland, still had nearly a year and a half of life left, and in August 2004 John Paul made one of the most memorable pilgrimages of his later years, to the Marian shrine of Lourdes in the French Pyrenees.

On the face of it, the event should have been strictly for Catholic connoisseurs. The occasion for the trip was the 150th anniversary of the Promulgation of the Dogma of the Immaculate Conception – the belief that 'from the moment of her conception the Blessed Virgin Mary was . . . kept free from all stain of original sin' – by that doughty opponent of all things modern, Pio Nono. And Lourdes is – rather like the Polish Marian shrines John Paul had known as a young man – the kind of place guaranteed to mystify or irritate non-Catholics; the Church claims that since a young French peasant girl had a vision of the Virgin in 1858 there have been sixty-six full-blown miracles and 7,000 'inexplicable cures' associated with the shrine. But the way John Paul conducted himself gave this pilgrimage a resonance well beyond the Catholic community. He was very ill indeed by this stage; a cardinal who travelled with him told me that at times during the pilgrimage he was unable to speak at all, and would demonstrate his frustration by making a cutting gesture across his throat. But he seemed if anything more determined than ever to show himself publicly. There were some 200,000 people in the field outside the town where he celebrated mass, and the scene was described by John Allen of the *National Catholic Reporter* as 'a massive hospital ward, with tens of thousands of pilgrims on canes, in wheelchairs, even on gurneys with IVs attached'. John Paul struggled through his sermon, muttering 'Jesus and Mary' and 'Help me' under his breath in Polish. He had to be reminded to raise the Host at the consecration, and was heard willing himself on with the words, 'I have to finish.' It is not just miracles that bring pilgrims to Lourdes; it is said to be a town where 'the sick are royalty', and many go in the hope of spiritual reinvigoration as much as a physical cure. John Paul was dramatising the message that their sickness was something that can be celebrated.

The pilgrimage demonstrated his continuing capacity to take an apparently unpromising aspect of the Catholic message and transform it through the alchemy of will-power and performance, bringing it alive for a world audience. It was a kind of preview of the spectacular *grand finale* he was to offer us the following spring. Dying well on stage is a notoriously tricky challenge in the acting profession; when John Paul did it for real he carried it off *con brio*.

12

The Last Days

I arrived in Rome on the evening of 2 April 2005 – it was a Friday – together with a team from the *Today* programme. While waiting at the luggage carousel we picked up the rumours that John Paul was in the final moments of his life – or, according to some versions of the story, had already died – so a producer and I abandoned the luggage and took a taxi into Rome. It may have been unwise to tell the driver why we wanted to get to St Peter's so quickly – he had a television on his dashboard, and he kept his eyes fixed on the live transmission from the Vatican while driving at a hair-raising speed into the city, turning in his seat from time to time to offer us updates in broken English.

St Peter's Square was full when we arrived – although not yet so densely packed as to prevent one walking through the crowd. A group of senior clergy was leading the recitation of the rosary from the steps in front of the basilica, and the image was projected onto two giant screens placed close to the junctions where Bernini's colonnade balloons out into two vast encircling arms. The pure theatricality of the scene was a reminder of one of the reasons why John Paul had seemed so at home in the Vatican; St Peter's Square is perhaps the greatest stage in the world, both intensely intimate and impossibly grand. Like the ancient and elaborate architecture of Krakow, it offered a perfect *mise en scène* for the actor-pope.

At around 8.30 p.m. the Italian television network SkyItalia reported that John Paul had died – Fox News in the United States soon followed. The reports turned out to be false, but the day had been rich in evidence that the end was near. At a briefing that afternoon Joacquin Navarro-Valls, the pope's personal spokesman, had announced that John Paul had received the Sacrament of the Anointing of the Sick (the last rites, as it used to be called) and, though he was usually the most composed of men, cried openly in front of journalists as he left the room. Cardinal Camillo Ruini, who acted on the pope's behalf in the administration of the diocese of Rome, said at an evening mass in the basilica of St John Lateran (the pope's cathedral church in his role as the Bishop of Rome) that 'The Holy Father can already touch and see the Lord.'

Stories that John Paul did in fact die that Friday evening have persisted. One experienced Vatican correspondent, Robert Mickens of *The Tablet*, claimed in an interview for this book that he had 'a contact who was part of the security operation who said he was dead on Friday' and that he was 'told by a person who was on the medical detail that no one saw the Pope on Saturday except through a doorway of the apartment'. The history of the way past papal deaths had been handled provided fertile ground for conspiracy theories to flourish; it used to be said that 'a pope is never sick until he dies', and memories of the shoddy manner in which the details of John Paul I's death had been cleaned up were bound to foster scepticism about official church statements. It was perhaps with that in mind that, some six months after John Paul's death, the Vatican published a special edition of the *Acta Apostolicae Sedis* – the official bulletin of the Holy See – which described the last days of John Paul in exhaustive clinical detail.

The document is fascinating because it is at one and the same time absolutely packed with detail and completely lacking in any convincing insights into the way the man who was Pope John Paul approached his passing. We read of the 'pink chasuble' he wore as he celebrated mass in the Gemelli Hospital chapel, of his 'functional stenosis of the trachae', 'nutritional deficiency' and 'elective tracheotomy'. But of what he actually felt, looked like or communicated to those around him during his last days and hours there is almost nothing, save for two stories which somehow seem too good to be true. Mass was said in his room two days before he died, and the *Acta* notes that 'This he celebrated with his eyes closed but, at the moment of the consecration he weakly lifted up his right arm twice, that is to say over the bread and wine. He also made as though to beat his breast during the recitation of the *Agnus Dei.*' The document also reports that John Paul's last words, spoken in 'a weak voice and mumbled words', were 'Let me go to the house of my father.' Mickens dismisses that as 'total baloney'. Sandro Magister, the senior 'Vaticanista' at the Italian newspaper *L'Expresso,* expresses his doubts in a slightly more measured way: 'It is not,' he said, 'necessarily the absolute reality, but it might be that he tried to say things like this over the last days. It would have been very hard for him to speak at all after all the treatments, so they probably had to interpret what he was saying.'

But at one level the account in the *Acta Apostolicae Sedis* does give us a very illuminating narrative indeed: it is the story of the final stages of a metamorphosis during which the last vestiges of Karol Wojtyla the man disappeared and John Paul the pope became all icon. The papal spokesman Joacquin Navarro-Valls had often referred to the ailing pope as 'a soul dragging a body'; the manner of his death, both as it was described in the official account and as it was 'managed' while it happened, seemed designed to show the world the process of the body falling away altogether, so that the soul could be revealed to us in all its grandeur. I am not, for the record, suggesting there was some kind of conspiracy, in which Cardinal Ratzinger or the Polish Mafia cruelly exploited their best public relations asset; John Paul needed no puppeteers to pull his strings.

In the words of Fr Gerald O'Collins, a professor of theology at the Gregorian University and veteran interpreter of matters papal, John Paul 'almost died on camera'. From the moment of his emergency admission to the Gemelli Hospital with flu and throat spasms several weeks earlier – on the evening of 1 February – even the smallest changes and developments in his condition became the focus for overwhelming media attention. 'The cameras of the world's media were trained on his hospital window,' says Fr Gerald. 'It was as though everyone was gathering round his bed.' It was a little like those early days of his pontificate when almost everything he did made a headline, and when he was declared fit enough to return to the Vatican on 10 February he did so in inimitable style. The time – around 7.30 in the evening – was, in

Fr Gerald's view, chosen to maximise the number of people who would be at home to watch the live television coverage as he made his triumphal progress down the Via Gregorio VII through eastern Rome. From the back of his popemobile, 'alert and engaged', John Paul enjoyed the enthusiasm of the crowds who had gathered along the route to wish him well.

After the scare of early February it did for a while seem that John Paul had once again made fools of those predicting his imminent demise. In the week of 13 February the Curia held its annual Lenten Retreat, so there was a natural explanation for the lack of any papal public appearances for a while. When he did finally appear at his window overlooking St Peter's Square on 23 February he seemed stronger and spoke with greater clarity. However, we now know from the detail recorded in the *Acta* that his 'respiratory problems' had come back quite soon after his return from hospital, and he then began to suffer 'repeated episodes of acute breathing problems'. John Paul was back in the Gemelli on the morning of 24 February, and agreed to a tracheotomy. Dr Joan Lewis, recently retired as the head of the English section of the Vatican Information Service and an out-and-out John Paul fan ('Personally I was in love with John Paul,' she volunteered cheerfully in an interview for this book) immediately saw the implications of the operation on the pope's throat. 'When I heard that he had a tracheotomy I thought, "Oh no! He won't be able to communicate."' There was a particular poignancy about the way the pope who had made communication such a hallmark of his reign was reduced to silence at its end.

The silence was not immediate; John Paul celebrated mass in the Gemelli on the fourth Sunday of Lent – 6 March – and was, according to the *Acta*, able to give the final benediction 'in a feeble voice'. And on the day he left hospital for the last time he thanked the crowds outside for coming and wished them 'a good Sunday and a good week'. Thereafter John Paul communicated more through images than words; but he was a master minter of the wordless symbol, as he had demonstrated in Ali Agca's cell and later at the Western Wall of Jerusalem, and he gave us some truly memorable moments during his final days.

Because those days coincided with the approach to Easter, the analogy with the Passion of Christ which the Church celebrates during Holy Week was inevitable; Vatican officials began to talk of John Paul's *Via Crucis* or Way of the Cross, and the phrase is given official blessing in the *Acta*. Holy Week begins with Palm Sunday, the day the Church marks the story of Jesus' triumphal progress into Jerusalem; John Paul's *Via Crucis* began the previous Sunday, 13 March, when he made that final journey home to the Vatican. 'Cries of "*Viva il Papa*" were once again heard along the route,' John Allen recorded in an instant book on the death of John Paul and the election of his successor. 'In another piece of media savvy, a television camera was actually positioned in the back of the popemobile, so all along the route viewers saw the scene from John Paul's point of view.' According to one of Robert Mickens' contacts it was John Paul himself who asked that a television cameraman accompany him in the vehicle 'because he felt it was so important to show himself'.

RAI, the Italian public broadcaster, announced that John Paul would, as usual, be appearing in its coverage of the Stations of the Cross procession which takes place each Good Friday at the Colosseum – no one thought he would be able to attend himself, but he was expected to send a recorded blessing, and his name was there in the opening credits of the programme. The image that actually appeared was extremely odd, although somehow fitting after a pontificate which had relied so heavily on the power of the electronic media: the television coverage of the procession mixed through to a picture of John Paul watching the television coverage – and the picture was broadcast on screens at the Colosseum so that the crowd whom he was watching could watch him watching them. His head was nodding vigorously – because of his Parkinson's – but the scene was shot entirely from the back and the side, and we never saw his face.

There were two final, wordless appearances. On Easter Sunday a microphone was placed at the open window overlooking St Peter's Square, and John Paul tried again and again to say something to the crowds beneath him; he could manage nothing but meaningless sounds, and at one point raised his hand to point to the source of his difficulties in his throat. It was the same the following Wednesday, 30 March, and this time his frustration with the body which refused to obey his will was palpable. Joan Lewis was among those watching and called the expression on his face 'that God-awful look'. When she was giving a television interview later that day she broke down. 'I felt like I was losing my dad for a second time,' she said, 'and I think a lot of people connected with him in that way. They didn't want him to suffer . . . He was a parent or a friend, people couldn't bear watching the suffering.' The *Acta* described the Wednesday appearance as 'The last public "station" of his painful *Via Crucis*'; later on Wednesday the Vatican announced that John Paul was being fed through a tube, and on Thursday night he suffered 'a grave sceptic shock with cardio-circulatory collapse that was diagnosed as a urinary infection'.

John Paul's determinedly public suffering earned him friends in the secular media again; for the first time in many years his press was overwhelmingly good. Not all his critics in the Catholic Church were won over, however. During John Paul's final days I spoke to a friend of the late Cardinal Hume (whose desire to die with 'no fuss' contrasted so strongly with what we were witnessing) who saw an obstinate refusal to accept the will of God where others saw a heroic willingness to offer the world a lesson in the meaning of pain. It prompted her to tell me a story which must rank as the most tantalising I have encountered while writing this book.

Cardinal Hume, she said, had told her that he sometimes struggled with his faith, and that in his darker moments he found the disciplines imposed by the religious life and the demands of his office a helpful crutch of support; others have confirmed to me that the cardinal endured difficulties of this kind, and there are hints of it in his clever children's book, *Basil in Blunderland*. She further reported that the cardinal had described a conversation with the pope which revealed that John Paul himself struggled with his faith sometimes, and that he too used the disciplines imposed by his duties as a defence against doubt. I reflected a good deal on this story – partly because it offered an intriguing new explanation for the high value John Paul placed on church discipline in everything from thought and writing to matters of clerical dress, and partly – if I am honest – because a newspaper headline along the lines of 'New biography claims late pope did not believe in God' might generate some attention for this book. Journalistic rigour compels me to admit that what may or may not have been said in a private conversation between two men who are both dead is ultimately unverifiable.

But the story prompted me to look again at the way John Paul formed relationships, and to ask whether he was the sort of man who would sit down alone with a friend and talk frankly and on terms of equality about questions like personal faith. The way this most sociable of popes crammed his days with guests at almost every meal was in marked contrast to the simpler life favoured by his successor, who greatly scaled back the level of papal entertaining, but there are in fact very few accounts of memorable *tête-à-têtes* with John Paul. People almost always remember him in larger groups; Fr Gerald O'Collins described him as a 'lonely figure', wonderful with a crowd (of course) and 'okay' in groups of ten or so, but slightly difficult as a dinner companion. 'I once had the privilege of sitting next to him at a supper for theologians who had been asked to come and discuss redemption,' he recalls. 'The Pope just listened and when I tried to engage him on his trip to Albania that he had just returned from he wouldn't engage, he just wanted to listen.' I have written earlier about the way the office of the papacy tends to isolate those who hold it, but there is evidence that John Paul always kept a slight sense of distance between himself and those around him. As part of its obituary coverage, *The Tablet* published a reminiscence by one of the group of students who used to join the young Fr Karol on his hiking expeditions. 'He wasn't accustomed to entertain us; he never told jokes or anecdotes. But nor did he extinguish our happiness with seriousness. And he maintained a humorous detachment on many matters,' she remembered. 'I can picture the scene during an excursion to Turbacz in the Tatra Mountains. We're talking, eating, laughing; and our professor is sitting a few paces from us, reading his breviary. It seems that nothing can disturb his concentration.'

And what we know of John Paul's death suggests that it may, paradoxically, have been a somewhat lonely one – despite the way it was shared by so many millions. The appropriate cardinals and officials trooped through the papal apartments to say goodbye, but we know nothing of what was said at these farewells; the *Acta* tells us that on the morning of Saturday 2 April, for example, the pope 'received, for the final time, the Cardinal Secretary of State', but no more than that. Access to the deathbed was controlled by the ever-faithful Stanislaw Dziwisz, and he presided over a final mass, an hour or so before John Paul died, with two other Polish associates and a cardinal from the Ukraine who had served as a priest with John Paul in Poland. The Polish nuns who ran the pope's household were there at the end. But the pope of course had no close family at all by the time he died, and there is a very moving passage at the end of his Last Will and Testament, written in 2000, which suggests he felt his early losses especially keenly when he contemplated death. 'As the end of my life approaches,' he wrote,

> I return with my memory to the beginning, to my parents, to my brother, to the sister (whom I never knew because she died before my birth), to the parish of Wadowice, where I was baptised, to that city I love, to my peers, friends from elementary school, high school and the university, up to the time of the occupation when I was a worker, then in the parish of Niegowic, then St Florian's in Krakow, to the pastoral ministry of academics, to the milieu of . . . to all milieux . . . to Krakow and to Rome . . . to all the people who were entrusted to me in a special way by the Lord.

The way his mind turns to memories of his youth rather than the big events of his time in office is affecting, and it is one of those relatively rare passages where John Paul writes as a man, and not just as a pope.

I had slipped off for dinner near the Piazza Navona when John Paul's death was announced – the news spread through the restaurants and late-opening shops in the narrow streets of medieval Rome. Returning across the Tiber to the Vatican City, I found a vast, silent crowd keeping vigil, many of them praying with eyes fixed on the windows of the papal apartment. St Peter's Square was almost entirely lit by candles. It can hold vast numbers in its shallow bowl, but at moments of high drama in the Church's life – which that spring evening undoubtedly was – everyone there feels as much actor as spectator.

For all the unanswered questions about the papal death, the overwhelming balance of probability must be that John Paul died when the Vatican said he did – at 9.37 on that Saturday evening. To be serious a conspiracy theory needs a motive, and the idea that the 'Old Guard' around John Paul wanted time to dress the set before announcing his exit from the stage does not quite hold water – Dr Guido Bertolaso, who, as head of the Italian government's Protezione Civile, was responsible for managing the logistics of the lying-in-state and the funeral, described it in an interview for this book as 'ridiculous'. He flew to Naples on that Saturday morning to help organise a contingency plan for a future eruption of Vesuvius and discussed the pope's condition with Vatican officials before he left. 'I . . . saw their concern about his health,' he said, 'but I would have known if they were lying. Anyway, I met the religious authorities from Saturday evening, and seeing how difficult it was for them to organise themselves anyway, an extra twenty-four hours would not have been any use.' Even more convincing for me was a piece of anecdotal evidence that came my way as the result of a BBC2 programme I was helping to make about the transition between popes; a member of our production team was with the official papal photographer that Saturday morning when he was called to say goodbye to John Paul, whom he had served throughout his pontificate. He returned in tears, and reported that John Paul was slipping in and out of consciousness – a description of the pope's condition which is consistent with that in the *Acta*.

Poland was convulsed with grief. *The Tablet* has quoted surveys which reported that four million Poles took part in vigils and marches, a third of the population placed flags and portraits of John Paul in their windows and more than half lit candles. In an echo of the emotions inspired by his early visits, one in ten Poles said they had experienced 'an exceptional, unprecedented sense of community' during the period of national mourning. The Polish parliament later declared a 'John Paul Day' which was to be celebrated on 16 October, the day of his election. Across the Atlantic, the *New York Times* commissioned a report on the reaction to John Paul's death in Boston, and found the two million Catholics in and around the city struggling 'with how to reconcile the respect and warmth they felt for John Paul with what they saw as too little attention to the problem of sexually abusive priests'. The paper interviewed Dr James E. Post, a professor at Boston University and leader of a group of lay Catholics. 'I think it is fair to say that John Paul had a kind of love affair with Boston from the time he was Archbishop of Krakow and made a trip here,' he told the paper, but he added, 'His behaviour in response to the sex abuse crisis disappointed many Catholics . . . His personal relationship with the Cardinal [Law] seemed to stand in the way of his being willing to address the problems of the archdiocese.'

In Rome the story – from the point of view of a professional journalist – just went on getting better and better. Pilgrims poured into the Eternal City – Dr Bertolaso had originally estimated that a million people would arrive in the run-up to the funeral, but afterwards concluded that the true figure was three times that. Demand for coverage from those of us lucky enough to be there became unceasing as the secular newsrooms of Europe were driven to appreciate the dimension of the story that was unfolding. And John Paul's flair for the dramatic was apparently undiminished by death; 'When they carried the pope's body from the Sala Clementina to St Peter's,' Fr Gerald O'Collins remembered, 'it was like a Viking king being carried through his people to his final burial ground.'

John Paul's funeral offered the world a magnificent expression of what I once heard a priest refer to as 'the great consoling mystery of the Roman Church', and as his body was taken into the basilica for burial the pall-bearers turned so that it faced the crowd for a moment, and tipped it towards the people in a final valedictory nod. John Allen of the *National Catholic Enquirer*, admirably hard-edged in so much of his reporting of the Vatican, later remembered the gesture in a way that echoed the emotions of Joan Lewis when she watched the dying John Paul's final appearance at his window: 'the one thing I never anticipated is that I would have a personal, emotional response' to his death, he wrote, but 'At that moment I had to choke back tears, realising in an instant that I would never write another sentence about John

Paul in the present tense. I flashed on memories of burying my own grandfather not long ago, and once again I felt I had suffered a loss that was in some sense irreplaceable.'

The 'Old Guard' of John Paul appointees did very well indeed out of the so-called 'funeral effect'; there is no doubt that Cardinal Ratzinger's brilliant tribute in his homily played a significant part in securing his election as Benedict XVI, and the fervour for John Paul's memory which surrounded the event must surely have been in the minds of the 115 cardinals who processed into the Sistine Chapel for their conclave at half past four on the afternoon of 18 April. John Paul had 'created' – the technical term for what popes do when they appoint a cardinal – almost all those who elected his successor, and he also created the climate in which they made their choice.

One of the complaints one often heard in the last years of John Paul's life – and it sometimes came from senior churchmen – was that his infirmity meant that the Church was effectively being run by a cabal of figures at the top of the Curia. Those who made that charge certainly had in mind Cardinal Ratzinger, who, as the Prefect of the Sacred Congregation of the Doctrine of the Faith, was the most powerful man in the Church next to John Paul. The only figure who came close to the same level of influence under the last pontificate, the Vatican's 'prime minister', Cardinal Angelo Sodano, remained in his job under the new regime. At the time of writing Cardinal Trujillo, the scourge of Liberation Theologians and the BBC, also seems secure in his curial employment – and in the autumn of 2005 a leak suggested he played a pivotal role in persuading other cardinals from Latin America to swing behind Cardinal Ratzinger during the conclave. Whether or not John Paul's Old Guard were running the Church during his last years alive, they were certainly doing so after his death. It is perhaps also worth recording, by way of a footnote to the roll-call above, that Stanislaw Dziwisz, John Paul's long-serving secretary, was appointed to his master's old job as the Archbishop of Krakow.

The other complaint which was often voiced about the administration of the Church in John Paul's last years was that big problems which urgently needed to be addressed were being left to fester. In the last few chapters I have tried to identify those areas where I think John Paul has left challenges for his successor to face – such as the Church's relationship with Islam and the nature of the priesthood – and those where he has set in train a permanent shift in the Church's position – on the death penalty, for example, or the morality of war. At the time of writing it is difficult to identify any of those issues where Pope Benedict has taken the discussion forward – with the possible exception of his *Instruction* on homosexuality and ordination, which was widely criticised as a misguided and inadequate answer to the crisis in the priesthood which the Boston paedophilia scandal revealed. Even the one big foreign trip by Pope Benedict in his early months in office – to Cologne for the 2005 celebration of World Youth Day – was dictated by the papal schedule John Paul left behind.

Benedict has taken one innovative step: in May 2005, in response to the crowds who had chanted '*Santo Subito*' at John Paul's funeral, he suspended the rule which requires a five-year waiting period before a beatification process can begin. The late pope's 'cause' was formally set in train on 28 June, and at the beginning of November a 'Rogatory Tribunal' to examine his life before his election opened in Krakow. Bishop Tadeusz Pieronek, chairman of the tribunal, said their work would be done in 'a few months only', because 'We're talking about a life which was very harmonious and consciously devoted from its first years to God. It is an exceptional case.' The new Archbishop of Krakow, Stanislaw Dziwisz, added that Karol Wojtyla had 'spent his whole life, from childhood to the last period, on his knees before the majesty of God and the majesty of humanity'. He had already said, in an interview with the Italian daily *Avenire* the previous month, that he personally knew of 'many miraculous healings' through John Paul's intercession and that beatification 'only awaits official confirmation'. In October a French nun said she had been cured of cancer after she and her community prayed for John Paul's help.

I spent much of my time in the days between John Paul's death and the election of his successor writing a script in a rented television suite in Rome. Watching the editing of a television programme can distort one's memory of events because the process often involves seeing the same image over and over again, and after looking repeatedly at a particular picture of John Paul lying in state in St Peter's my colleagues and I realised that it showed – distressingly but unmistakably – a small black creature, possibly a cockroach, crawling across his face. On reflection I found it perversely comforting, because it was a reminder that in death he was a human being like the rest of us, something in danger of being forgotten amid the supercharged adoration of that extraordinary period. The image also stayed in my mind because of the contrast between the frail, corruptible body laid out beneath the altar – it looked oddly small now that it was no longer animated by the formidable will that made him who he was – and the massive magnificence of its surroundings. St Peter's is a monument to the human yearning to create things that will survive our deaths, and the tableau beneath its dome perfectly expressed the tension between what we are and what we dream of being. It brought home the truth that drama and poetry are at the heart of the way Catholicism calls to people, and there can have been few popes who understood that as well as Karol Wojtyla.

Bibliography

The material for this book has been drawn from a shamelessly unscholarly journalistic *pot pourri* of sources: papal documents, newspaper and magazine articles, personal reminiscences, original interviews, specialist and general works of twentieth-century and church history, interviews on radio and television, a handful of unpublished papers and the more reliable pieces of ecclesiastical gossip which have come my way over the past two and a half decades. But there should be no doubt at all about the debt I owe to those who have produced earlier biographies of John Paul; I have not always found myself in agreement with their views, but they provided the central structure upon which everything else hangs. I have listed them below, together with other books which I found particularly helpful.

Accattoli, Luigi, *When a Pope Asks Forgiveness: The Mea Culpas of John Paul II*, trans. Jordan Aumann OP, Alba House, New York, 1998.

Allen, John L., *Opus Dei: Secrets and Power inside the Catholic Church*, Allen Lane, London, 2005.

Allen, John L., *The Rise of Benedict XVI: The Inside Story of How the Pope was Elected and What it Means for the World*, Penguin, London, 2005.

Ascherson, Neal, *The Polish August: What Has Happened*, Penguin, London, 1981.

Ascherson, Neal, *The Struggles for Poland*, Michael Joseph, London, 1987.

Balasuriya, Tissa, *Mary and Human Liberation: The Story and the Text*, Mowbray, London, 1997.

Bernstein, Carl and Politi, Marco, *His Holiness: John Paul II and the Hidden History of Our Time*, Bantam, London, 1997.

Blazynski, George, *John Paul II: The Man from Krakow*, Weidenfeld and Nicholson, London, 1979.

Bolton, Glorney, *Roman Century 1870–1970*, Hamish Hamilton, London, 1970.

Boniecki, Fr Adam, *Kalendarium of the Life of Karol Wojtyla: The Making of the Pope of the Millennium*, Marian Press, Stockbridge Massachusetts, 2000.

Boston Globe (Investigative staff of), *Betrayal: The Crisis in the Catholic Church*, Little Brown and Company, Boston, New York and London, 2002.

Burns, Monsignor Charles, *The Election of a Pope*, Catholic Truth Society, London, 1997.

Buttiglione, Rocco, *Karol Wojtyla: The Thought of the Man who Became Pope John Paul II*, trans. Paulo Guietti and Francesca Murphy, William B. Eerdmans Publishing Company, Grand Rapids, Michigan, 1997.

Carey, George, *Know the Truth: A Memoir*, Harper Perennial, London, 2005.

Chadwick, Owen, *Britain and the Vatican during the Second World War*, Cambridge University Press, Cambridge, 1986.

Chinigo, Michael (ed.), *The Teachings of Pius XII*, Methuen, London, 1958.

Coppa, Frank J., *The Modern Papacy since 1789*, Longman, London and New York, 1998.

Cornwall, John, *A Thief in the Night*, Penguin, London, 1990.

Cornwall, John, *The Pope in Winter: The Dark Face of John Paul II's Papacy*, Viking, London, 2004.

Davies, Norman, *God's Playground: A History of Poland*, Clarendon Press, Oxford, 1981.

Dziewanowski, M. K., *Poland in the Twentieth Century*, Columbia University Press, New York, 1977.

Formicola, Jo Renee, *Pope John Paul: Prophetic Politician*, Georgetown University Press, Washington DC, 2002.

Frossard, André, *Be Not Afraid: André Frossard in Conversation with John Paul II*, trans. J. R. Foster, The Bodley Head, London, 1984.

Fukuyama, Francis, *The End of History and the Last Man*, Hamish Hamilton, London, 1992.

Godden, Gertrude, *Poland, Yesterday, To-day, To-morrow*, Burns and Oates, London, 1940.

Gromyko, Andrei, *Memoirs*, Hutchinson, London, 1989.

Gutierrez, Gustavo, *A Theology of Liberation: History, Politics and Salvation*, SCM Press, London, 1974.

Hastings, Adrian (ed.), *Modern Catholicism: Vatican II and After*, Oxford University Press, Oxford, 1991.

Hebblethwaite, Margaret and Peter, *The Next Pope*, HarperSanFrancisco, California, 1999.

Hebblethwaite, Peter, *The Runaway Church*, William Collins, London, 1975.

Hebblethwaite, Peter, *The Year of Three Popes*, Collins, London, 1978.

Hebblethwaite, Peter, *In the Vatican*, Oxford University Press, Oxford, 1987.

Holmes, George, *The Oxford Illustrated History of Italy*, Oxford University Press, Oxford, 1977.

Hotchkiss, Christine, *Home to Poland*, Eyre and Spottiswoode, London, 1958.

Howard, Anthony, *Basil Hume: The Monk Cardinal*, Headline, London, 2005.

John Paul II, *Crossing the Threshold of Hope*, trans. Jenny McPhee and Martha McPhee, Jonathan Cape, London, 1994.

John Paul II, *Gift and Mystery: On the Fiftieth Anniversary of My Priestly Ordination*, Image Books/Doubleday, London, 1996.

John Paul II, *Rise, Let Us Be On Our Way*, trans. Walter Ziemba, Warner Books, London, 2004.

John Paul II, *Memory and Identity: Personal Reflections*, Weidenfeld and Nicholson, London, 2005.

Katz, Robert, *Fatal Silence*, Weidenfeld and Nicholson, London, 2003.

Kwitny, Jonathan, *Man of the Century: The Life and Times of Pope John Paul II*, Henry Holt, London, 1997.

Lernoux, Penny, *People of God: The Struggle for World Catholicism*, Viking, London, 1989.

Longley, Clifford, *The Worlock Archive*, Geoffrey Chapman, London and New York, 2000.

MacEoin, Gary, *The Inner Elite: Dossiers of Papal Candidates*, Sheed Andrews and McMeel, Kansas City, 1978.

Malinski, Mieczyslaw, *Pope John Paul II: The Life of Karol Wojtyla*, trans. P.S. Falla, Image Books, New York, 1982.

O'Brien, Darcy, *The Hidden Pope*, HarperCollins, London, 1998.

O'Connor, Garry, *Universal Father: A Life of Pope John Paul II*, Bloomsbury, London, 2005.

Oddie, William (ed.), *John Paul the Great, Maker of the Post-conciliar Church*, Catholic Truth Society and the Catholic Herald, London, 2003.

Pepinster, Catherine (ed.), *John Paul II: Reflections from The Tablet*, Burns and Oates, London, 2005.

Pirie, Valerie, *The Triple Crown: An Account of the Papal Conclaves from the Fifteenth Century to Modern Times*, Spring Books, London, 1965.

Rees, Thomas J., *Inside the Vatican: The Politics and Organisation of the Catholic Church*, Harvard University Press, Cambridge Massachusetts and London, 1996.

Rittner, Carol and Roth, John K. (eds), *Pope Pius XII and the Holocaust*, Leicester University Press, London and New York, 2002.

Roberts, J. M., *A History of Europe*, Helicon, Oxford, 1996.

Robinson, William (ed.), *August 1980: The Strikes in Poland*, Radio Free Europe Research, Munich, 1980.

Roos, Hans, *A History of Modern Poland*, trans. J. R. Foster, Eyre and Spottiswoode, London, 1966.

Rowland, Christopher (ed.), *The Cambridge Companion to Liberation Theology*, Cambridge University Press, Cambridge, 1999.

Ruffin, Bernard, *Padre Pio: True Story*, Our Sunday Visitor, USA, 1991.

Salter, Cedric, *Flight from Poland*, Faber and Faber, London, 1940.

Sienkiewicz, Henryk, *The Deluge*, trans. Jeremiah Curtin, J. M. Dent, London, 1895.

Sienkiewicz, Henryk, *With Fire and Sword*, trans. Jeremiah Curtin, J. M. Dent, London, 1898.

Sienkiewicz, Henryk, *Fire in the Steppe*, trans. W. S. Kuniczak, Copernicus Society of America, 1992.

Snow, Jon, *Shooting History: A Personal Journey*, HarperCollins, London, 2004.

Stourton, Edward, *Absolute Truth: The Catholic Church in the World Today*, Viking, London, 1998.

Svidercoschi, Gian Franco, *Stories of Karol: The Unknown Life of John Paul II*, Gracewing, Leominster, Herefordshire, 2003.

Syrop, Konrad, *Poland between the Hammer and the Anvil*, Robert Hale, London, 1968.

Tombs, David, *Latin American Liberation Theology*, Brill, Boston, Massachusetts, 2002.

Walsh, Michael, *John Paul II: A Biography*, HarperCollins, London, 2005.

Weigel, George, *Witness to Hope: The Biography of Pope John Paul II*, Cliff Street Books (HarperCollins), New York, 2001.

Wilkins, John (ed.), *Understanding Veritatis Splendor: The Encyclical Letter of Pope John Paul II on the Church's Moral Teaching*, SPCK, London, 1994.

Willey, David, *God's Politician: John Paul at the Vatican*, Faber and Faber, London, 1992.

Williams, George Hunston, *The Mind of John Paul II; Origins of his Thought and Actions*, Seabury Press, New York, 1981.

Wojtyla, Karol, *Love and Responsibility*, trans. H. T. Willetts, Ignatius Press, San Francisco, 1991.

Wojtyla, Karol, *The Collected Plays and Writings on the Theatre*, University of California Press, Berkeley, Los Angeles, London, 1987.

Index

Index